INSIDE GHQ

Orlo, later in life (Print, 1962, Robert Lutyens, © Candia Lutyens Peterson/ National Portrait Gallery, London).

INSIDE GHQ

THE GALLIPOLI DIARY OF CAPTAIN ORLO WILLIAMS

EDITED BY

Rhys Crawley, Stephen Chambers
& Ashleigh Brown

L.G.P.

Published May 2025.

ISBN 978-1-7636268-3-6 (hardback)
ISBN 978-0-6459276-9-6 (paperback)
ISBN 978-1-7636268-2-9 (ebook)

Little Gully Publishing
littlegully.com

NATIONAL LIBRARY OF AUSTRALIA

A catalogue record for this book is available from the National Library of Australia

‘The history of the
Gallipoli campaign,
rich in military lessons,
should also serve as a
general warning to all who
at crises place
undue confidence in
Cabinets.’

O.C. WILLIAMS
1929

Private
Diary. Opened. March 13/15

of O.C. Williams Capt.
G.H.Q.
British Mediterranean E.F

CONTENTS

Abbreviations and acronyms

AA&QMG	Assistant Adjutant and Quartermaster General
ADC	Aide-de-Camp
ADMS	Assistant Director of Medical Services
AG	Adjutant-General
AHQ	Army Headquarters
ANZAC	Australian and New Zealand Army Corps
APM	Assistant Provost Marshal
ASC	Army Service Corps
BGGS	Brigadier-General, General Staff
BGRA	Brigadier-General, Royal Artillery
Bn	Battalion
CB	Companion of the Order of the Bath
CEO	*Corps Expéditionnaire d'Orient*
CGS	Chief of the General Staff
CID	Committee of Imperial Defence
CIGS	Chief of the Imperial General Staff
COO	Chief Ordnance Officer
CRA	Commander, Royal Artillery
CRE	Commander, Royal Engineers
DAA	Deputy Assistant Adjutant
DAA&QMG	Deputy Assistant Adjutant and Quartermaster General
DAG	Deputy Adjutant General

DAQMG	Deputy Assistant Quartermaster General
DAS	Director of Army Signals
DDOS	Deputy Director of Ordnance Services
DIGC	Deputy Inspector General of Communications
DMO	Directorate of Military Operations
DOW	Died of wounds
DQMG	Deputy Quartermaster General
DSO	Distinguished Service Order
EMS	Eastern Mediterranean Squadron
FO	Foreign Office
GC	General Commanding
GHQ	General Headquarters
GOC	General Officer Commanding
GS	General Staff
GSO	General Staff Officer (Grade 1, 2, 3)
HE	High Explosive
HMS	His Majesty's Ship
HQ	Headquarters
IGC	Inspector General of Communications
KCMG	Knight Commander of the Order of St Michael and St George
KIA	Killed in action
KM	King's Messenger
KOSB	King's Own Scottish Borderers
KRRC	King's Royal Rifle Corps
MA	Military Attaché
MC	Military Cross
MEF	Mediterranean Expeditionary Force

MLO	Military Landing Officer
MP	Member of Parliament
NZ&A	New Zealand and Australian Division
OC	Officer Commanding
OIC	Officer in charge
PMO	Principal Medical Officer
PNTO	Principal Naval Transport Officer
psc	Passed Staff College
Q	Quartermaster General's Branch (GHQ)
QMG	Quartermaster General
RA	Royal Artillery
RAMC	Royal Army Medical Corps
RE	Royal Engineers
RFA	Royal Field Artillery
RMLI	Royal Marine Light Infantry
RMSP	Royal Mail Steam Packet
RN	Royal Navy
RND	Royal Naval Division
RNVR	Royal Naval Volunteer Reserve
SS	Secret Service (i.e. Secret Intelligence Service, MI6)
SWB	South Wales Borderers
TBD	Torpedo Boat Destroyer
TF	Territorial Force
VA	Vice Admiral
VC	Victoria Cross
WO	War Office

Orlo excelled at Eton College (Reproduced by permission of the Provost and Fellows of Eton College).

Introduction

Dr Orlando Cyprian Williams CB, MC (1883–1967), known affectionately as Orlo, was a man of many and varied interests, talents and titles: son, brother, husband, father, grandfather, and friend; birdwatcher, pianist, motorcycle enthusiast, and sportsman; civil servant, military officer, linguist, literary critic, scholar, author, translator, and diarist.

Born on 4 May 1883 in Paddington, London, Orlo was the eldest child and only son of Thomas Cyprian Williams (1854–1932) and Helen Rosalind Campbell (1856–1939), who had been married on 13 July 1882. Their other children, Orlo's younger sisters, were Gwendolen Meta Williams (1884–1975) and Joan Violet Helen Williams (1886–1977). Known professionally as T. Cyprian or personally as Cyp, Orlo's father followed his own father, Joshua Williams QC (1813–1881), into law. A conveyancing solicitor and barrister at Lincoln's Inn, as well as a law professor and an avid art collector, Cyp was best known for writing numerous law books. His eldest brother (Orlo's uncle), Sir Joshua Strange Williams (1837–1915), similarly practiced law and, after spending much of his adult life in New Zealand, rose to a position representing the Dominion on the Judicial Committee of the Privy Council. Orlo's mother, Helen, was the eldest of the seven children of Alexander Copse Campbell (1822–1916) and Elizabeth Henrietta Drummond (1833–1900). Two of her brothers were senior officers in the Indian Army: Colonel Colin Powys Campbell (1859–1923) and Brigadier-General Alan James Campbell (1865–1944), who was awarded the Distinguished Service Order in 1917.

A well-known artist and philanthropist, apparently with 'volatile temperament', Helen was a patron of artists such as Philip Wilson Steer (1860–1942) who, in 1891, did an oil painting of Helen, Gwendolen and Joan titled *Mrs Cyprian Williams and her Two Little Girls.*

Orlo's mother, Helen, and sisters, Gwen and Joan (*Mrs Cyprian Williams and her Two Little Girls*, 1891, Philip Wilson Steer. Tate).

Orlo was first educated at Ashdown House preparatory school, Forest Row, East Sussex. From there, between 1897 and 1902, he attended the prestigious Eton College as a King's Scholar. In addition to his academic achievements and role as Editor of the *Eton College Chronicle* and President of Eton's Musical Society, Orlo played tennis and golf, represented the College in the Wall Elevens, and won fencing and boxing competitions. Continuing his sporting endeavours, including cricket and field hockey, at

Balliol College, Oxford University, 1902–1906, he excelled in humanities and languages, obtaining proficiency in Latin, classical Greek, German, French and Italian.

Orlo balanced studies and sports at Balliol College, Oxford (Reproduced by permission of Balliol College).

Orlo returned to university later in life, earning a Doctor of Civil Law from Oxford in 1946. Many of those with whom Orlo attended Eton and Balliol appear throughout his diary. After graduating from Oxford, in 1907 Orlo commenced as a clerk in the House of Commons; it was the start of a long career in the civil service.

On 15 June 1912, at the age of 29, Orlo married 36-year-old Alice Isabella Pollock (1876–1953), daughter of Privy Counsellor, Sir Frederick Pollock, 3rd Baronet of Hatton (1845–1937), and Lady Pollock, Georgina Harriet Deffell (1847–1935). Alice's brother, Sir Frederick John Pollock (1878–1963), was a noted historian. Alice was married previously in 1902 to British diplomat Sydney Waterlow (1878–1944). Curiously, Orlo and his close friend, Bernard Wallis, were visitors at Sydney and Alice's house in Hillyfields, Rye, Sussex, during the 2 April 1911 census. Shortly after, in June 1911, Alice filed for divorce from Waterlow on the grounds that the marriage had never been consummated. The divorce was granted on 10 June 1912, and five days later Orlo and Alice were married. The following year, on

Orlo with Alice and Rowan (Family collection).

their first wedding anniversary, Orlo and Alice's only child, a daughter, Elizabeth Mary Williams (later known as Rowan Mary Williams), who Orlo called Betty, was born (1913–2004). Together, the family lived at 4 Campden Hill Gardens, Kensington, London.

When Britain entered the First World War in August 1914, Orlo had spent almost eight years working in the House of Commons. He didn't immediately enlist in the military, but he did transfer to the War Office, where, for seven months, he worked as a civilian in C2: the Parliamentary and Legal Section within the Department of the Secretary. Reporting to the Permanent Under-Secretary at the War Office, Sir Reginald Brade, C2's—and Orlo's—duties included drafting answers to Parliamentary questions, enciphering and deciphering the War Office's Secret and Foreign telegrams, editing the Government's code book, and maintaining custody of and distributing Secret documents. It is not surprising, then, that when Orlo enlisted on 11 March 1915—originally with the intent of joining the Royal Naval Division—he was instead appointed cipher officer for the newly-formed General Headquarters (GHQ) of the Mediterranean Expeditionary Force (MEF).

Just 28 hours after his appointment, having been assigned the temporary rank of captain, Orlo, standing 6 feet 3 inches, departed London for the Dardanelles with other members of General Sir Ian Hamilton's staff. It is here that Orlo's Gallipoli story, and his diary, begins. 'For each of us', Orlo wrote of those on the train from Charing Cross station, 'the whole course of his future had been changed in the twinkling of an eye. Our kit, in various degrees, had shown signs of hasty improvisation, especially my own, which was off the peg from A to Z and fitted nowhere'. A 'sense of boyish enthusiasm for adventure' infected all, from the most senior to junior of officers. As we will learn in the following pages, Orlo worked as part of GHQ's Operations section, initially as its cipher officer—responsible for encoding and decoding sensitive and important messages between London and Gallipoli, or between General Hamilton and his fellow officers—and, from November 1915, as a staff officer in General Sir Charles Monro's GHQ, where he drafted and distributed orders, and wrote the General Staff war diary.

After Gallipoli, Orlo moved to Egypt where, in March 1916, along with many of his colleagues from GHQ MEF, he transferred to General Sir Archibald Murray's new

GHQ of the Egyptian Expeditionary Force. Serving in Egypt and Palestine, first under Murray and then General Sir Edmund Allenby, Orlo continued to perform the duties of a General Staff Officer (Grade 3 until June 1917, when he was made GSO2). His signature can be seen on the General Staff war diary for most months between March 1916 and December 1917. In early 1918, following the successful battles at Beersheba and Jerusalem, he returned to London and the War Office where, from 1 February 1918, he was GSO2 in the Directorate of Staff Duties, Office of the Chief of the Imperial General Staff. His superior officer, as it had been for a time at Gallipoli and in Egypt, was Major-General Sir Arthur Lynden-Bell. Promoted Major on 25 February 1918, Orlo served in this Directorate beyond war's end. He had his 36th birthday at the War Office, and shortly after, in May or June 1919, returned to his pre-war role in the Palace of Westminster, where he remained until his retirement in 1948.

Although never considering himself as a military man, Orlo's war experiences were nonetheless a defining experience for him, and a matter of pride for his family. His mother followed the war closely, regularly corresponding with soldiers and officers from her parish, pasting articles, notices and photos of those killed in a family album, and volunteering as Village Registrar for the Women's Land Army in Oxford County. Like Helen, Orlo's sisters and Alice corresponded and sent packages to some of Orlo's friends in uniform. Orlo's father, shortly before his death, was proud to attend a dinner at Lincoln's Inn with Orlo, his son's left breast adorned with a Military Cross (for his staff work at Gallipoli), 1914-15 Star, British War Medal, Victory Medal with Oak Leaf (Orlo was mentioned in despatches four times), French Legion of Honour (Chevalier), and Italian Silver Medal of Military Valor. Four more medals followed in later years. For his service to the House of Commons, which included seven years as Principal Clerk in the Committee and Private Bill Office, Orlo received the 1935 Silver Jubilee Medal, 1937 Coronation Medal, and in 1941 was invested as a Companion of the Order of the Bath (CB). Lastly, for his service as a lieutenant in the Home Guard's Palace of Westminster Detachment during the Second World War, Orlo received the Defence Medal.

Orlo with his sisters (Family collection).

A prolific writer and friend of other authors including Compton Mackenzie (who dedicated *Gallipoli Memories* to Orlo), Katherine Mansfield and T.S. Eliot, Orlo was a regular essayist, reviewer, critic, editor, translator, and author in his own right. Drawing on his wartime experience, Orlo wrote articles dealing with the Gallipoli campaign, frequently referring to his diary entries to lend authority. These publications include 'The evacuation of the Dardanelles' (*The National Review*, 1920), 'The Gallipoli tragedy: part one' (*The Nineteenth Century and After*, 1929, which was a review of Cecil Aspinall-Oglander's first volume of the Official History), and 'Memories of a gallant adventure' (*Radio Times*, 1931). His name and views adorned the pages of *Blackwood's*, *London Mercury*, *Monthly Criterion*, *National Review*, *The Listener*, *The Times* and *Times Literary Supplement*. From his first in 1908, to his last in 1954, Orlo produced no fewer than 17 books: translations of Louis de Launay's *The world's gold: its geology, extraction, and political economy* (1908), Riccardo Baccheli's *The devil at the long bridge: a historical novel* (1929), and Paolo Monelli's *Toes up: a chronicle of gay and doleful adventures of Alpini and mules and wine* (1930); editorship of the *Minute book of James Courthope* (1953); and his own books, *The Officials of the House of Commons: A History* (1909); *Lamb's friend and the census-taker: life and letters of John Rickman* (1912); *Vie de Bohème: A Patch of Romantic Paris* (1913); *Giosuè Carducci* (1914); *The Good Englishwoman* (1920); *Three Naughty Children* (1922); *Contemporary Criticism of Literature* (1924); *Some great English novels: studies in the art of fiction* (1926); *Charles Lamb* (1934), *The Historical Development of Private Bill Procedure and Standing Orders in the House of Commons* (2 volumes, 1948-9), *The Topography of the Old House of Commons* (1953), *The Clerical Organisation of the House of Commons, 1661–1850* (1954). The diversity of these publications—including English translations of Italian books, a collection on classical English novelists, a volume of children's fairytales, and many academic works—show the breadth of his knowledge and interests.

What else Orlo's life involved is mostly lost to history. A man who seemed more comfortable behind the scenes, only occasionally did he crack the curtains to reveal himself.

Alice died in London on 28 June 1953. Orlo followed 13 years later, aged 83, on 10 March 1967. They left behind one daughter and three grandchildren. 'His tall, erect figure, white hair and vivacity in conversation made him stand out in any company', said Orlo's obituary in *The Times*. Combining his many talents and accomplishments 'with gaiety of manner', Orlo was credited with maintaining until the end 'an unquenchable zest for living a full life.' His career had spanned an impressive four decades in the House of Commons, interrupted only by his wartime service. Through his wide collection of publications, Orlo left behind his knowledge and thoughts on an array of topics ranging from literary works to the British political system, and Britain's First World War experience. Importantly for our purposes, he provided a view of the Gallipoli campaign both on an individual level and through the strategic lens of his privileged position within GHQ (made more colourful by his relationships with and opinions of key figures) in his, until now, unpublished diary.

* * *

Although not written for publication, Orlo anticipated that his 'very full diary... may see the light' one day. Possibly towards that end, Orlo deposited his diaries and wartime photos with the Imperial War Museum in 1952. Known as the Private Papers of Dr O.C. Williams, with small snippets regularly quoted by historians, it remains one of the strongest collections concerning the Gallipoli campaign.

Arranged in two volumes, Orlo's diary provides an almost day-by-day account of life inside GHQ for the entirety of the Gallipoli campaign, from 13 March 1915 to 10 January 1916. Written under great pressure of work and in haste at the end of each day, always using every spare space on the page (indicating how scarce paper was), Orlo's small, sometimes illegible handwriting, is terribly difficult to decipher. Still, its value as a primary source meant it was worth persevering. Indeed, Orlo's diary is undoubtedly the best insight into GHQ; how it functioned, its problems, its personalities, and what they thought of each other and the situations they found themselves in. As GHQ's main cipher officer, Orlo was responsible for sending and receiving sensitive information pertaining to matters of tactical, strategic, and political import. Deciphering encoded messages from London before they got to Gallipoli's Commander-in-Chief, and enciphering responses to the War Office, Secretary of State for War, Prime Minister or the King, Orlo had privileged, real-time access to Secret information—most of which he recorded in his diary—often before anyone else. Because of his access to news from home, Orlo was up to date with significant political and military events in Britain, other capital cities, and on the Great War's many fronts.

To read Orlo's unique diary is to better understand what the key players, politicians and generals alike, knew, thought, or decided at the time. On such matters, Orlo is often critical—sometimes downright damning—of those in positions of power. 'The history of the Gallipoli campaign, rich in military lessons, should also serve as a general warning to all who at crises place undue confidence in Cabinets', he later wrote of the negative influence politics, and politicians, had on the Gallipoli campaign from its inception to end. Through his own observations and words, as well as conversations with his close friends and colleagues in GHQ—plus excerpts from Secret telegrams and a healthy dose of GHQ gossip—Orlo treats us to an insight like no other into how Gallipoli was conceived, planned, and conducted.

Ian Hamilton's *Gallipoli Diary* (2 volumes, 1920) and Compton Mackenzie's *Gallipoli Memories* (1929) provide the views of others in GHQ, though, being secondary sources written for a public market and aiming to shape the narrative one way or another, neither is as reliable or perceptive as Orlo's account.

Inside GHQ: The Gallipoli Diary of Captain Orlo Williams takes much of the difficulty out of both accessing and understanding Orlo's diary. In transcribing Orlo's handwriting and adding relevant context and biographical details, this book brings his incredible insights into the Gallipoli campaign—as well as this uniquely detailed primary source—and makes them available to a wider audience. In doing so, it adds to the unpublished efforts of American Nelson Jonnes, who, we learned late into our own efforts, had also transcribed Orlo's diary. A comparison of his typed version with the original handwritten diaries, however, reveals many inaccuracies and editor insertions (due, no doubt, to the fact that Jonnes read the diaries into a tape recorder and then typed them on return to the USA, without the benefit of double-checking the original source).

In editing Orlo's diaries, we have endeavoured to avoid, as much as possible, making the same mistakes. As such, our editorial touch has been light. Our only changes have been the occasional insertion of commas or the expansion of abbreviations and military ranks, so that 'K' and 'WO' become 'Kitchener' and 'War Office', and 'Col' becomes 'Colonel'. We inserted ellipses (...) where we were unsure of a word or phrase. Where the meaning was obvious but the original words not clear, we inserted a replacement word or phrase in [parenthesis]. Where we believed some additional explanation was required, including when the identity of a person was not obvious (such as when only their first name was given), we have given the information in a footnote. Most people in the diary, however, are referred to by their surname, and therefore no footnote was required. Readers should consult the Biographies section towards the end of the book, arranged alphabetically based on surname, for fuller details of the nearly 300 individuals mentioned in the diary.

Our short introductory histories that begin each chapter provide the wider context necessary to understand Orlo's remarks and will help anyone who needs a refresher of the Gallipoli campaign's main events. For those wishing to learn more about the structure and responsibilities of GHQ, we recommend Chapter 7 of Rhys Crawley and Michael LoCicero's edited volume *Gallipoli: New Perspectives on the Mediterranean Expeditionary Force, 1915–16* (Helion & Co., 2018). For another reflection on some of the issues Orlo mentions, using the words of one of his friends and fellow officers (with expert analysis by a leading historian of the First World War), we recommend Aimée Fox's edited book *The Military Papers and Correspondence of Major General Guy Dawnay, 1915–1919* (Boydell & Brewer, 2024). Those wanting a detailed analysis of Gallipoli's strategic failures should read Robin Prior's *Gallipoli: The End of the Myth* (Yale University Press, 2010). For an excellent and accessible history of the campaign, it is hard to go past Peter Hart's *Gallipoli* (Profile Books, 2011). For soldiers' perspectives of the campaign see Richard van Emden and Stephen Chambers *Gallipoli: The Dardanelles Disaster in Soldiers' Words and Photographs* (Bloomsbury, 2015). Finally, for an excellent history of the Ottoman victory we recommend Edward J. Erickson's *Gallipoli: The Ottoman Campaign* (Pen & Sword, 2010).

* * *

INTRODUCTION

Inside GHQ has been a labour of love for a long time. We must, of course, first thank Orlo Williams for keeping—and then making public—such a detailed and exceptional diary. We persisted because we believe it to be the best diary and most interesting insight into the machinations of the Gallipoli campaign. Our next thanks go to Orlo's granddaughter, Janet Bettesworth, for permission to publish Orlo's diary and photographs, and for allowing us access to the family albums created by Orlo's mother. We acknowledge the efforts of Nelson Jonnes, who clearly saw in Orlo's diary the same things we did. We would like to thank the Imperial War Museum, London, where Orlo's diaries and wartime photographs still reside, for their support and provision of materials. Eton and Balliol Colleges were helpful and responsive in tracking down details of Orlo's younger life, and we are thankful for their permission to reproduce the photos they supplied. Similarly, we thank Tate Britain for permission to publish Philip Steer's painting of Orlo's mother and sisters, and the National Portrait Gallery, London, for permission to reproduce Robert Lutyens' 1962 print of Orlo. The University of New South Wales and the Australian War Memorial provided an institutional base while we undertook this project. Personally, we are grateful to Dr Aimée Fox and Peter Hart, whose encouragement kept the project going. Likewise, each other and our families, without whom *Inside GHQ* would not have been possible. Finally, we would like to thank Bernard de Broglio and Little Gully Publishing for their assistance, interest and excellent work in publishing this book.

Rhys Crawley, Stephen Chambers, Ashleigh Brown

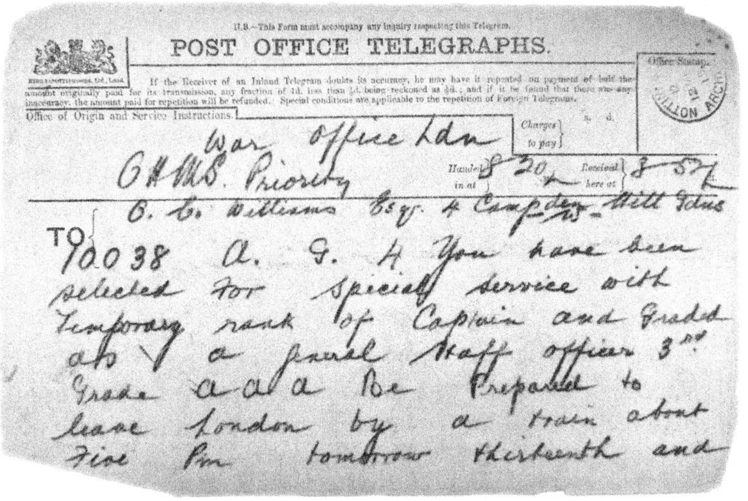
N.B.—This Form must accompany any inquiry respecting this Telegram.

POST OFFICE TELEGRAPHS.

If the Receiver of an Inland Telegram doubts its accuracy, he may have it repeated on payment of half the amount originally paid for its transmission, any fraction of 1d. less than ½d. being reckoned as ½d.; and if it be found that there was any inaccuracy, the amount paid for repetition will be refunded. Special conditions are applicable to the repetition of Foreign Telegrams.

Office of Origin and Service Instructions. War Office Ldn

OHMS. Priority

Charges to pay s. d.

Handed in at 8 20 p Received here at 8 57 p

Office Stamp.

TO O. C. Williams Esq. 4 Campden Hill Gdns W.

10038 A. G. 4 You have been selected for special service with temporary rank of Captain and Graded as a general Staff officer 3rd Grade aaa Be prepared to leave London by a train about Five pm tomorrow thirteenth and

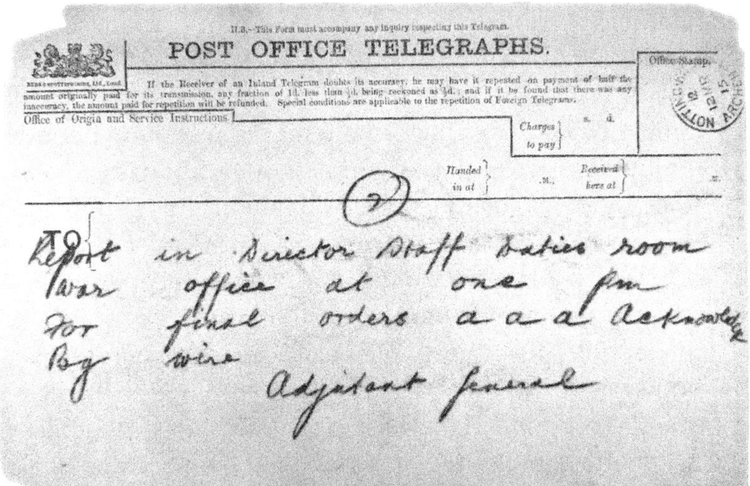
N.B.—This Form must accompany any inquiry respecting this Telegram.

POST OFFICE TELEGRAPHS.

If the Receiver of an Inland Telegram doubts its accuracy, he may have it repeated on payment of half the amount originally paid for its transmission, any fraction of 1d. less than ½d. being reckoned as ½d.; and if it be found that there was any inaccuracy, the amount paid for repetition will be refunded. Special conditions are applicable to the repetition of Foreign Telegrams.

Office of Origin and Service Instructions.

Charges to pay s. d.

Handed in at .M. Received here at

(2)

TO Report in Director Staff Duties room War office at one pm for final orders aaa Acknowledge by wire

Adjutant General

The War Office telegram received 12 March 1915, confirming Orlo's selection for special service with the Mediterranean Expeditionary Force, to leave London the next day (O.C. Williams, IWM).

Prelude

'DAMN THE DARDANELLES'

ORIGINS OF THE GALLIPOLI CAMPAIGN

The outbreak of the First World War in 1914 was triggered by a complex web of political tensions, militarism, alliances, and nationalistic fervour in Europe. The immediate catalyst was the assassination of Archduke Franz Ferdinand of Austria-Hungary on 28 June 1914, by a Serbian nationalist. In response, Austria-Hungary issued an ultimatum to Serbia, and when Serbia's reply was deemed unsatisfactory, Austria-Hungary declared war on 28 July 1914. The intricate system of alliances in place quickly drew in other major powers: Russia mobilized to defend Serbia, Germany supported Austria-Hungary, France and the United Kingdom were drawn into the conflict as the situation escalated. Within weeks, what began as a regional dispute transformed into a full-scale global war, engulfing Europe and eventually many other parts of the world.

The Ottoman Empire's entry into the war was marked by a combination of strategic decisions and diplomatic manoeuvres. Initially neutral, the Ottomans were keen to regain lost territories and bolster their weakened state, seeking alliances that could protect their interests. In late 1914, the empire aligned itself with the Central Powers of Germany and Austria-Hungary. The decision was influenced by a desire to counter Russian expansionism and internal nationalist movements. On 29 October 1914, the Ottoman Navy, with German support, launched a surprise attack on the Russian Black Sea ports, prompting Russia to declare war on the Ottoman Empire. The Ottomans, seeking to secure their territorial integrity and strengthen their position in the conflict, closed the Dardanelles, strengthening the Straits defences with mines and artillery. For Britain this was a particular blow, as the loss of this warm-water link with Russia was compounded by the Ottoman threat to British imperial possessions and influence in Egypt, southern Arabia and the Persian Gulf. Turkey then put into effect plans to attack Russia in the Caucasus, to regain her former territory, and to attack British interests in Egypt (the Suez Canal) and the Persian coast. The threat to Suez could severely impede Britain's communications with India, whilst an attack on British assets on the Persian coast would threaten oil supplies on which the newest British warships depended. Britain had little choice but to respond.

On 3 November, in a rapid response to the Ottoman's unprovoked attack on the Black Sea ports, the First Lord of Admiralty, Winston Churchill, ordered the navy to bombard the outer forts that guarded the mouth of the Dardanelles. This was to be a demonstration only and, to reduce risk to the Anglo-French fleet, it would be conducted at long range. The British fleet targeted the forts at Sedd-el-Bahr on the European side, whilst the French aimed for the forts at Kum Kale on the Asiatic side. After ten minutes of negligible return fire, a lucky shot detonated the magazine at Sedd-el-Bahr, killed eighty-six Ottoman defenders and destroying large parts of the fort. On 5 November 1914 Britain and France declared war on Turkey, but operationally little would happen at the Dardanelles for some months.

On 2 January 1915, Russia asked Britain and France for a diversionary attack to help release the pressure on the Caucasus Front which had been a strain on Russia's war machine. It was the Entente's aim to see Russia focus on Germany, not Turkey. It was this request that brought the Dardanelles back to the attention of the War Council. Kitchener immediately latched onto the idea of a tactical naval attack in the Dardanelles, if no troops were involved. France supported the idea and offered a naval squadron to help. Sir Edward Grey, the British Foreign Secretary, stated: 'The attack on the Dardanelles was agreed on the express condition that it should be a naval operation only; it was under no circumstances to involve the use of troops... If it did not succeed, it was to be treated as a demonstration and abandoned.'

The plan was to send the fleet up through the Dardanelles and into the Sea of Marmara from where it would create havoc, paralysing all Ottoman movements in the area. The fleet would then proceed to Constantinople, the country's capital. It was hoped that the sight of this great armada would be enough to force the belligerent Turks to capitulate and then transfer their allegiances to the Entente. If not, the navy would bombard the capital and await the white flag to be hoisted.

Strategically the plan made sense, although it did have its flaws, based as it was on false assumptions. Political and military leaders in London believed that the Turks lacked the ability and determination to put up much of a fight: a naval bombardment alone could destroy the Dardanelles defences and once the fleet had arrived off Constantinople a coup d'état would occur. Putting that aside, no thought was given to sustaining an operation even if the Ottoman army did withdraw its forces from Thrace. Military land support to keep the Dardanelles open for re-supply would be needed but it was not planned. Cooperation with Russia would be necessary, so that control of the Bosporus could be affected. Putting all this aside in the short term, these were risks that Britain and France were willing to take to quickly knock Turkey out of the war and re-establish the warm-water route to Russia, along which she exported half of her goods, including nine tenths of her grain. With the Russian bear re-focussed on Germany, it was hoped that further German resources would be moved to the east, thus allowing the deadlock to be broken on the Western Front. Doubtless, it was felt, this show of might would influence Greece, Bulgaria and possibly Romania to join a Balkan coalition against the Central Powers. If it all went wrong, however, the effect could be dire.

Demonstrations apart, the elderly First Sea Lord, Admiral Sir John 'Jacky' Fisher and Churchill devised a major naval attack. Vice Admiral Sackville Carden was asked if he thought the scheme was practical by using naval gunfire against the forts. He thought it was so long as he had sufficient ships and time. In London, Fisher soon had second thoughts and was concerned how quickly the operation had gathered pace. 'Damn the Dardanelles! They will be our grave.' The more concerned he was, the more uncooperative he became, eventually falling out with Churchill and resigning. Carden's support for it remained resolute and, because of this, the War Council allowed the operation to continue.

Carden's plan was to destroy the outer forts and then reduce all defences, permanent and semi-permanent, up to and including the forts at the Narrows; sweep the minefields from the entrance of the Straits as far as the Narrows and silence the forts above the Narrows and then proceed into the Sea of Marmara. This would be achieved by long-range bombardment, direct and indirect, followed by a bombardment at closer range with secondary armament. There was a likelihood of mines, especially floaters, which would be dealt with by rifle fire or by being netted and towed away. Moored mines would be cleared by minesweepers.

Using a mix of British and French ships, a long-range bombardment began on 19 February 1915 against the three forts guarding the entrance of the Dardanelles: Sedd-el-Bahr, Kum Kale and Orkanieh. The shelling was from seven miles away, which kept the fleet out of range of the forts' guns. The guns of the fleet were powerful enough; their fire could blow away huge chunks of earth and stone but was not so good at destroying the guns that were positioned behind. There were also concerns with accuracy and indeed only a small proportion of the armour piercing and high explosive shells hit their targets. This was hardly surprising as the targets were barely visible at such a long range. Many shells missed and sank into the soft earth, whilst the damage of those that did hit was difficult to assess at that range. The fleet closed in to survey the damage and even though all three forts were in ruins the Turks still fired back. With failing light and facing an enlivened defence, Carden withdrew the fleet for the day.

Bad weather then frustrated the operation. It was not until 25 February that the bombardment could be recommenced. This time the ships of the fleet, under the command of Rear-Admiral John de Robeck, were brought in closer to target the batteries between Kum Kale and Kephez, but success was limited. Parties of sailors and marines landed the following day to survey the destruction and to destroy any remaining guns, mountings, munitions and searchlights in the Kum Kale, Orkanieh and Sedd-el-Bahr forts. Whilst these raids were initially successful, a repeated raid on 4 March was met with stiff Ottoman resistance causing an early withdrawal of the raiding forces.

Although hampered by the weather the plan was progressing, with at least three of the outer forts put out of action. Carden optimistically reported that he hoped to be in Constantinople in two weeks. This encouraging news of an impending victory was supplemented when a German wireless message was intercepted indicating that the Ottoman forts were running low on ammunition, which subsequently proved to be inaccurate.

During the first week in March, Commodore Roger Keyes, Carden's Chief of Staff, concentrated efforts on sweeping the minefields. These efforts were frustrated by the Ottoman defenders and despite the best efforts by the British and French, little headway was being made. Churchill was getting impatient with the lack of progress since operations started and urged Carden on. Kitchener now appreciated the need to send troops to the Dardanelles.

On 12 March General Sir Ian Hamilton was appointed as the commander of this new Mediterranean Expeditionary Force, who would arrive on the eve of the main naval assault, scheduled for 18 March. Before this, however, there would be another setback. Admiral Carden, suffering a nervous breakdown, announced that he could not continue. Although Rear-Admiral Rosslyn Wemyss succeeded Carden, he willingly allowed Acting Vice-Admiral John de Robeck to continue the operation as commander of the fleet.

The next day, 13 March, the allied minesweepers began a series of attempts to clear a path through the minefields under the cover of darkness. Despite the brave and almost suicidal efforts of these men they all failed. Only a dozen mines were destroyed, far from enough to allow safe passage for the fleet.

It is here that Orlo's diary begins.

1

'NAVY CAN'T DO IT ALONE'

PREPARING FOR BATTLE

On Saturday 13 March Orlo Williams, Cipher Officer, joined General Sir Ian Hamilton's hastily improvised General Staff officers at Charing Cross Station to be waved off by the First Lord of the Admiralty, Winston Churchill. Arriving at their destination during the afternoon of 17 March, Orlo and his fellow officers were to witness the Anglo-French fleet anchored off the island of Tenedos, readying themselves to go into battle the following day.

After dropping anchor Hamilton had little time to appreciate the view as he proceeded on board HMS Queen Elizabeth for a conference between Admirals de Robeck, Wemyss, Guépratte, Commodore Keyes and General d'Amade. The generals were brought up to date by de Robeck who, fully aware of the challenge ahead, was still confident that large-scale army assistance may not be needed. Hamilton and General d'Amade left the following morning aboard HMS Phaeton to reconnoitre the Gallipoli coast and to get a lie of the land. There was little question for having boots on the ground, come success or failure of the naval assault on the following day.

The all-out naval assault began as planned on 18 March. Three waves of ships, four to five abreast, went into battle against the Dardanelles defences, and into disaster they went. The fleet lost three battleships sunk and another three put out of action. Whilst de Robeck was convinced that the

Ottomans had expended vast quantities of ammunition to the extent that some of the main forts were down to their last rounds, this was against the loss of a third of the fleet. With the current rate of loss, the attack could not be sustained for more than another day. Both Wemyss and de Robeck had no other option than to cancel the attack. Orlo remarked that it was 'not altogether joyful day' following the big naval battle, concluding in his diary entry that the general impression was that the 'Navy can't do it alone.'

Now it was recognised that the battleships could not force the Straits until the minefields had been cleared; but the minefields could not be cleared until the defending guns had been destroyed. These guns could not be destroyed until the army was ashore. No longer would the Aegean be the preserve of the Admiralty alone. It was a predicament with one clear answer. On 22 March, de Robeck told Churchill that for the fleet to be successful it needed the army to take the forts. Kitchener was also of the same opinion now, although he wanted an early conclusion to the operation. He could not afford for it to turn into a long-winded campaign and a further drain on military resources that he knew were best placed on the Western Front. The fleet stepped back from the limelight. All hopes now rested with the army to execute what would be the largest amphibious operation the world had known.

This chapter contains Orlo's diary entries from joining Hamilton's staff on 13 March to 24 April, the eve of the Gallipoli landings. We are introduced to some key characters in the Gallipoli campaign from someone inside GHQ. His vivid descriptions of his time in Egypt: the people, the GHQ lifestyle, all hardly the grand mansions that one would expect. We get an insight into the five weeks of planning Hamilton and his staff were focussed on, knowing that each day of delay allowed the Turks to strengthen their defences.

Life within GHQ is a different view to that we know of from troops; it's thanks to Orlo that we get this valuable insight into the gears behind this tragic campaign.

* * *

Saturday 13 March 1915

Appointed as cipher officer on GHQ Mediterranean Force only suggested to me Thursday 8pm, confirmed 1pm next day with orders to be ready to leave England 5pm Saturday 13 March. After getting some instructions and uniform grant at the War Office on Friday afternoon I joined Alice[1] at Harrods and got practically everything by closing time. Dined with her, poor brave dear, at the Carlton. The whole thing seeming a dream coming so suddenly when I had already settled to join the RND at Blandford. Harrods came up to scratch wonderfully and all my kit was ready by 11.30 Saturday, today.

After making various purchases, returned to put on my uniform at 11.30. Then reported at War Office, met Alice again..., returned to finish packing. Mother and the 2 girls[2] came at 3.30 and stayed till I left at 4.15. Feelings in the course of the day were very mixed, *abbandonare tanto subito la piccina moglie e per in incerto tempo era straziante per me e per her. Era grande il suo sacrificio.*[3] Off in cab at 4.15 to Charing Cross where a small special awaited us behind our ordinary train. Winston[4] and his wife to see us off also Lord Midleton whose son[5] is on the staff.

1 Orlo's wife, Alice Isabella Williams (née Pollock).

2 Orlo's sisters, Gwen and Joan.

3 Translation: 'so just leave the little wife and in uncertain weather was heartbreaking for me and her. Great was his sacrifice'.

4 Winston Churchill.

5 Lieutenant George Brodrick.

There were only 14 of us altogether including Sir Ian.[6] A few acquaintances made in the saloon going to Dover; the CGS is General Braithwaite, whose son a Subaltern is with him. Also Captain Aspinall from S.D.2,[7] Major Fuller from H.D.1,[8] Lieutenant-Colonel Ward from M.O.8,[9] and Major Churchill, came over that morning from France, looking a regular campaigner with a most vicious bludgeon in his hand and huge revolver sticking out of his holster.

Arriving at Dover we went straight on board the Scout *Foresight* which soon weighed. The Commander welcomed us most cheerily with a collation in his cabin. We were due to arrive Calais at 8 and leave at once, but were very tiresomely delayed outside the harbour for nearly two hours till the examination service let us in. Sea was glassy calm and very odd to be sailing with lights out under White Ensign. Hear we are to have a record journey to our destination. We are to embark at Marseilles on one of the fastest cruisers and arrive on Tuesday. No chance of inoculation till we do. When we arrived left Calais very quickly in great comfort. Special train with Wagons-Lits and restaurant. Good dinner and stayed up smoking and talking till 12. Did not sleep very much. Still excited and suffering from indigestion. Also engine whistled most abominably. Everybody exceedingly kind and pleasant to me. Major Churchill sharing my compartment. Have a servant called Ashley, 20th Hussars, sharing him with one Powell who has not yet turned up. It must be great fun for

6 General Sir Ian Hamilton.

7 S.D.2 was the Principles, Co-ordination, and War Organization Section within the Directorate of Staff Duties, Department of the Chief of the Imperial General Staff.

8 H.D.1 was the Home Defence Section, Directorate of Military Training, Department of the Chief of the Imperial General Staff.

9 M.O.8 was the Cable Censorship Section within the Directorate of Special Intelligence at the War Office.

them and the clerks. In fact it is quite extra ordinary for us all who have suddenly been rushed off at such short notice on this expedition with its incalculable possibilities. One could dilate at large on this, especially if that one were I, a civilian. Aspinall said all the rest of the WO were green with envy. Sir Ian greeted me very kindly on my being introduced and said I should be worked off my head.

Sunday 14 March 1915

Writing in my diary at 11 a.m. We reached Paris soon after 7 a.m. and went to the Gare de Lyon where we stayed 15 minutes. Nothing very striking to observe on the platforms. Algerian soldiers in a train opposite. How odd for me to set foot in Paris in khaki, a captain! Breakfast, read papers and then shaved and washed, having by a determined effort yesterday got my haversack and bits of things out of my valise. Idling away the day as the train goes south, reading at intervals Eugène Labrich's comedies. Stopped to change engines at La Roche where two French officers came to greet the General. Also enciphered one telegram. Train all day with a few halts. Sun came out at Dijon as we were having lunch and scenery down Rhone Valley beautiful. The chef of the train was splendid and we were exceedingly comfortable. Major Churchill our Camp Commandant sharing my compartment. He, as all of them, seems a very good fellow. When we had a short holt at Avignon, a little soldier in French uniform came up and shook hands saying he recognized I was English, and that he was Italian and wanted to join English army. I said "*Siete Italiano*",[10] whereupon he addressed me at length in his native tongue, explaining that he had fought with 'The Garibaldians' in the Argonne, and now had either to go back to Italy (reserves being called out) or join the Foreign

10 Translation: 'you are Italian'.

Legion, which he did not want to do: but he wanted to fight somewhere. He was very excited and a large crowd gathered to hear the speech which they could not understand. Some sensation caused among our party.

We reached Marseilles about 10 p.m. and went straight on board HMS *Phaeton*, which has woundily little accommodation for so many. I had to send off 3 cipher wires on arriving, and when that was done came aboard, and into the wardroom where some of junior officers simply poured whisky and soda down us. Only the seniors among us had cabins the others slept either in sick bay, or in cots slung in the gangways. I have a cot, and no other accommodation of my own at all. Luckily for our first night, the ship stayed in harbour, for they told us very frequently that the vibration aft was tremendous when she was going. The *Phaeton* is one of the newest fast light cruisers, with the lines of a yacht, two 6-inch guns, and eight 4-inch, very narrow, and much cut away under the stern. All the officers very kind in doing what they could for us. Most of us slept poorly and were up early.

Monday 15 March 1915

On deck by 6, when we weighed. Lovely morning and when finally dressed and washed began to enjoy life a bit. Heard we were bound for Toulon to take on oil. Arrived Toulon soon after 9; wonderful harbour, with rocky hills all round. They sent us all ashore at 9.30 in the motor boat till 1 (NB. We do not observe proper naval etiquette about precedence of CO in entering and leaving ship). Weather continued perfect, and our party made some sensation in Toulon. First act of some was to order lunch at restaurant on the quay. Then off to send telegrams, post cards etc. Some who had come away at still shorter notice than I bought kit. Bolton, Grant and I had our hair cut, and then glass of beer at café. I joined the CGS's lunch at the café! Fresh moules and excellent spaghetti. Off at one, and so on through Mediterranean; sea perfectly calm and warm sun. Lazed on deck with walks all the afternoon. Sunset gorgeous, and shot colours mauve, orange, and deep indigo in sea quite indescribable. Of course there is a certain amount of discomfort here. No accommodation, and if we have bad

Orlo at sea (Family collection).

weather it will be ward room or nothing. The quarter deck is very small and that is the only place to walk in. Still we had little to complain for and are enjoying ourselves.

One advances in acquaintance with the others. I had a sunset walk with Dawnay whom I found very attractive. He had been at Oxford, then army and staff college, was a financier when war broke out, and since then working in MT2.[11] We talked chiefly about literature of which we found much common ground. Bolton is very good fellow

11 Training Section, Directorate of Military Training, Department of the Chief of the Imperial General Staff.

too. He was at Oxford a year. Also made acquaintance with Colonel Williams in the train. He has been nearly all his active life in India, and had come home to take a training appointment in Wales. Since war has been at Cambridge with Welsh Territorial Division. He came away so quick that he was in the Mediterranean before his wife could get a letter saying where he was. He is another very charming person, who knows Colin Campbell. Very pleasing to have him say how he had enjoyed living at Cambridge, and how interesting he found the young dons. Very creditable to both parties.

Tuesday 16 March 1915

Perfect weather continues. I slept splendidly through right over the propeller which roared and rumbled all night. We passed Straits of Bonifacio last night and Stromboli about 11.30 this morning. Up on deck since breakfast, watching gun drill etc. and now writing this. Also reading *Manual of Combined Naval and Military Operations* which we are all supposed to study. Lazed on deck all afternoon. Passed the Straits of Messina 1–1.30 pm. Rather pathetic to see the General propped up most uncomfortably against a casemate dozing and reading a magazine. After tea had a long pace up and down with the Captain—a very charming person, good looking, tall, thin and clean shaven, Cameron by name. After first dinner stood on deck with Dawnay and Aspinall without coat or muffler. Before bed down to see the engines with Chief Engineer. Marvel of compactness and fearfully hot. 40,000 H.P. in 3000-ton ship.

Wednesday 17 March 1915

Up before 7 to see Greek coast to port. Weather still perfect. All morning sailing up the islands past Gulfs of

Nauplia, Aegina, and foot of Euboea. Due Lemnos at 1 pm or so. Unknown after that.

Nothing eventful till just after 3, after gradually approaching the Turkish coast, we rounded the southern corner of Tenedos and then with extraordinary suddenness, instead of sailing on a lonely sea, we came into a world full of life. In the roadstead of Tenedos lay a whole fleet, two liners hospital ships, French and English, then two French battleships, and then our own fleet. Among others were the *Vengeance, Indomitable, Blenheim, Albion, Swiftsure, Agamemnon*, and *Queen Elizabeth*, and *Dartmouth* came in with General d'Amade the same moment as we did. The *Queen Elizabeth* with her enormous beam and eight 15-inch guns a wonderful sight. The scene was magnificent. A brilliant sun which gradually sank lit up the opposite coast. Through glasses one could plainly see the entrance to the Straits, with the forts of Kum Kale on one side and Sedd el Bahr on the other. Destroyers and other ships came and went in the offing. The coast there comparatively low with hills rising inland. One or two little villages visible. To the north Imbros ran straight across, a dark hilly mass. To the east the low island of Tenedos with its antiquated fort and windmills and all the rest of the fleet. There was the *Ark Royal* there too, and a seaplane from her sailed round us. Also a submarine. There were innumerable things to stare at through glasses, especially the opposite shore where lay the field of battle. It was almost impossible to believe the enemy was there waiting for us. No scene was ever more beautiful and serene. The General went off to a conference on the *Queen Elizabeth*, and we sat about. At 7 a boat from her came for me, and off I went with a cipher. I immediately set to on a long message giving results of conference. Admiral de Robeck in command. I.H. [Hamilton] great confidence in him. Difficulties the good preparations of enemy. Only time to snatch a hasty bite before I had to be off, the others having dined while I was working. Saw where shrapnel shell came through into ward room. The *Queen Elizabeth* off to bombard tomorrow. *Phaeton* taking our party and General d'Amade to see northern coast. Brodrick, Braithwaite Jr and I to stay behind and take up gear and quarters in *Franconia* where we shall all be. It will be odd to meet the Marquis[12] as I suppose I shall. Have just been on deck, to see in the distance the Turkish searchlights and to hear guns from time to time. Almost impossible to believe this is only Wednesday, and I was in London on Saturday.

Thursday 18 March 1915

Woke up to find ourselves in Mudros Bay, Lemnos Island, among all the transports of the RND, the French division, and the Australian brigade on shore. Lemnos a picturesque island with low hills, a few villages, a large bay practically encircled by land. The days' plan to take General d'Amade on board and General Paris and sail over to look at Gallipoli peninsula.

Braithwaite Jr and I to come aboard *Franconia* where GHQ to be established. Churchill, Brodrick and Braithwaite Jr went off early with servants and baggage to get accommodation: got us all private cabins, and turned some of the RND out, which must have been a bore for them. After breakfast General Paris came on board with Captain Deedes, one of the neatest little men I ever saw, Lt. Col Doughty-Wylie and others. General Paris not a very impressive man; Marquis says too good natured. Then Admiral Wemyss arrived; a hearty rather choleric

12 Lieutenant Harry Bernard Wallis, Royal Marines. Orlo, who attended Balliol with Wallis, refers to him throughout the diary as both 'Marquis' and 'Wallis'.

individual with an eyeglass rather like George Grossmith. Talked like anything. Then General d'Amade and staff. The general a good looking man in blue uniform. Some delay in getting off owing to need to draft a telegram for me to send. Admiral Wemyss detained to take me back, got rather annoyed and when he finally did get me off fell foul of a boat's crew alongside. I to *Franconia* where did 3 telegrams and then looked about for means to get to the telegraph ship *Hussar*. Found General Mercer, brigadier of RND, and got loan of general's steam launch.

Orlo's sketch, 18 March:
'General impression from deck of *Fanconia*'

Lunch time. Went into saloon. Eustace Fiennes recognized my face and made me sit by him at Captain's table. General conversation; our voyage a matter of universal astonishment. Half way through lunch caught sight of half familiar face a little way off. It had a horrible moustache and stared like one who saw the devil. It was the Marquis. I winked and he expired. He came up after lunch and we had a long talk over coffee. Also met Cherry, Bill Farrer, Charles Lister. Heard of other Balliol men about. Comfortably unpacked kit after hearing what Mercer had to say, all grumble about RND, and enjoyed this luxurious hotel with its gymnasium and ale. HQ and 2 battalions of RND on this ship. Introduced to Lord Bangor, their divisional ordnance officer, Major Peel, APM, and so on. Long talk with Marquis about their voyage and his complaint of want of ginger in RND. No doubt that will be set to rights. We shall soon all be off to Egypt. No doubt of that from telegrams.

General not back by dinner. Dined at Bangor's table. Party returned about 8.30 having had interesting but not altogether joyful day. The Navy had had a big fight: 4 ships very badly damaged by mines. *Gaulois* ashore on Island of Rabbits,[13] *Ocean* and *Irresistible*, latter practically done for, *Inflexible* mined just got back to Tenedos escorted by *Phaeton*. *Phaeton* herself shelled by field guns 1 mile up the Straits. General impression Navy can't do it alone. More talk and so to bed.

Friday 19 March 1915

At 7.30 joined Marquis in gym did Swedish exercises with instructor and riding on machine, shave and bath. Two ciphers in just as sitting down to breakfast. Delayed meal till 9.30. Then one out, and other details. Staff organising office and setting to work. Nothing doing at present. General Birdwood expected. We have taken the library as GHQ. Very comfortable. RND lively looking men; all very cheery. Officers mostly young and inexperienced. Not particularly exciting day. A few telegrams. Just marking time. Determined to move Alexandria, but need to get Admiral's agreement. General military impression down on the Navy for trying to do too big a job without preparation. Also the sending out of 6 transports of RND last night to make a demonstration by Admiral condemned as silly.

Saturday 20 March 1915

Blowing a gale, and rough in harbour. Still no news of General Birdwood coming from Alexandria on *Doris*. Hardly possible to walk deck forward. Certain number of

13 Rabbit Island.

wires which had to come and go by flag from and to *Hussar*. First one woke me out of bed at 3.30 a.m. Rather sore owing to blister from riding machine. Lot of rather useless hanging about. Chief event of the day was a Balliol dinner which was a very cheery business. We were the following: H. M. Farrer, F. R. Henley, P. Kershaw, C. Lister, H.B. Wallis, Brodrick and self. We drank Lanson,[14] which you get here at 6/ a bottle and was most excellent. Port followed. Then we went to the saloon and captured the piano and made a godless row singing till after 11. The ribald ditty about the hedgehog, sung to the tune of the Tarpaulin Jacket, had an immense success. Very merry and hearty time.

Sunday 21 March 1915

Admiral Wemyss to see the General. Gen. Birdwood on *Doris* outside. Fine day with some wind. Navy ships boats blown ashore last night very careless work on somebody's part. Beautiful weather till 3.30 then came on to blow hard and got cold. A few telegrams but nothing much decided. General Birdwood and Major Wagstaff arrived on board and I discarded to cabin on D deck without port hole. Birdwood a neat little man with cheery face. General impression from conversations with others that Army has little faith in strategy of Navy, and that to do things as they have been being done is impossible. Naval guns can't touch the howitzers, and whenever Navy cease bombarding enemy make new defences and put down more mines. The chief loss of Thursday the *Bouvet*, who sank in 45 seconds. Only 66 saved out of 750. An officer observing her says she dived straight under water like a submarine. The *Queen Elizabeth* fired 170 rounds. Navy say that scheme went very well at first: i.e. 4 heavy ships did preliminary bombardment, then *Ocean* etc. came in closer and did well; only

14 Champagne.

Members of General Sir Ian Hamilton's staff, Mudros, March/April 1915.

Above, left to right: 2nd Lieutenant Braithwaite ('Braithwaite Jr'), Captain Pollen and Major John 'Jack' Churchill, brother of Winston Churchill, then First Lord of the Admiralty and instigator of the Campaign.

Lieutenant Brodrick at ease with a book in Mudros Bay.
In the background, the five thin funnels of Russian cruiser *Askold*.

(O.C. Williams, IWM)

the mine sweepers would not face it when their turn came to go up. They don't fear mines, but they can't stand shell and rifle fire. General I.H. says the leading mine sweeper retiring was firing hard at the others to make them return. Army anyhow going to reorganize at Alexandria and load transports properly. 29th Division to reorganize at Malta and come straight here. We are hung up till French Government are persuaded to order French Division back to Alexandria. D'Amade won't go without orders.

Spent afternoon playing chess with Bolton and won. It will be a good thing for the RND when they return to shore. It is too soft a life here and too many cocktails drank.

Monday 22 March 1915

Still blowing and still waiting. Telegraphing to a certain extent. General d'Amade called in the morning while Sir I[an] on board *Queen Elizabeth*. Poor old chap had a long wait, and we all took turns at talking to him. A charming and distinguished man. Signalling here very bad and shortage of boats. We meant to go over the *Queen Elizabeth*, but several including myself got tired of waiting. I had tea at the General's table. He most affable. I introduced subject of *Sinister Street*[15] of which he is reading Volume II. Sir I[an] said he knew Monty,[16] and when I told him he had tried for a commission in Egypt, he told me at once to write to him and tell him that if he would get into communication with Eddie Marsh and get set out as a Marine or what not, he would give him a job. Sir I[an] would write to Marsh. Came in for a very jovial dinner. General dinning aboard *Queen Elizabeth*. Doughty-Wylie, a jovial ... ex consul Addis Ababa, and one of [the] intelligence officers, dinning General Paris, and stood fizz to all at same table. I was

15 A book by Compton Mackenzie.

16 Orlo's name for Compton Mackenzie.

inspired thereafter to write the ditty "Staff Duties", to pull the leg of Aspinall and Dawnay. Poem had a great success.[17]

Tuesday 23 March 1915

Began ciphering 7 a.m. and had quite a busy morning of it. At lunch the General said he had noticed a great change in me since I first came; said I must have put on 6 or 7 lb already. Must be weighed tomorrow. In afternoon fenced with foils and sabres in gym and rode for ¼ of an hour. Major Grant told me at tea that he and Fuller propose to give me some regular staff work to do. This is very good news and just what I hoped for. Cipher all very well but not enough for me. Five ships of RND start today. We still held up through not hearing about the French. Shall all be very glad when we start.

Must again express my appreciation of the pleasantness and comradeship of colleagues of the other officers on the staff. What I should have missed had I only been in the RND. Perhaps a selfish point of view, as they will do the fighting. But one can't help liking what one likes. Churchill,[18] of course, is rather a loud talker, with some of Winston's weak points without his cleverness. But that's all. I should say a bold front would always knock him out.

People at home would perhaps not believe how officers on service talk of their families, their children in particular, and how obviously that is their great joy in life. I had a long talk with Colonel Williams yesterday about children's education, apropos of his daughter of 5 and mine. Today Pollen talked to me quite lyrically of his 3 children, saying they were far the best thing that ever happened to him, and how they played and how different they were. He told me to try one experience on them. One fine night tell them

17 The poem is at Annex 1.

18 Major John Churchill.

you were going to show them something they had never seen before. Then at 10.30 wrap them up in blankets and show them a starlit sky... a good idea.

Captain Deedes and Captain Lloyd MP
(O.C. Williams, IWM).

Sunday 28 March 1915

In the train. Have been lazy at my diary for 4 days partly owing to having had a good deal of work to do on the ships and subsequently to the crowd of events.

Up to Friday 26th events may be briefly recorded.

Having had a satisfactory reply from London we sailed *Wednesday 24 March* from Lemnos about 1 p.m. bound for Alexandria, whither we are going together with RND and the French, who received orders from Paris, so that

Captain Mitchell RN, liaison officer, and Major-General Braithwaite, Hamilton's Chief of Staff.

Captain Dawnay, Lieutenant-Colonel Aspinall and Major Grant.

(O.C. Williams, IWM)

the troops may be disembarked and the transports re-arranged so that units may be able to land on [Gallipoli] peninsula complete. Harbour of Lemnos too primitive for this work. The 29th Division to do the same at Malta. Cold wind was still blowing when we started but sun came out, and very pleasant to feel the ship moving. Was inoculated against typhoid at 9 p.m. for the 1st time by Fleet-Surgeon Gaskell RND, together with Aspinall and Dawnay. Slept well but felt pains all *Thursday 25 March* with sore chest, where I was pricked. No worse symptoms and hardly any fever. Kept quiet most of the day and played a good deal of chess. Several telegrams came to us by wireless and on Thursday night was aroused several times because our course was changed by wireless and I had to do the deciphering of message and enciphering of answer. We were told to go Port Said instead of Alexandria. I had to wake up the Captain and tell him. We made one protest, but having again received same order, proceeded to Port Said. It was then 5 a.m. bright stars and the Pharos of Alexandria stirring in the offing. Warm enough to go on bridge only in overcoat and pyjamas.

Friday 26 March felt perfectly well again and did my exercises. Busy morning enciphering long wire which was afterwards cancelled. The plan was that the General [Hamilton] and Pollen, with CGS [Braithwaite] and his son, Ward and Aspinall were to go up to Cairo for 2 days to visit Maxwell and see various others. Doubtful at first whether I was to go too, but finally decided that I was. It turned out that we were switched off to Port Said because Malta was unable to undertake rearrangement of 29th Division, they were going on to Alexandria. We arrived off Port Said breakwater about 3 p.m. My first view of the real east: Lateen sails, Arabs in cassocks, whatever they call them, and palm trees. Our party went ashore at once and left at 4 in a special [train] for Cairo with Birdwood, Majors Wagstaff and Hancock and Captain Mitchell. Very comfortable journey with ten on board. The line goes for considerable distance along the canal with the desert on both sides. There was an excellent mirage for my inexperienced eyes, and later on a most gorgeous crimson sunset which gave the eastern sky and the desert wonderful tints. Very interesting to see the trenches and gun emplacements for the [Suez] Canal defences, also the Indian soldiers and their camps, especially at El Kantara where [there is] a large camp. Also saw from the window the remains of the famous lines of Tel el Kebir. Arrived at Cairo about 8. Railway station gave one impression of being in the White City...

Were met by motors and taken to the famous Shepheard's [Hotel] where Birdwood has his HQ. Had a comfortable room, bed with mosquito curtains; dined at table reserved for Birdwood's staff. General impression of the hotel after 2 days that it was a beastly place, of course, there are no fashionable people in it. Only a few rusty looking civilians and the HQ. A good many troops of all ranks come in to meals. The waiting shocking: nearly all done by Egyptians in picturesque costume, red jackets, white baggy trousers and tarboosh, but no earthly use at waiting and smell of garlic. Chief time when hotel filled was Saturday tea, when band played from 4.30 to 6.30, and all kinds of odd nuts and impossible females turned up to sit in the verandah which looks on to one of the main streets. Still for the first night dinner was good enough and Pollen stood a bottle of Mouton Rothschild. After dinner saw George Lloyd MP in hotel—he was serving in Intelligence Department—and Keeling (late King's Scholar of Eton) who, being in diplomatic service, is now in Residency. He wants to be Turkish interpreter with us and I was able to introduce him next day to Colonel Ward who may be able to put it through.

After dinner up some time helping Ward with Secret Service ciphers from Athens. Very difficult to get over the oddness of the situation. Here was I, Captain Williams, doing Secret Service ciphers in Cairo, where I had never dreamed of going, in a hotel I had never expected to know except by reputation.

Conversation with Onslow, Birdwood's ADC, at dinner revealed to me the fact that soldiers in Egypt were not over-pleased at the passive resistance made a few weeks ago to the big Turkish attack.[19] No effort, as I knew, was made to pursue and round them up, but what I didn't know was that people in Egypt were disgusted about it, and nobody knew where the blame lay. No cavalry went out, and a mysterious order seems to have gone all down the line, originating nobody knows where, that there was to be no counter attack. There has been a little fighting off and on since, but the Turks always get away with all their wounded.

Saturday 27 March (yesterday) was a lovely morning, too much of which was spent in hanging about till wires came in from the General, who was staying with Maxwell. Meant to go out and do a bit of shopping but only got off at 12.30 and then wasted ½ an hour waiting while the CGS and his son were photographed together. After that straight back to lunch. After lunch went with Pollen, Ward, and young Braithwaite to pay official call at Residency. As Braithwaite had a photo for Lady McMahon we were asked in and shook hands with her. Then passed out on to very pretty garden overlooking the Nile. Back to tea and band at hotel. Then set out with CGS and son, Aspinall and Ward in one of Birdie's[20] cars to Pyramids, about 10 miles off. A camp of Australians at the bottom of the pyramids

19 This refers to the Ottoman attack on the Suez Canal, 3 February 1915.

20 Lieutenant-General Birdwood.

and hosts of them along the road. Found Pyramids more impressive than I expected, though disappointed in hoped for sunset effect, as heavy cloud coming up. Walked towards Sphinx. A guide of course attached himself to us and an army of rascally Arabs followed us with camels and donkeys. I stopped to try and take a photo and when I got up to the others found them in the midst of a hawking mob, all the Arabs yelling, all the camels braying like diseased trombones, and donkeys and drivers jostling the party to get them into the saddle—all because the CGS had got on to a donkey. So there was nothing for it—a camel knelt down for me to [get] on and nearly threw me off when it knelt up again. So jogged on to Sphinx and dismounted to see underground Temple of Cephus—really very remarkable with its enormous monoliths of stone and alabaster. Back on camel to the car and drove back in the dark. After dinner went with jolly party of officers, Aspinall, Wagstaff, Hancock, Mitchell, and the Australian APM to Kursaal. Usual French music hall show good gymnasts, 4 Cockney girls who clogged, and a French chanteur[21]—he excellent—sang Tipperary in French and an impassioned ditty about "*Vive le roi Albert, vive le bon roi*".[22] Heat intense, and intenser at 2 dancing halls where we went later. Rather disgusting and mournful places. Dreadful collection of worn tarts doing bunny hugs with tarbooshes and a few officers. Don't like to see a uniform doing that kind of thing. Back very thirsty 1 a.m. Cairo seemed a pretty dirty, smelly kind of place by then.

Today (28th) out for a walk with Ward to take photos. Spent some time in Egyptian WO Intelligence Department where George Lloyd and Major Newcombe [are

21 Singer.

22 Translation: 'Long live King Albert, long live the good king'.

based]. Saw Turkish deserter brought in and questioned as to whereabouts of Turkish regiments. He looked a pretty good ruffian. Question how to use him without letting him see too much. Lloyd and Newcombe don't think much of WO Intelligence. Walked over Kasr el Nil bridge and took one or two photos of garden on opposite side. Back to hotel to lunch and lazy afternoon. Finally off by 6.35 train to Alexandria. Dined on train.

Just been talking to Aspinall who has apparently done a certain amount of writing on military subjects. Was correspondent of [the London] *Standard* in Ashanti and did Bulgar-Turkish War for *The Pioneer* in India. Would it do to collaborate with him over this show? Possibly could get good terms from a big publisher.

Another feature of Cairo—fresh cigarettes. Certainly very good, but got rather a throat yesterday smoking too many. Must not give up pipe.

Monday 29 March 1915

Alexandria. Staff quartered at Savoy Palace Hotel, Rue de la Porte Rosette. GHQ address, Hotel D'Angleterre, 18 Rue.

Chief business of today settling into our new GHQ and getting things straight. The ASC people here have taken for us a large, bare house just off Place Saint Cathérine, quite 15 minutes walk from the Hotel.[23] It is an old house, not inhabited for some time, its doors and windows and shutters rattle and are decayed. The drainage system quite impossible, no light laid on or water, and the first day some of the staff visited the place they were severely assailed by fleas. However by today it had been scrubbed out, the local ASC had supplied tables with blankets for cloths, and our clerks had produced their stationary. Things gradually got

23 Orlo sidelined it: 'Subsequently heard it was a well known disorderly house'.

into shape, and the O[perations] branch of the GS settled into one large room on the first floor. Maps of Gallipoli set out in middle of room, and I artistically erected 2 maps (large scale and small) of Alexandria on the walls.

There being no light laid on, when 7 o'clock drew near the poor staff had to work by candles stuck on to envelopes. I was busy all day getting the cipher telegrams in order in the files and their right jackets, and for an interlude drove ... to the Arsenal to get a wire sent off by Admiral's staff.

Bareness and want of fittings matters little here because the climate is so perfect. Hot sun, beautifully cool wind all day and intense blue sky. They say it is exactly like Indian cold weather. Only regret that so much time is spent in office instead of out of doors and sea bathing which would be the pleasure seeker's programme now. But work has begun in earnest now. We reach the office soon after 9 and continue with intervals for lunch and tea till nearly 8. ... This evening the C in C having reviewed the A&NZ AC[24] arrived at Alexandria. Told me he had written to Eddie Marsh about Monty so I posted my letter to the latter [see below].

C in C is going to have Rupert Brooke the poet, now in RND, as his 3rd ADC.

Have been very lame owing to boots rubbing ankles (This led to my first getting a pair of French boots that didn't do, and then a pair of English shoes, very extravagant).

Naturally there are degrees of enlightenment on the staff. Dawnay, Deedes and Fuller on highest plane, I should say. Dawnay said to me that 10 years ago he never thought he should ever sit with 2 soldiers like Deedes and Fuller one on each side of him: said it still always surprised him to find an intelligent soldier, but things had progressed a lot in our generation. Aspinall is a very good man at his job and no

24 An early version of ANZAC.

fool at all, and seen a good deal, but far less cultivated intellectually. He amused me tonight at dinner by declaiming against politics as a game and a pretence, by denouncing Lloyd George for his land schemes when he knew nothing about land and at the end of all calmly saying "But I'm a soldier and have no politics". What *do* people mean who say that especially when they have a most obvious sentimental bias in one direction? I suppose if pressed they would deny that they didn't care how their country was governed, but it really comes to that. It was my own attitude once, but interest in politics, though I am still more a spectator than anything, has come to me in spite of myself.

* * *

Compton Mackenzie, having returned to Capri from England after failing to get a commission, received a letter from 'my old friend Orlo Williams' on 4 April 1915. The letter was dated 23 March 1915, and was written whilst on board RMS Franconia. It read:

'I don't know when this will get to you, but I am writing to you by order of Sir Ian Hamilton, Commander-in-Chief of the Mediterranean Expeditionary Force. I'm cipher officer on his Staff with the rank of Captain, having left London at twenty-eight hours' notice. Well, I noticed a day or two ago that he [i.e. Hamilton] had brought Vol. II of Sinister Street to read. So when I was in conversation with him I told him I knew you, etc., and that you had tried for a commission in Egypt. So he said at once, 'Write to him and tell him to get into communication with Eddie Marsh and get sent out to me as a Marine or anything, and I will find him a job of some kind, sub-cipher officer or something like that.' He says that if I write to you, he will write to Marsh. So there you are. He told me to write to you again to-day, so I am doing it. Our mail went the day before yesterday when the next will go

I can't say. But if you take the opportunity and feel up to it do come. The General Staff are a charming set of people, and the possibilities of this show are romantic to a degree.'[25]

* * *

Tuesday 30 March 1915

Perfect weather as usual and [I spent] all day in the office where a fair number of telegrams [were sent]. Also I am taking over the War Diary which is a summary of chief events, telegrams and letters. The chief business at GHQ is on the part of O(a), Colonel Williams, Aspinall, Dawnay and Bolton. They have got a tremendously complicated and difficult piece of staff work before them to do very quickly. They have got to work out very carefully exactly how the force is to be embarked, how its supply etc. is to be managed, what special fittings and arrangements are necessary in view of the special problem of the Gallipoli peninsula. Also there is the problem of the landing of the covering force, to be formed by the 29th Division. Captain Mitchell RN is attached to the staff to assist in naval matters and they are all deep in details of tugs, tows, lighters and horse boats. How many men each will hold, how long the round trip will take, how horses, bicycles, transport, guns and ammunition are to be landed and in what order. The plan is to land on the point of Cape Helles I believe. I rather gather that Aspinall and Co. find Colonel Williams the GSO1 rather in the way.

Half the 29th Division have arrived with their HQ. General Hunter-Weston in command. The camp is at [El] Mex about 10 miles away along the narrow spit between

25 Compton Mackenzie, *Gallipoli Memories*, Cassell and Company, London, 1929, pp. 7-8.

the lake and the sea. HQ live at the Savoy, and have office at the Excelsior Hotel. Hunter-Weston, whom all call a thruster and who has done very well in France, is a vivacious loud voiced man with lots to say: hook nose, large moustache and wide mouth and bushy brows. His GSO1 is Colonel Wolley-Dod. Our A&Q[26] staff still not arrived. We are all longing for the arrival of the *Arcadian*.

The French division is encamped at Ramleh, about 8 miles away NE, where I much hope to go and see them. The RND have remained at Port Said rearranging. Some ½ battalions sent for 3 nights to bridge head camp at Kantara.

Alexandria strikes me as a much pleasanter place than Cairo: a wealthy commercial city well built and ideally situated. The streets much cleaner and less scamps and pimps about. Far less oriental than Cairo.

The gallant [Jack] Churchill has come out in a GHQ brassard of red and blue, and is very proud of himself. Aspinall says he is not really entitled to one. The ADC's have followed his example, and I don't believe they are either.

Wednesday 31 March 1915

Not very much to record.

Aspinall went to see his regiment today (the Munsters) and was much amused to find his pals sick as mud. On enquiring why, they said "It's damnable being switched off here. We wanted to go to the Gallipoli show. Hear we're to be here 6 months". They will know it alright when they form the covering force.

... an amusing censorship episode on the *Fanconia*. A telegram presented for a feminine recipient: "It must be all or nothing. I don't want friendship".

26 The Adjutant General's and Quartermaster General's Branches of GHQ.

Written 9 April 1915 9.30 pm on deck of SS Arcadian

Have done no more than keep my note book going since the 31st owing to having a good deal of work while we were at Alexandria. The average office day at GHQ was from 9.30 am till 8 pm with intervals for meals and one only felt inclined to sit round and talk in the lounge of the Savoy after dinner. Now we are nearing Mudros again in the *Arcadian*, and I have had practically 48 hours respite, though my 2nd inoculation has prevented its being quite as pleasant a rest as it would otherwise have been.

Thursday 1 April. The A&Q staff arrived. General Woodward with Major Gascoigne and Captain McLeod. General Winter QMG. A project for destroying viaduct and railway near Balikesir and Azizich was sanctioned by wire to Doughty-Wylie, who thereupon asked for rifles and ammunition.

It was settled that A&NZ AC were to start embarking on 4th [of April] and 29th Division on 6th. General Staff to leave in *Arcadian* on the 7th and use the ship as GHQ.

There was some idea of getting a permanent office waiter for some of us on the GS and today a man recommended by the Hotel waiter came to GHQ. I struggled with him in Italian, and after some time arrived at the fact that he wanted too much and was not at all the kind of man we wanted.

Walking back from office Colonel Williams said to me "if you write a book, mind you rub it in that though all the books insist that surprise is the chief factor in all operations of this kind, here we have been slogging away for 6 weeks and all possibility of surprise is gone. All the work we are doing now ought to have been done in England, and though we have gained valuable experience by rearranging the transports locally, I believe if it had all been properly done in England we should have done the whole thing (i.e. the landing) in a day".

Other arrivals. Powell the Censor, Etonian, and Maxwell, the *Daily Mail* correspondent as his assistant. The latter a *good appointment.*[27] Rather amusing that for 12 years Northcliffe had been paying him a retainer of £1000 a year to do this war, and has got nothing out of it. Also arrived General Roper CRE and General Fuller CRA.

Saturday 3 April. Wire from WO that Russian Expeditionary Force to be one AC [Army Corps] under General Istomine; Russian fleet to be under Admiral Eberhardt.

The landing scheme getting more or less settled. Main objective [is the village of] Krithia. Attack further along at same time. Other arrivals. Captain de Putron, very pleasant being who is liaison officer with French division and Major Bigham our Provost Marshal.

This evening with Fuller, Grant and Mitchell to the Opera in a box. Not at all a bad little Italian company from Milan. They did 2 acts of Don Pasquale (Donizetti) and then Pagliacci. The baritone in the latter, and the basso comico and tenor in former were excellent.

Sunday 4 April. The weather changed to stuffiness with overcast sky which made work rather unpleasant. Met Walter Cheatle at the Union Club at tea. He in 1 KOSB's. Had heard of my job. Thought Sir Ian's was divisional command and that d'Amade was boss of the show. Corresponds with Apsinall's account of ignorance of his regiment and Colonel Williams who said that *his* had not the vaguest idea where they were going.

Apropos of the plan. A long wire arrived from K[28] last night suggesting an idea which is ours in every detail. In answering, General [Hamilton] pointed out that ammunition, especially for destroying barbed wire, was our chief deficiency.

27 Next to this Orlo wrote: 'Subsequent events did not justify this remark'.

28 Lord Kitchener.

The French expeditionary force. *Chasseurs d'Afrique* in camp at Alexandria (O.C. Williams, IWM).

Settled that Keeling to come for additional cipher [with the] rank [of] lieutenant.

Monday 5 April. Stuffy again. Easter Monday and most shops shut. Streets dusty owing to people driving out to races. General reviewed French troops and told me later the *coup d'oeil* was splendid. In afternoon motored out with Ward and de Putron to the French HQ. They have the Victoria College at Ramleh, a splendid building, large and airy. French troops encamped all round it. Present at interview between Ward and [a] Colonel who was head of *Bureau de Renseignement*[29] about censorship, press correspondents, ciphers etc. The 2 colonels a great contrast. The French vivacious and dramatic, suggested shooting all correspondents etc., Ward stodgy to a degree, and at the end I had simply to push his hand into the French colonels. My first letter from England (mother) arrived today.

29 Bureau of Intelligence.

Tuesday 6 April. Chief event, my first letter from A[lice].

Wednesday 7 April. Spent most of morning shutting up the GS office and hanging about. Missed my chance of getting hair cut. Then, after nearly leaving my letter case with £5 in it behind, drove a long way to the Timber Quays where the *Arcadian* was lying. Truly a wonderful sight at the docks. Transports crowded side by side and troops and baggage embarking the whole time. To think that few know where they are going and where they will, so many of them, meet their fate.

In many ways the *Arcadian,* RMSP, is a comfortable ship. She is fitted only for 1st class passengers and is used for the Norway cruises. The deck is really good for walking, and we have got proper offices. But there are drawbacks. The ventilation is bad in cabins etc. and the food beastly as I expected. Very few stewards, so our servants have to look after cabins. Also on board HQ Signal Company, and 1 printing section, and General's escort of 100. With one or two others had 2nd inoculation. Sore arm. The A&Q staff [to] come later. Very nice Colonel Manifold, DAS and Major Evans of Signal Company. Also George Lloyd and Keeling with us.

3 letters from darling A[lice] and 1 from Gwennie.

Thursday 8 April. Sailed all day. Same motion which did for Bolton and young Braithwaite. Self rather rotten with sore arm and stupid head.

Friday 9 April. Same as 8th. Still very sore. Weather rather hazy and cloudy. Not very good for Greek islands.

Saturday 10 April 1915

Arrived about 6 a.m. in Mudros Bay where we anchored in a much better berth opposite Mudros village. The morning was extraordinarily beautiful with a silvery haze rising off the hills and the sun just breaking through and lighting up the impressive cluster of shipping in the harbour. Besides a good number of transports, store ships etc. there were then in the bay 8 British ships of war and 4 TBDs, including *Queen Elizabeth*, *Implacable*, *Cornwallis*, *Minerva*, *Ark Royal*, *Grasshopper*, and *Fouvette*. The *Lord Nelson* and *Dartmouth* arrived later in the day... There were also the French battleships *Henri IV* and *Jauréguiberry*. The latter with her very odd shape lying very near the *Arcadian*. Today 33 British transports in the bay, and 11 French. At the close there will be 109 British ships altogether. Wonderful exhibition of sea power.

HMS *Arcadian*, Mudros, April 1915 (O.C. Williams, IWM).

4 naval officers, Captain Dent PNTO and 3 others came to live on board today and confer with the GS about the landing. They were conferring in the GS room all the afternoon, and it was an interesting conversation to listen to.

Heard of the two dummy battleships *Tiger* and *Invincible* which have been rigged up near the Dardanelles.

Sunday 11 April 1915

Lloyd at lunch told some interesting things of his work in the Intelligence at Cairo. On one occasion 2 agents told him of presence of a Turkish officer at a cinema. So he sent for police and went to cinema, all dark, and no means of seeing the man, *entr'acte* due in 5 minutes and several exits. They got on to stage and waited till lights went up. Then they saw another agent sitting behind the man and trying to point to him most cautiously. Both agents very frightened of being seen, as they had been in Turkish army, and went about with their handkerchiefs up to their faces. Man safely arrested. Another time, when they wanted the Turks to come on, a pocket book was filled with official looking papers, and a bogus letter from General Maxwell to the Intelligence saying that for next 3 weeks Egypt would be greatly denuded of troops, and that they must keep him extra well informed. This pocket book was carefully dropped, and an Arab deputed to see that other Arabs took it to the Turks. A great fuss was made about the loss, and a search party sent out. The ruse was successful, and brought on the Turks.

At 3.30 Colonel Ward, Major Delacombe, Lloyd, Pollen and others including myself went ashore at Mudros. Mudros itself full of activity, as Australian camp there, also French Senegalese troops and French base. Greek traders had set up wooden booths near the landing where they sold all manner of things. We walked on to another village

Mudros, 11 April 1915. View from the sea, Greek traders in the town and French colonial infantry (O.C. Williams, IWM).

about 3 miles off, and there, it being Sunday, come on a fiesta. In the open space round the village well, a group of men were dancing in a chain, very much as they danced in Corfu, to the sound of mandolins and other instruments. The village priest and a few veterans sat outside a house in the centre on rough wooden stools, and away on the other side of the well sat the women and children. We came and

Major Delacombe, Army Pay Corps officer, GHQ, walking on Mudros (O.C. Williams, IWM).

sat down on the stones of the well. Then the priest signed to us to come up and sit with him, which we did. Lloyd and he conversed in Turkish, and he had coffee brought for us. There we sat for ½ an hour. As we returned we met a Major and Havildar of an Indian Mountain Battery. The Indian much intrigued the village people. We found our boat had gone when we got to the landing stage, but did not mind waiting a bit amid the bustle. We saw Admiral Guépratté go off in his own cutter, manned by matelots with their picturesque red pom poms. The Admiral after a tremendous deal of saluting got aboard, seized the tiller himself, ordered the sails to be hoisted, and so sheered gallantly off, though a little difficulty involving the main sheet and the tiller rather spoiled the effect. We saw a seaplane going round the harbour, and it was said that a Taube was sighted.

Monday 12 April 1915

The *Bacchante* and *Euryalus* arrived. The *Queen Elizabeth* took out a large number of officers to look at the northern coast of the peninsula though the real reason of the voyage was to test her engines.

Several more officers, beach masters, came to stay on board [the *Arcadian*].

Before dinner talked [while] pacing the deck with Lloyd. Asked him what he thought of probable effects of war. He settled on the near Eastern part of it. Expressed strong view that this expedition a great mistake, and that we should have strengthened the Red Sea force and advanced on Bagdad, at the same time seizing Alexandretta, which could have been easily done. Lloyd, however, does not impress me as a very sound thinker. He jumps rather hastily at conclusions, and seems to see only the side of things that especially interests him.

Deedes, who knows much more about the east than he, thinks we are doing the right thing.

Tuesday 13 April 1915

The first really wet day since we left London. Only cleared up at sunset. The wind has blown incessantly, which will be very tiresome if it continues.

Wednesday 14 April 1915

Weather beautifully fine again, but still the annoying fresh breeze from the South. Coaling begun on this ship which necessitates promenade deck being all covered in

Loading coal into HMS *Arcadian* (O.C. Williams, IWM).

with canvas, which is stuffy. My digestion, owing to too little exercise, suffering rather. Saw Pirie-Gordon after dinner. He is intelligence officer on the *Doris* and seems to have been having a splendid time since November, filibustering on the Syrian coast. He gave a very amusing account of the ultimatum to Alexandretta which resulted in the blowing up of 2 engines on the railway. It was all very like comic opera apparently, for they had no explosives and had to borrow the ship's, and they had nobody who knew explosives, so it was decided that a ship's officer as representing His Britannic Majesty should lay the charge, and the same officer, temporarily representing the Sultan, should apply the match. The Turks tried a good deal of delay and finesse, but they were frightened out of their lives with a 10 minute ultimatum, and sent the engines down the line. The party in the cutter had to go after them and took the harbour master, whom they put into the sea, minus boots and swords, to go and stop the engines. When all was finally done and the harbour masters got back, he said meekly "populacy much excited: please do go away".

Orlo took many pictures of the Allied fleet in Mudros Bay (O.C. Williams, IWM).

Top: *Cressy*-class armoured cruiser, either HMS *Euryalus* or *Bacchante*, with HMS *London* and troopships in the distance. Centre: HMS *Cornwallis* (right) with seaplane carrier HMS *Ark Royal* (left). Bottom: French destroyer *Coutelas*.

Today the force orders at which O(a) have been so desperately working were issued, minus dates and times, to those they concerned. Very interesting reading they make, and it is to be hoped they will be successfully carried out.

Sunday 18 April 1915

Work during last few days has been considerably heavier. A batch of cipher telegrams always arrives about 11 p.m. keeping me out of bed. But I should say nothing to what is to come when field ciphers begin. The *Southland* with A&Q staff have arrived. *La Provence* also came with General d'Amade. The *Royal George* with HQ RND turned up yesterday evening bringing 300 stokers for landing purposes, and coming aboard to ask a few questions. Their rendezvous is Trebuki [Bay] as well as of French.

On the 15th HMS *Triumph* cruised out to shell barbed wire at extremity of peninsula. Grant and Brodrick aboard. In Morto Bay rather a shock for them to be hit 3 times by batteries, and the Captain's messenger wounded.

Wire from Marsh that Monty appointed lieutenant Royal Marines. Orders sent him to report BC [Base Commandant] Alexandria who was to send him to RND.

On the 16th came grave news that the *Manitou* with 147th Brigade RFA on board had been torpedoed by the Turks, one of their torpedo boats [*Demirhisar*] that had got to Smyrna having unexpectedly broken through the blockade. Luckily for us the affair turned out much better than it might have been. The *Manitou* arrived on 17th and Colonel Peel made his report. What happened was that at 10 a.m. a Turkish torpedo [boat] came alongside and Captain said he would give them 2 minutes to abandon ship. They said they had not enough boats, so were given 10 minutes. All boats lowered though 2 capsized and every available bit of wood thrown over, about 400 men got off

Allied fleet at anchor, Mudros, April 1915
(O.C. Williams, IWM).

ship one way or another. The TB fired 3 torpedoes all of which missed, and the SOS signal having been sent out and our ships coming up enemy made off. She was headed off and run ashore on Chio. The men were picked up, but there were 51 deaths from exposure and drowning. The same day one of our E submarines went ashore and was lost off Kephez Point. A sad loss. Expedition sent off to make sure she was destroyed. Turkish tug who tried to pull her off was blown into the air. Submarine finally destroyed by picket boats one of which was sunk.

Today went ashore with Fuller and Colonel Manifold the DAS and clambered up a hill. Very beneficial. Weather is getting much calmer, though cloudy and hazy at times. Morning and evening glassy calm in the harbour which is just what we want. We don't see much of Birdwood, but Hunter-Bunter,[30] as he is familiarly called, is often here. All say we are very lucky to have him. He is a very enthusiastic, energetic, determined man: more popular with men than officers. He has a striking face with very hooked nose and bushy eyebrows.

30 Major-General Hunter-Weston.

Birdwood a quiet looking little man, rather quaintly dressed with a very short tunic; in mufti he would look very insignificant. He is a Kitchener man and has been very well pushed by K who would have liked him to have this show to himself. There is a lot of jobbery and jealousy in the Army. Pollen was declaiming about it to me at tea the other day. He very annoyed at General [Hamilton]

General Sir Ian Hamilton and Lieutenant-Colonel Doughty-Wylie confer on deck (O.C. Williams, IWM).

sending for Monty. Told me it was true General only got the job definitely on March 11, Thursday, but it was the result of 10 days or more intriguing, cabinet meetings etc.

The Australian Division all here now (22 ships) and 14 out of 19 NZ&A Division. Also 13 of 29th Division out of 20.

Mails have come to us lately (chiefly arrears) so we have an indigestion of newspapers. Began lunch today with foie gras. What price hardships of campaign?

Monday 19 April 1915

The most lovely day we have yet had here: a summer day, still hot. Left off woolly waistcoat, though at 1 p.m. heard barometer was falling. Did little all day: dozed on deck and read Cornhill. Vaccinated. After breakfast composed poem 'The PNTO [pronounced 'Pinto'] and the PMLO [pronounced 'Pummelo']' which had a great success.[31]

Today conference on the *Queen Elizabeth* at which day of landing was, weather permitting, fixed for April 23 which means preliminary movement to begin on 21st. Staff to be broken up temporarily. Colonel Williams and Bolton go on to V Beach, also Doughty-Wylie who shares the great adventure of the *River Clyde*. Lloyd and Smith go up to Z [Beach].

Tuesday 20 April 1915

Still fine but blowing all day and bad sky in the evening. Not much in the way of events to record. All busy making ready for the moves. Hear with pleasure that with General, CGS, Ward, Fuller, am to go on board *Queen Elizabeth* when the day comes. After a lot of talk, especially from Hunter-Bunter instructions for 29th Division are altered.

Covering force to consist of 86th Brigade, half 87th and half battalion of 88th. Landing to be made in 4 trawlers on S, and also party in tows on Y besides all the others.

S [Beach]. 4 trawlers, 2 companies SWB.

Y [Beach]. KOSB and 1 company SWB and Plymouth Bn.

Rest divided between X, W, V ... First parties to land in tows and *River Clyde*. Remainder of covering force get on board fleet sweepers and so into tows.

Had hair cut, good short crop. General meeting me on deck before dinner exclaimed "Hello Cipher, you get younger every day".

31 The poem is at Annex 2.

SS *River Clyde* in Mudros Bay. On her port bow are clearly seen two of the eight sally ports cut into her side (O.C. Williams, IWM).

Wednesday 21 April 1915

As we feared. Gale and rain from NE, preliminary operations impossible. All off for at least 24 hours. Impossible to tow provision lighters to Tenedos today. Various people busy drawing mess tins, field dressings, water bottles, haversacks, and pistol ammunition. In drawing latter heard quite by chance my case sent off by Alice was resting with the COO at Alexandria. Promptly wired for it, and hope I shall get it soon. It is fairly obvious once we get going mails won't be very regular either way.

Thursday 22 April 1915

Fine day but still blowing sturdily. Postponed another 24 hours.

Friday 23 April 1915

Less wind and decided to proceed with things. At noon the *River Clyde,* called the Wooden Horse, left the harbour for Tenedos. Colonel Doughty-Wylie on board. At 4 three transports of ANZAC move outside the boom, and B1, B2, B3 sail from Mudros at 5. The excitement begins to get higher. People have drawn iron rations, field dressings, pistol ammunition etc. Bolton has gone off, fully accoutred, haversack and all on board the *Alannia* to join the *Implacable*, as he is [to] go with Colonel Williams on the beach. Lloyd and Smith will also leave soon. The *Queen Elizabeth* party are making preparations to go aboard tomorrow, prepared to land if necessary with iron rations and all completed and valises to sleep in on deck. We hope only to be a day or two but impossible to foresee anything. At the worst it might be for ever.

Will here make a summary of the landing scheme and events up to now.

The delay since we left England has been due 1st to slow arrival of troops in transports. 2. Necessity for reloading transports so that units could land complete. There was also delay in leaving Mudros 1st time owing to waiting for War Office sanction to go Alexandria, and for orders to d'Amade to go there. Since we have been here the transports have been rolling up. At Mudros there is the 29th Division—the last regular division of the British army—that is 10 regular battalions, 2 special reserve, under General Hunter-Weston. The A&NZ AC of which the 1st Australian Division is complete, the… NZ&A Division minus its mounted rifles brigade. There is also a battery of 75mm French guns here. At Trebuki assemble the RND and the French division which is partly *troops metropolitaines*, partly colonial.

The idea, which has been worked out in all detail between army and navy is to land on the Gallipoli peninsula and gain the heights of Kilid Bahr, so as to take the forts that command the Narrows and let the fleet get up. Two actual landings are to be made. The chief landing is given to the 29th Division on the point of the peninsula. Landings will be made on several beaches; at Y on NW coast, on W, V and X the principal beaches and a small landing of 2 companies somewhere about Morto Bay. The objective is the village of Krithia and the heights of Achi Baba about 500 ft high. The covering force consists of 86th Brigade, half 87th, half battalion of 88th, and 1 battalion of Anson (Marine) Battalion, RND. Most of the landings will be in tows from trawlers and Gun Boat Destroyers in the first instance and later from fleet sweepers. The most exciting show is the running ashore of the Wooden Horse with 2100 troops, Munsters, Royal Dublins. She is commanded by Captain Unwin and going to run it at speed of 10 knots.

The ANZAC covering force lands between Kaba Tepe and Fisherman's Hut, to gain a strong position further up the NE coast on the heights to prevent arrival of reinforcements. This all done from tows.

A demonstration to be made at the same time by the RND who are to feint at landing Kavajali on East Coast together with fleet bombardment of Bulair. Meanwhile French will land at Kum Kale with fleet demonstration in Besika Bay to prevent Asiatic forts from shelling if possible.

The main bodies of 29th and ANZAC will disembark immediately after covering force: RND and French await further orders.

The British fleet at present here: 15 battleships, 5 cruisers, 20 TBDs, some submarines; 2 French battleships, several TBDs and submarines.

1st Squadron and 4th under Wemyss

Euryalus—flag
Implacable
Cornwallis
Swiftsure
Albion
Vengeance
Lord Nelson
Prince George

Talbot
Minerva
Amethyst
Sapphire
8 TBDs
12 trawlers

2nd Squadron under Thursby

Queen—flag
London
Prince of Wales
Triumph
Majestic
Bacchante
Ark Royal
Manica
8 sweepers

3rd Squadron

Canopus
Doris
Dartmouth
2 TBDs and 6 trawlers

4th Squadron

Agamemnon
12 TBDs

6th Squadron

Jaureguiberry
Charlemagne
Henri IV
Askold

Saturday 24 April 1915

At 1 p.m. the General and Pollen, CGS and son, Aspinall, Dawnay, [Major] Fuller, General Fuller, Deedes, Churchill, self and Commander Douglas went on board *Queen Elizabeth*. She weighed at once and steamed slowly through all the transports and warships waiting in the outer harbour.

Aboard HMS *Queen Elizabeth*—four of her eight 15-inch guns (O.C. Williams, IWM).

HMS *Queen Elizabeth*, 24 April 1915 (O.C. Williams, IWM).

Top: General Sir Ian Hamilton (hands in pockets) with Major-General Braithwaite and Vice-Admiral de Robeck. Bottom: De Robeck and Hamilton.

It was a fine day and it was stirring slight. We made for Tenedos and just before we got there some excitement because the *Queen Elizabeth* made a sudden swerve having sighted a floating mine. This was fired at by a 3-pounder gun and sank without any explosion after several shots. Vicious yellow smoke came out of it. We anchored for a bit and then went on to Imbros where we arrived about 7.40 p.m.

HMS *Queen Elizabeth* drops anchor off Tenedos, 24 April 1915 (O.C. Williams, IWM).

Dined in the wardroom where all very cheery. The Staff Surgeon—a fat man rather like a comedian said to be the Lambeth Coroner—took me about, to bridge, engine room etc. Very difficult to find one's way about the ship. CGS sleeping in captain's cabin, Braithwaite [Jr] and I on the floor of his day cabin in our valises. Others in valises in other parts of ship. We had to be up early the next morning and did not have an over good night.

firing time stayed with Majestic Triumph, C
is over Sari Bair. The blast of 15" just und
t was fearful & blew my cap off every tim
y very unpleasant. After breakfast out
E. had stopped firing by 9. Rifle fire very
s of Sari Bair & shrapnel bursting in a
ed down to Cape Helles coming off Y &
ut 10 am.

report f. 29th div. that the troops on V. b
g in Seddel Bahr but d. not advance.
ath reported situation of Y force desperat
to wade to reembark them wh. was
e with all wounded stores & ammn.
oliath, Dublin, Amethyst & Sapphire. We
agement on Y from deck of Q.E. and
ps retiring. 400 casualties reported. R
div. reported not strong enough to ta
d V. beach. Arranged to order D'Amade
transports f. Tenedos & disembark
llowed by rest of brigade. This actually
ight of 26th.

QE steamed back to Kaba Tepe, & l
ch. On deck again at 2 we shooting
Sari Bair. Attack progressing left of
[illegible]

2

'BATTLE OF THE BEACHES'

THE LANDINGS AT GALLIPOLI

Having decided to use the Army and working out the plans, favourable weather finally arrived to allow the commencement of the first major amphibious operation of modern war on 25 April. In what was a fairly busy day for Orlo, stationed on HMS Queen Elizabeth, he was able to observe much of the 'battle of the beaches' from the sea. First, off what became known as the Anzac sector, he witnessed the charge and the popping of shrapnel shells, and then off Cape Helles he saw firsthand the actions of the British and French forces landing.

To facilitate the landing of as many troops as possible, and to confuse the enemy as to where the main assault would be, Sir Ian Hamilton decided to split his force into two main attacks. His plan was to land Major-General Sir Aylmer Hunter-Weston's 29th Division across five beaches, codenamed S, V, W, X and Y, around the tip of Cape Helles. The day one objective for this force would be the capture of the vital high ground of Achi Baba. Landing approximately 15 miles to the north of Cape Helles, Lieutenant-General Sir William Birdwood's Australian and New Zealand Army Corps (ANZAC) would land at Z beach. This force had the task of engaging the Ottoman reserve in the area, before advancing towards Maidos, thereby cutting off any Ottoman reinforcements that may be moving south towards the British forces at Cape Helles. Birdwood and Hunter-Weston's forces would then capture the Kilid Bahr plateau, the key high ground which overlooks the forts at the Narrows. Once taken the MEF would then neutralise the defences below, thus allowing the Dardanelles to be opened to allow the navy through. Of course, plans rarely survived contact with the enemy.

To support these main thrusts a diversionary feint attack would be affected on the Asiatic shore by the landing of a French division at Kum Kale, whilst the remainder of Corps Expéditionnaire d'Orient (CEO), under the command of General Albert d'Amade, would appear in their transports off Besika Bay. Similarly, at Bulair, in the Gulf of Saros, the Royal Naval Division (RND) would carry out a similar demonstration, although not a landing, with the hope to hold the Ottoman troops in that area. This complex plan was designed by Hamilton to confuse his German opponent (who commanded the Ottoman Fifth Army), General Otto Liman von Sanders, as to where the main attack would be taking place. The date chosen for the landings was 23 April 1915; due to bad weather it was postponed for forty-eight hours. It was not until Sunday, 25 April, over a month after the failed naval attack, that the land campaign could start.

On board the battleship HMS Queen Elizabeth Orlo was at the centre of GHQ's operations that gave him a rare holistic picture of the landings. His first mention of the ANZAC landing was when HMS Queen Elizabeth arrived off Kaba Tepe about 5.30 am, about an hour after the first 4,000 Australians had been landed. This was the 3rd Brigade, the selected covering force that spearheaded the landing on Z beach. Only some of this first wave landed in good order, most arrived mixed up and clustered together around the headland of Ari Burnu. This was partially due to what

Orlo alluded to in his diary where he mentioned the boats landing about 1 mile north of where they intended. The first ashore found themselves in disarray, fragmented in small groups all over the area. Chaotic as it was, a landing on a hostile shore had been made.

Orlo refers again to this landing about 3 hours later when a message was received at 8.39 am reporting 8,000 men having been landed, and 400 Plateau being captured. The main body of the 1st Australian Division by this stage were in positions all along the Second Ridge, which included 400 Plateau. Some had even reached the Third Ridge, which still lay undefended at this time. However, the Ottomans were about to counterattack and push them back to the Second Ridge. The day's fighting was confused. Thick scrub meant that men lying prone were invisible, which made it difficult to maintain contact with adjacent units. Lacking any coherent organisation, small groups of men would advance, either following the original orders to reach the Third Ridge or the new orders to reinforce the firing line on the Second. When Orlo received another message at 4.30pm reporting that 13,000 men were ashore, the battle was all but over. Facing repeated Ottoman counterattack and heavy shrapnel fire the Australians and New Zealanders, despite fierce fighting, were forced to pull back from their forward positions on 400 Plateau, and the heights at Baby 700, which had changed hands five times. With this key ground lost, the ANZACs withdrew back to a defensive line that would change little for the next 8 months of the campaign.

HMS Queen Elizabeth returned once again to Kaba Tepe about midnight when Orlo wrote that Brigadier-General Robert Carruthers came aboard to report the dire situation ashore. 'They had pushed on too far and not dug in, so that shrapnel shook them badly and they wanted to reembark.'

This is when Hamilton gave his famous 'dig' order:

> *Your news is indeed serious. But there is nothing for it but to dig yourselves right in and stick it out. It would take at least two days to re-embark you. Make a personal appeal to your men and Godley's to make a supreme effort to hold their ground.*
>
> *P.S. you have got through the difficult business; now you only have to dig, dig, dig, until you are safe.*

With this order all remaining doubts were settled. From that moment, there was no further talk of evacuation, the ANZACs were there to stay.

The situation at Helles brought little encouragement despite some initial success. Under gunfire support from HMS Cornwallis, three companies of the 2/South Wales Borderers (SWB) landed at S beach and captured Eski Hissarlik, an old Ottoman gun battery. The SWB quickly set up a defensive perimeter and waited for the main advance from V beach to meet it. At X beach the 2/Royal Fusiliers, supported by the guns of HMS Implacable, landed with no initial opposition. They threw out a similar defensive perimeter before they linked up with the W Beach landing on Hill 114. Similarly at Y beach, two battalions: 1/King's Own Scottish Borderers (KOSB) and Royal Marines from Plymouth Battalion landed with no opposition, and as per the orders waited for the main force to join them from W beach.

Whilst the landings at S, X and Y were a surprise to the Ottomans, the beaches codenamed V and W were not. As these were the larger beaches the Ottomans were certain that they would be used for a landing. Because of this both beaches were well defended. Taking advantage of the natural amphitheatre and steep sandy banks of these beaches, the Ottomans had wired their full length. Well concealed trenches had been dug into the cliffs above where the defenders commanded from both sides and in front. In addition, on V beach was an old castle and a gun battery. Whilst all the heavy guns had been destroyed by the Royal Navy, the stone structures, including those of Sedd-el-Bahr village, provided good cover for the defenders.

Orlo was witness to the disaster that befell V beach, recording that 'the River Clyde was ashore, and lighters round her. Under the cliff was a body of men crouching and nearer the sea many more lying who must have been dead. There was an incessant fire of rifles and machine guns. Perfectly obvious they could not advance an inch.' Orlo was referring to the 1/Royal Dublin Fusiliers that were pinned down on the beach by Ottoman rifle and Pom-Pom fire.[1] *Some of the Irishmen were hit in the boats, others on the beach or in front of the barbed wire. The River Clyde, a converted steam collier, beached herself as planned, but the ferocious Ottoman fire prevented the main body of men, consisting of the 1/Royal Munster Fusiliers and 2/Hampshire Regiment, from exiting the ship through purpose cut sallyports. Nine Victoria Crosses were awarded for valour for the V Beach landing, which incidentally took until 26 April for the beach, the forts and village to be secured. The naval gunfire support that Orlo describes in the diary as 'terrific', proved to be largely ineffective against entrenched positions. With heavy officer casualties and the men being shot whenever they tried to approach the wire, it was decided to halt this landing and divert the rest of troops to W beach.*

W beach had also been a bloody landing. The 1/Lancashire Fusiliers were the spearhead force landed at W beach. To give them the best chance of success a short but intensive thirty-minute bombardment by HMS Euryalus and HMS Swiftsure was to precede the landing, to lift some ten minutes

1 The Ottomans had both 25mm and 37mm Nordenfelt quick-firing guns in their defences at V and X beaches.

before the boats hit the shore. Unfortunately, this lull in the bombardment was to give the Ottoman defenders ten unmolested minutes to meet the landing. Like V beach, the Ottomans withheld their fire until the boats had entered the kill zone, and then they unleashed their deadly fusillade of fire. Those that had not been killed or wounded in the boats gallantly jumped into the water. The men struggled waist-deep, exacerbated by the weight of their equipment, and defences such as trip wires and land mines, to get to cover. The Ottomans continued to fire down from the cliffs into the battalion, who were now held up by a deep belt of wire. Through valour of the highest order some of the men managed to fight their way off the beach and push the defenders back. W beach, later renamed Lancashire Landing, was the scene of 'Six VCs before breakfast', an indication of the bravery shown that morning. By later morning W beach was secured and a link-up was made with 2/Royal Fusiliers on Hill 114. Now W beach was open the follow up waves made up from the 1/Essex Regiment and 4/Worcestershire Regiment were able to push out from the beach. It took until late afternoon to capture Hill 138, the link to those still pinned down on V beach.

The night of 25 April ended with uncertainty for the British at Cape Helles. Fierce Ottoman resistance had contained the various landings, preventing any from really being exploited that day. During the morning of 26 April the force at Y beach had erroneously been evacuated, and V beach, Sedd-el-Bahr and Hill 141 had yet to be captured. The whole effort was now directed to capture of Sedd-el-Bahr and Hill 141. It was then that two staff officers, Captain Garth Walford and Lieutenant-Colonel Charles Doughty-Wylie, were instrumental in breaking the impasse, capturing the fort, village and hill. Both were posthumously awarded the Victoria Cross for their actions in securing V beach.

The Battle of the Beaches had come to an end, but the struggle for Achi Baba was only beginning.

The First Battle of Krithia began on 28 April as the British made their way forward from the beaches in an advance to contact operation. They were joined by the French who, after their diversionary attack at Kum Kale, had now landed at Helles. This battle allowed the allies to push forward about two kilometres inland, over a five-mile front, but it was not without heavy casualties. What turned out to be an overly complex and poorly communicated battle, led to uncoordinated advances and loss of cohesion of troops. The casualties to date had been colossal, a rate that could not be sustained without reinforcements. Any thought that carrying Achi Baba by a coup de main were over when the battle ended that same day.

Whilst the British and French were left licking their wounds the Ottomans took advantage of the situation and thew a series of unsuccessful counterattacks during the nights of 1-3 May. The outcome of these attacks had been a close-run thing, leaving both Hunter-Weston and d'Amade deeply worried. On 4 May both generals sought to make the case for reinforcement and relief to Hamilton, whose own account shows how deeply concerned everyone was. On 4 May Orlo even records an anxious Secretary of State for War, Lord Kitchener, as the situation in the Dardanelles was not going as expected.

The situation in the Anzac sector had become equally desperate. Exhausted from the continuous fighting since the landing, Birdwood's forces also needed reinforcements. Hamilton despatched four battalions from the RND who quickly found themselves in action. On 2 May it was the turn of the ANZACs to attack and test the Ottoman resolve once more. A joint New Zealand and Australian attack, supported by the RND brigade, was launched. Its objective was not to breakout of the beachhead, but to improve the local tactical positions by capturing the Chessboard and Baby 700, both of which overlooked the Anzac positions. The attack was an unmitigated disaster. By 3 May it was apparent that a stalemate had developed and a series of 'Western Front' style trenches was quickly being established, with neither side having the resources to break the deadlock. Focus from Anzac then moved to Helles where Hamilton hoped that one more attack would allow Achi Baba to be taken before trench warfare had also set in. Orlo wrote:

'Others more worthy than I may commemorate the titanic battle which opened before dawn on the 25th. I shall not forget those six weird days on board the Queen Elizabeth, the glimpses of the battle, the colossal blast of the QE's 15-inch guns, the pathetic boat of wounded soldiers that drifted alongside one morning, and the sight of those all but impregnable defences on April 30, when most of the enemy wire was still standing, there were still dead Turks in the trenches, and the concealed pom-poms which had made such a sinister noise on V beach were still in position, two dummies inviting our fire between them. But some roads had already been made and a few tents pitched, and the beaches were stacked with cases of rations and crowded with mules, Indian and Zionist mule-drivers, working parties and all kinds of odd details. At a bare camp table on the bare top of Hill 138 sat General Hunter-Weston, voluble and determined, consulting with Sir Ian and his Chief of Staff.'[2]

* * *

2 Williams, O.C., 'Memories of a Gallant Adventure', *The Gallipolian: The Journal of the Gallipoli Association*, No. 71, Spring 1993, pp. 12–13.

Sunday 25 April 1915

First day of Battle of Beaches. Up at 4 a.m. Shaved and out on deck by 5. All kit had to be stored below deck under the armour and we were all told off to various battle stations. Deedes, young Braithwaite and I were stationed in 6″ battery, a large flat where four 6″ guns were on each side. Anyone who stayed there saw nothing at all. We steamed up to Kaba Tepe where we arrived about 5.30. The sun was shining brilliantly but low in the east, and there was a slight mist, so that one's view was a little impeded. Nevertheless, we plainly saw HMS *Minerva* and HMS *Talbot* firing and shrapnel bursting on the slopes of Sari Bair. Orders then came to go to stations which meant that doors on to quarter deck were closed. Not knowing the ropes, we stayed very bored in 6″ battery. Then the word came for battery to break off and all went on upper deck. There while smoking a pipe I saw all that was to be seen. The sea was clam and the sun shining brilliantly. There were puffs of smoke everywhere and continuous rattle of rifle fire. The *Minerva* and *Talbot* away plastering the hill and a battery on a low slope to the south. By 5.35 a.m. 4000 Australians had landed on Z beach and rushed up the steep slope. The Sari Bair landing a terrific place. A narrow strip of sandy beach under a massif of sandy bluffs cut about by nullahs into a series of steep bastions with here and there a grassy slope. The upper slopes of the hill are scrub. The Australian boats drifted by tide about 1 mile north of where they were intended to land and where Turks were expecting them. As the boats came up, the Turks came out on to the beach, running towards them, fixing bayonets and shooting from the hip. The Australians kept their rifles between their knees and waited for the word ... when they rushed out silently and straight up the steep slope opposite with the bayonet. During the day they worked right up the

V beach seen through the slit of the after torpedo control of HMS *Queen Elizabeth* during the landings.

Left of picture is the 'Wooden Horse', SS *River Clyde*, while Sedd el Bahr fort is straight ahead. On the skyline beyond the fort is 'Old Castle', where Lt-Col. Doughty-Wylie VC's grave can be seen to this day.

(O.C. Williams, IWM)

hill but were later driven back and had to dig in in semicircular position on lower slopes.

We steamed down towards Cape Helles about 6.30 where firing and ships' bombardment grew heavier and heavier. As we neared the point one plainly saw the pinnaces towing their 4 boats into the shore. Above Beach Y you could plainly see a party of our men advancing by rushes. These were the KOSB's and Plymouth Battalion, RMLI who had landed with practically no opposition on this beach, which is due west of Krithia, and clambered up the steep sandy cliff above it. About 7 a.m. the upper deck was cleared and I went below to have breakfast in the 6″ battery, the centre of which is galleys etc. We sat at long tables alongside the gun emplacement with the gun's crew lying all around and the layer standing by with his telephone fastened to his ears. After breakfast up into the after torpedo control. One ascended to this from the flat below the 6″ battery. One inserted oneself into a hole just big enough to take one human body and climbed up a perpendicular steel ladder till one came to a trap door on which one knocked. It was opened and one came out into a circular armoured pillbox containing a range finder, telephones, etc. Several snotties[3] in there, the padre and Deedes.

One looked through a narrow slit which ran all round the armour. The view excellent. I stayed here without lunch, just a few biscuits, till about 2 o'clock, off V Beach, though we could see something of W and the barbed wire covering the redoubt on Hill 138. Also we could see the French advance against Kum Kale on the other shore. What we could actually see of V Beach was its shape and the sandy bluff. The *River Clyde* was ashore and lighters round her. Under the cliff was a body of men crouching

3 Slang for midshipmen.

and nearer the sea many more lying who must have been dead. There was an incessant fire of rifles and machine guns. Perfectly obvious they could not advance an inch. A heavy bombardment of the beach from the *Queen Elizabeth* and *Bacchante* took place all this time, the *Queen Elizabeth* both 6" and 15" [guns], my first experience of gun fire. The shell bursts all along the ridge, in the upper part of village and in barracks of fort No. 1 were terrific, but it did not assist the troops to advance. A boat containing 6 wounded SWB from Morto Bay was picked up. The French hard at it all this while obviously advancing well.

At 8.39 ANZAC reported landing of 8000 men, capture of ridge 400[4] and extending right towards Kaba Tepe.

By 1.30 p.m. D'Amade reported all well. All infantry disembarked and artillery to follow. He was occupying Kum Kale and advancing on Yeni Shehr. The bursts of shell on Yeni Shehr, which is right on a hill on coast line, easily seen.

2.10 p.m. Report troops on Y Beach reached 175 U.Z, 168 D.[5] 4 battalions and 18 pounder battery at W Beach attacking Hill 138. 1000 men on V Beach unable to move. The Royal Fusiliers at X Beach forced to return owing to fire of troops landed after them. Holding a line 800 yards round beach.

From 2–3.15 p.m. I was with Deedes deciphering wires in wireless lieutenant's cabin, where heat was disgusting. At 3.20 p.m. out on deck watching in blazing sun. Saw Worcester's [Regiment] gallant attack on the barbed wire and saw them all lying under eastern crest under heavy fire. Very stirring to see one or two little black figures go forward and kneel down by the wire. 4.30 p.m. ANZAC reported 13,000 men ashore but being heavily shelled.

4 400 Plateau

5 Eski Line to Pink Farm.

Queen Elizabeth went on heavily shelling till dark. All the upper part of Sedd el Bahr set on fire and blazed magnificently in the night. Report that all brigadiers and 2 brigade majors of 29th Div had been hit, 2 brigadiers wounded, rest killed. A counterattack on Y Beach that was repulsed.

8.45 p.m. A long wire from Birdwood saying position not so good as it might be. Very difficult country heavily entrenched and field guns no good. Bombarded for several hours by shrapnel and unable to reply. About 2000 casualties.

Had a very hurried dinner and hard at work ciphering till 12. Meanwhile *Queen Elizabeth* had come up to Sari Bair and when I went on deck at 12, rifle fire still very heavy. No doubt a good deal of this due to nerves. General Carruthers came aboard and reported situation of Australians serious. They had pushed on too far and not dug in, so that shrapnel shook them badly and they wanted to reembark. General [Hamilton] said they must dig themselves in, and *Queen Elizabeth* and other ships would ease their task in the morning. Roused at 1.30 to send wire to Kitchener reporting this which was luckily never sent off.

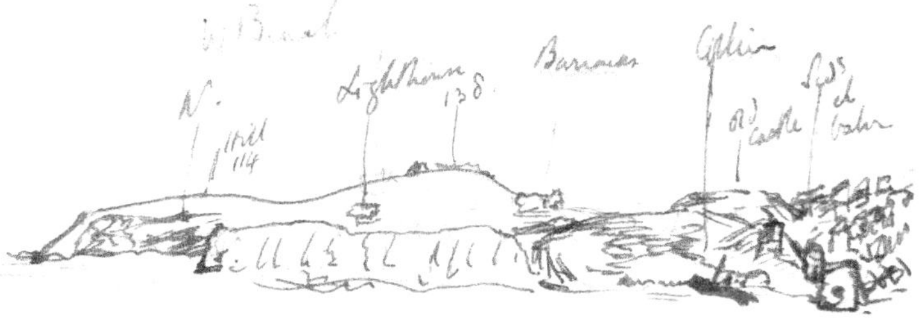

Orlo's sketch, 25 April.

From left: W Beach, Hill 114, Lighthouse, Hill 138, Barracks, Collier, Old Castle, Sedd el Bahr.

Top: Vice-Admiral de Robeck (left). Hamilton (right) hears from Major-General Paris, GOC RND, during the landings. The battleship behind them is HMS *Lord Nelson.*

Bottom: High Command aboard HMS *Queen Elizabeth* during the landings. General D'Amade, GOC French Corps, is seen third from left.

(O.C. Williams, IWM)

Monday 26 April 1915

Up very early again and in torpedo control till 7.30. *Queen Elizabeth* firing like blazes with *Majestic*, *Triumph*, *Canopus* and *Doris* over Sari Bair. The blast of 15" just underneath turret was fearful and blew my cap off every time it went off. Really very unpleasant. After breakfast out on deck. The *Queen Elizabeth* had stopped firing by 9. Rifle fire very heavy on slopes of Sari Bair and shrapnel bursting incessantly. We moved down to Cape Helles coming off Y and X beaches about 10 am.

By 6 a.m. report from 29th Division that the troops on V [Beach] had got a footing on Sedd el Bahr but could not advance. And at 7.25 *Goliath* reported situation of Y [Beach] force desperate. Arrangements made to reembark them which was successfully done with all wounded, stores and ammunition under fire of *Goliath*, *Dublin*, *Amethyst* and *Sapphire*. One could see the engagement on Y from deck of *Queen Elizabeth* and especially our troops retiring. 400 casualties reported. Meanwhile 29th Division reported not strong enough to take [Hill] 141 and make good V Beach. Arranged to order d'Amade to bring up his transports from Tenedos and disembark 1 regiment to be followed by rest of brigade. This actually took place on night of 26th.

12.30 p.m. *Queen Elizabeth* steamed back to Kabe Tepe, and I got to ciphers and lunch. On deck again at 2. We were shooting at intervals over Sari Bair. Attack progressing and left of ridge plastered with shrapnel from ships. An aeroplane spotting [for *Queen Elizabeth's* firing].

4.50 p.m.: Tea and ciphers. At 5 up on deck. *Queen Elizabeth* at Helles again. By this time V Beach was taken by Williams and Doughty-Wylie and Hills 138 and 141 in our hands, but thinly held and troops very exhausted. Very lucky Turks did not counterattack.

6.30 p.m. Bombardment of Krithia began which soon set

it blazing up till about 7.10. D'Amade reports 500 prisoners taken at Kum Kale. W Beach reports enemy retired all along the line. By 11.30 French were disembarking on V Beach and at day break they relieved our right on Hill 141. SWB meanwhile holding on to [Hill] 236.[6]

HMS *Swiftsure* firing (O.C. Williams, IWM).

Tuesday 27 April 1915

Up at 5. Nothing doing. By 8.30 came off Sari Bair where there was much rifle fire. Guépratte reported that French position at Kum Kale was excellent but that General d'Amade had already embarked. This was due to some misunderstanding and was a great misfortune. The Turkish morale was bad on that side, and the French could have easily kept silent the howitzer batteries on that side which subsequently shelled our beaches. At 2.30 a.m. 29th Division reported attacks had taken place all along the line previous afternoon and last night, which were repelled. Troops at S [Beach] maintaining themselves successfully.

6 De Tott's Battery.

This not a very pleasant day for me as, the War Diary being in arrears, Fuller and I worked for 6 hours in our shirtsleeves in the wireless man's cabins. The heat was sweltering and the 15" guns shook the whole place. During the morning *Queen Elizabeth* had 2 shots over the land at what was said to be the *Goeben*, driving her off, and also sank a transport in the Dardanelles. Meanwhile our southern force had all got into line from Hill 236 on the right to the stream mouth on left. The *Implacable* reported to have done great execution with her fire on a Turkish regiment.

12.30–1.30 p.m. and 2–2.45 p.m. on deck. *Queen Elizabeth* steamed down to Helles and we witnessed bombardment of Krithia and enemy's position by ships. During the afternoon CGS [Braithwaite] went ashore to see Anzac, and reported the men very cheerful.

2.25 p.m. 29th Division reported Turks who attacked about 11 a.m. on our left driven back. Troops now advancing north with 2 battalions of French troops on the right. This day the southern line advanced without opposition to line ... N. of [Hill] 138. Thence carried on by French to [Hill] 236. Early this morning 29th Indian Brigade under General Cox left Egypt for Tenedos.

Wednesday 28 April 1915

Had only 3 hours sleep again owing to getting to bed very late and then being up for 2 hours 3.30–5.30. Struggling with a very corrupt cipher from Anzac. Enemy made a determined attack on Birdwood's centre. By 6 a.m. 4 French battalions and battery of 75 [mm guns] landed and put under Hunter-Weston. At 3 a.m. Anzac reported having repulsed a determined attack: had to put beach parties and staff officers into firing line. Asked for reinforcements from Naval Division. One brigade RND ordered to him at 8 a.m.

9.30 a.m.: Wired Egypt to send [42nd] East Lancashire Territorial [Division] at once as soon as ships could be filled.

Queen Elizabeth supported flank of 29th Division all day, staying rather to the north of Y Beach, firing at intervals. Heavy engagement going on: our flanks advancing and Turks counterattacking. *Goliath* ordered to support our left flank which was getting disorganized. We distinctly saw the Border Regiment forced to retire and driven over the summit of cliff where they got cover. They gradually all got down on to the beach and filed along towards X Beach. The enemy's advance stopped by ships' fire. We distinctly saw a shell burst and blow a body of Turks into the air. Extraordinary how callous one is to scenes like that seen at a distance. Aspinall went ashore and reported very few wounded. *Sapphire* and trawlers ordered to take the men off. At 4.45 29th Division reported no progress being made and much ammunition expended. However, in spite of alarmist signals from certain units, he reported at 6.55 situation satisfactory in spite of local reverses but troops very tired. Reports holding line 176L–Y and French 169J–U.[7] Bolton reported only want of ammunition prevented capture of Krithia.

Got to bed very late, 2 a.m., and up again 4.30 a.m. Beginning to get very tired with tight feeling in the head.

Thursday 29 April 1915

Windy day and cold, but sun came out later. Had a quieter day and most refreshing sleep on wireless man's bed 10.30 a.m. to nearly 1 p.m. General [Hamilton] went ashore first at W [Beach] and then at Kaba Tepe and into the trenches at latter. No firing by *Queen Elizabeth* till after that.

7 This roughly equates to the British holding a line facing Krithia between what became known as Y Ravine and Horse Shoe; and the French in the Kereves Dere.

The firing of the *Triumph* set Maidos on fire: a great column of smoke rising from behind Achi Baba. Heard later 1st shell burst in hospital, and later a store was set on fire. Dawnay reported Anzac line very strong but a gap in the centre in front of a kind of steep bastion.

It was decided that Cox's brigade should join Hunter-Weston and the Marine brigade RND and 1½ other brigades remain with Birdwood. Also another French division to be asked for.

Line of 29th Division 175P–176Y. 169J–169U.[8]

Ciphers today stopped at midnight and I had quite a respectable night.

Friday 30 April 1915

It was decided that General [Hamilton] and GHQ should return to *Arcadian*. Our things accordingly sent off and I spent the morning ashore seeing W and V beaches. Visited HQ 29th Division which consisted a few tiny tents, some dispatch boxes, and a little table at which Hunter-Weston sat.

Later in the day ships set fire to Chanak from which came high cloud of black smoke.

Spent rest of day quietly in *Arcadian*. A most beautiful summery day with cool breeze. The sunset colours most magnificent especially just when sun is sinking below hills of Imbros which turn a gorgeous purple. Lately a great moon has been rising behind Eren Keui and this with lights of ships, winking of signal lamps and sweep of Chanak searchlight makes an unforgettable sight.

8 Gurkha Ravine – Horse Shoe, Kereves Dere to the coast.

29th Division HQ at Hill 138 on 30 April 1915 (O.C. Williams, IWM).

Top: Major-General Hunter-Weston (seated left) confers with Braithwaite.
Centre: Braithwaite seated, Hunter-Weston (left) with Hamilton.
Bottom: Braithwaite stands.

Horse lines and tents on W beach, 30 April 1915
(O.C. Williams, IWM).

View of V and W beaches, 30 April

Landed on W Beach which already cleared and made into rough camp. Roads made, a few tents up, many men and horses. Still saw the deep trenches cut all round it and commanding position of cliffs. Went on over Hill 138 and up through the stupendous barbed wire so gallantly cut by the Worcesters on 25th. On to Fort No. 1 with 2 guns (9.2″) put out of action by Navy. So on to edge of bluff looking over V Beach which [I] photographed. The defences of this beach look absolutely impregnable. It is shaped like a large amphitheatre, with Sedd el Bahr fort on one side and steep cliff on the other. Trenches all round and down the middle, with barbed wire very thick in several lines. On left hand side high up were 4 concealed pom-poms with 2 dummy pom-poms in between the 2 pairs. Sedd el Bahr on the other side was a nest of Maxims. On the summit in centre the old fort, surrounded by barbed wire and commanding all the steep slope.

Top: Fort No. 1. Centre: View from bluff overlooking V beach and Sedd el Bahr. Bottom left: deep trench with dead Turk. Bottom right: Braithwaite Jr and Deedes pictured against Turkish barbed wire. (O.C. Williams, IWM)

Some account of life on Queen Elizabeth. April 24–

Living on battleship under battle conditions for a military staff very uncomfortable. Most of us sleep on valises on floor of day cabins. …

Ship not meant for these continuous operations and very inconvenient. The after part of ship quite cut off when we are closed down: not armoured and communication between various stations very difficult. Officers continually sweating up and down ladders and bumping their heads along various flats to find one another. The atmosphere below intolerably hot and stuffy. No fixed place for us to work in. Fuller, Deedes and I make considerable use of wireless lieutenant's cabin which kindly put at our disposal. One day Fuller and I worked there 6 hours at War Diary which nearly did for me.

Meals for wardroom and gunroom during stations served at long tables in 6-inch battery. No casemates for these guns: but 6 on each side under amour: galleys, etc. in middle of deck. Watched crews working one day while salvos[9] being shot. Noise not very great. During stations hardly any facilities for washing, etc. and even in evening after opening up facilities small. I [am] lucky in being able to use lavatory of captain's cabin but no time for bath: no change of clothes etc.

Up to today have hardly had 3 hours sleep a night. When day over and dinner [is ready, there is] always a rush of ciphering and deciphering etc. which seems to go on till 1 or 2 a.m. Then most mornings up at 4 or 4.30. Also frequently roused in middle of night to do ciphers and so on 27th [April] lost the one long line. Field cipher sent by wireless proved quite impossibly corrupt.

Life therefore very tiring in spite of interest of watching

9 Simultaneous discharge of two or more guns, including artillery.

operations. Strain of standing so long peering through glasses. Also noise of gun fire.

The blast and noise of 15″ guns pretty terrific, especially when anywhere near muzzle. Worst time in torpedo control aft when turrets firing forward. Blew cap off every time. 6-inch salvos not so bad. The burst of shell wonderful to see, but observation of target usually impossible. Ships officers all very good fellows indeed.

Saturday 1 May 1915

Beautiful day. A bit more wind. On ship all day. Fairly heavy bombardment by ships all morning and part of afternoon. Shells still dropping on V and W beaches but doing very little harm because not bursting. The shipping off the point and the men on the beaches a very remarkable sight. Cox's Indian Brigade arrived and disembarked V Beach. Dawnay's story of French Colonials. 200 Turks came down to Kum Kale as French were coming away and implored to be taken off as prisoners. Reply "*Mais, messieurs, il n'y a pas de place*".[10]

Lovely moonlit night. About 11 a night attack begun by Turks. Continuous musketry and gun fire from *Swiftsure* and batteries on shore and star rockets at intervals. This was a heavy counterattack all along the front especially on French left, repulsed with great loss.

Sunday 2 May 1915

Woken at 6 by firing of ship's guns up on deck and found hot engagement going on. This was a counterattack by French right which advanced to ridge overlooking Kereves Dere. Hope to continue by French left and British right later in the morning.

The attack was chiefly where 29th Division joined

10 Translation: 'But, gentlemen, there is no room'.

Ruins of Sedd el Bahr village (O.C. Williams, IWM).

French left [flank on the] Sedd el Bahr–Krithia road. This repulsed, in spite of report that French left had gone back. At 6 a.m. French right advanced but Colonial Corps on left still unable to advance in to lines. On our left line had gone forward about 400 yards along cliffs 175 U4 to U2.[11]

Prisoners taken about 2 or 300. In afternoon ashore with Fuller and others. Saw beaches again and up through Sedd el Bahr village. Every single house ruined a rather remarkable sight. Battle still going on, and from Hill 138 saw gun fire and shrapnel. Turks attacked again after dinner tonight.

In counter attack lasting from 8–12pm Turks lost heavily, scores of reserves coming under searchlight and French 75s. We lost little. Anzac lost about 700 straightening out their left.

11 The cliffs above Y Beach.

Monday 3 May 1915

Wired to Kitchener we're waiting for brigade of East Lancashires to come up and then would go for Achi Baba with 2 brigades. ANZAC in sweepers. Two things noticeable.

Congestion of beaches growing. PNTO and Admiral beginning to get cross.

French rather trying continually asking for battalions from English to support them. Hunter-Weston being very canny however, and so GS have lent them 2 battalions temporarily.

Lovely day today and quiet.

G. Lloyd says Z Beach under continuous shrapnel, very trying.

Scene tonight very beautiful, strange. Water very calm and a starlit night with no moon. Ships all fairly dark but a few had twinkling lights and twinkling lights on shore. The winking eye of signals in the dark, and the great sweep over the sky of the Chanak searchlight. Now and again a flash like summer lightning. If close, soon followed by loud report from one of the ships. If just above Sedd el Bahr flashes in 3 or 4 followed by the short report and tearing sound of the [French] 75s; if in the distance by Achi Baba followed by the flash of bursting shrapnel, like a ball of fire.

The clerk of Kitchener in wiring "Your telegrams require very careful ciphering" etc. Answer... "The ciphering is done by Williams late of C2".

Tuesday 4 May 1915

My birthday. Lovely day but little else to record. From wire sent by General to Secretary of State it appears that French suffered rather in repulsing enemy's attack. Turks broke the Senegalese line. ... The moral[e] of these troops and of their officers gone. After serious talk with d'Amade, General gave him a smaller sector and 3 battalions for his left. The expenditure of ammunition has been alarming. Fairly obvious that French nerve not over good. They are always sending alarmist messages which are usually contradicted by 29th Division. General impression that French very difficult to fight with.

Wire from Russia today that they are vigorously bombarding Bosphorus.

Saw Wallis for 10 [minutes] on *Arcadian*. He looked well. Had been under shrapnel at Gaba Tepe.[12]

Life on board now very normal. Aeroplanes now and then try to drop things and one hears what firing there is. Otherwise one stays on board working at what work there is and longing for exercise. A game of chess now and then. I [am] very busy examining prisoners and translating Turkish orders of which a great many have been captured, which show their organisation is more thorough than would be expected.

A wire from Athens last night reports 6000 wounded at Constantinople and that General Weber[13] had died there in hospital. His HQ was in Krithia.

Lord Kitchener sending rather futile telegrams which obviously show he is rather anxious for us to get on.

Wednesday 5 May 1915

Pretty quiet day with little sound of firing: spent a certain amount of time trying to write up this diary. Bolton spent the night on shore at the French HQ. Says they had very poor food and were situated between two 75 mm guns with a heavy gun behind which fired at intervals all night and quite prevented all sleep on his part.

Instructions issued for the next big advance which is to

12 Orlo uses Kapa Tepe and Gaba Tepe throughout his diary.

13 This was incorrect. Weber survived the war.

take place tomorrow. Our southern force with 2 brigades from Anzac and 2 naval battalions and one brigade East Lancashires in reserve to advance on Krithia and Achi Baba.

The main attack to be undertaken by 29th Division by the left, who are to pivot round on a position 169D[14] which is to be held at all costs by the French. The left will advance up the stream from 176V8 to 176O8[15] and take Krithia and then sweep round in summit of Achi Baba from W. The right battalion of 29th will move with its left on the parallel stream 169B9-176T3[16] and then sweep round on Achi Baba. The gap to be filled by naval brigade in trenches of 88th Brigade. Motor machine guns RND to be in support. The French not to leave 169D till capture of Krithia assured. Then to move up to southern slopes of Achi Baba. The advance to be supported by ships to be placed at various points round the peninsula.

14 West of Quadrilateral

15 Krithia Nullah, roughly from what became known as Eastern Mule Trench to the southern edge of Krithia village.

16 Achi Baba Nullah.

3

'EVERYTHING LOVELY BUT THE WAR'

MAY 1915

Observing the Ottomans developing their defences at Helles provided a dilemma for Hamilton. Should he wait for sufficient reserves and ammunition, or attack before their positions had been strengthened?

As Orlo explains in his diary entry for 5 May, the 'next big advance', later known as The Second Battle of Krithia, would be undertaken yet again by 29th Division. In their support was 125th Lancashire Fusilier Brigade and 29th Indian Brigade. Together they would attack on the left, up Gully Spur and Fir Tree Spur, to capture the village of Krithia before sweeping round to take the summit of Achi Baba. The French 1e Division, together with the attached 2 (Naval) Brigade, RND, were to attack the formidable defences of the Bouchet Redoubt and Kereves Dere, before moving up the southern slopes of Achi Baba. In reserve for this attack, Hamilton had the loan of an Australian brigade and a New Zealand brigade that had been transferred from the Anzac sector, and 1 (Naval) Brigade, RND, which together formed a composite division. In addition, five Australian and one New Zealand field artillery batteries were landed at Helles, attached to 29th Division in support. This was a complex plan which would have kept Orlo and the staff busy, so it was not surprising that his diary has a gap for 6–8 May.

The three-day battle was a failure. The Allies had been ashore a fortnight and, apart from wrestling a slightly firmer footing from the Ottomans, they had little else to show from these costly daylight frontal assaults. Despite the Allies' initial plans for a coordinated attack, the battle was characterised by a series of poorly executed assaults, by already exhausted men, against unrealistic objectives. The Allies faced significant challenges due to logistical issues and indecisiveness in command. The terrain's rugged nature further complicated the operations, making coordinated movements difficult and reducing the attack's overall effectiveness. As the Allies moved toward their objectives, they encountered a stubborn Ottoman defence, with machine-gun and artillery fire inflicting heavy casualties. The Ottomans were proving themselves to be an organised, well-disciplined and efficient fighting force that had frustrated and delayed the landings and now blocked all attempts to take Krithia and Achi Baba.

These challenges would lead to a change in tactics. Hamilton realised that they had to revert to small scale trench warfare, an early example of 'bite and hold' tactics, until he had the resources to mount another major offensive. This proved successful when during the night of 12/13 May, Gurkhas from 29th Indian Brigade launched an imaginative attack to capture an Ottoman redoubt near Y beach. This position had been a thorn in the side of the British during both Krithia battles, but once taken, 29th Division was able to advance the line over 500 yards. Similarly, a series of four modest tactical night advances on 18, 23, 24 and 27 May resulted in the allied line moving forward almost a kilometre with little loss, barely fifty casualties; quite a contrast to the 6,000 casualties paid for a similar distance during the last battle of Krithia. Bite and hold tactics were usually successful at achieving a limited goal but their nature meant it was unlikely to create a breakthrough. The purpose of bite and hold meant you had to concentrate a lot of resources on a short section of the line, with a relatively narrow depth. To breakthrough, Hamilton needed more resources—men and artillery.

Achi Baba had not been captured after two battles, and on the Western Front the situation was not encouraging after the disastrous attacks at Aubers Ridge and Festubert. Kitchener had doubts about Britain's ability to fight on two fronts, but he needed to support both. He feared that a loss at the Dardanelles would lead to problems in the East, particularly Egypt. Kitchener looked to Hamilton to do whatever he could to produce a victory, or at worse prevent a defeat. Hamilton, even with the 42nd (East Lancashire) Division and the French 2e Division, which both landed in early May, and the promise of the 52nd (Lowland) Division the following month, would still be short of what he needed. Pressure to 'push on' was not helpful when the MEF didn't have the resources to do that. Kitchener did ask how many men were needed, if the troops could be made available, to bring the campaign to a successful end. Hamilton requested two Army corps, which left Kitchener with a challenge. It had also become clear to Kitchener that naval gunnery support was not the force multiplier that he had hoped it would be. It was no substitute to having more artillery ashore, especially heavier calibre guns and howitzers. Artillery was key to dominating the battlefield, but without sufficient shells it would not be affective. Ammunition re-supply was a major problem for Hamilton who became 'much irritated' when the War Council indicated that no one had calculated the supply needed for a prolonged campaign.

By this time, Orlo had become quite critical of Hamilton, remarking on his temperamental moods and weakness. His recent communications with Kitchener were evidence of this, some thinking Hamilton feared his political master, and too easily acquiesced when told more troops and ammunition were not available. Hamilton was there to command but it appeared to be his CGS, Braithwaite, that was running the show. Orlo had also formed strong opinions of others that he worked with, particularly their capabilities for the roles they were undertaking. It was becoming clear that all was not well amongst GHQ staff, particularly with Braithwaite, who was getting on people's nerves and had delegated much of the decision-making to Aspinall and Dawnay, which in turn alienated some of the other staff officers. Internal politics and friction were not restricted to just GHQ, as their relationship with the Navy was little better. It is interesting how honest Orlo is with his criticism, something only possible because this was a personal diary.

At Anzac the situation was little better. General Bridges, GOC 1st Australian Division, was mortally wounded on 15 May, hit by a sniper's bullet that severed his femoral artery. Hamilton visited him ashore, but he died three days later onboard a hospital ship. On 19 May, recently reinforced, the Ottomans launched a massive night attack which fell mainly on the centre of the line along the Second Ridge. It was repulsed with heavy Ottoman losses; of the 40,000 soldiers involved, 10,000 became casualties. ANZAC losses were a little over 600. By the end of the day ANZAC artillery had expended nearly 3,000 artillery shells and an astonishing 948,000 rifle and machine-gun rounds. Australia had also gained their first Victoria Cross of the war when Lance-Corporal Albert Jacka, single-handedly, recaptured a portion of trench that had fallen to the Ottomans at Courtney's Post. On 20 May, the smell of decomposing bodies meant that the front lines at Anzac had become almost uninhabitable. A burial armistice was arranged for 24 May so that soldiers from both sides could recover and bury their dead comrades. Orlo and Compton Mackenzie had come ashore to witness the truce, and for many this was the first time that each side had seen each other's faces. The following day the war re-commenced. Quinn's Post, the scene of some of the most dramatic events in the campaign, became the next focal area for attack, this time one from underground. At 3:30 a.m. on 29 May, an Ottoman mine was exploded under a section of Quinn's, the Australians losing a trench. Desperate fighting took place before a determined Australian counterattack eventually recaptured the position.

The month of May was a particularly dangerous time for those afloat, including GHQ, as Orlo recorded on 11 May when intelligence was received that German submarines had been sent to the area. Because of this GHQ, which until then was still onboard the Arcadia, set up a permanent camp on Imbros. The pre-dreadnoughts that remained offshore were not so fortunate. On 13 May an Ottoman torpedo boat, Muâvenet-i Millîye, made a bold and daring attack on HMS Goliath, sinking the ship with the loss of 570 crew. Then on 25 May the German submarine U-21 torpedoed and sunk HMS Triumph, and two days later HMS Majestic. The situation had become unsustainable for the navy, which was forced to withdraw its larger ships. This was a turning point for Hamilton who prior to the submarine scourge was full of confidence but knew the impact they would have on the fleet, which his forces were reliant upon for support, both logistical and for artillery.

On 15 May, First Sea Lord, Admiral John 'Jacky' Fisher, resigned. Fisher had never been keen on the Dardanelles and Gallipoli operations that were championed by Churchill, believing them to be ill-conceived and unnecessary diversions from the true theatre of war against Germany in the North Sea and the Baltic. When HMS Goliath was sunk, he demanded the withdrawal of the super-dreadnought Queen Elizabeth, the Royal Navy's most modern ship at the Dardanelles.

Kitchener accused the Navy of letting the Army down in its time of need. Fisher could not stand this denigration, and finally spoke up, saying he had been 'against the Dardanelles operations from the beginning... the Prime Minister and Lord Kitchener knew this fact well.' This uncharacteristic outburst was apparently received in silence. Churchill, his political master, had a tempestuous relationship working together, not made any easier by pressure on Fisher to deliver a 'second Trafalgar', to prevent the German submarines that seemed to be running amok, and their Naval Zeppelins from bombing the East Coast of England and London, and of course their clash over the Dardanelles.

Fisher's resignation led to Churchill's removal as First Lord of the Admiralty just over a week later. It was one crisis after another for Herbert Asquith's Liberal Government. Overwhelmed by scandal, the shell shortage, the growing casualties, a grieving population and now the publicly adored Lord Fisher going, the government collapsed. On 25 May a coalition government was created under Asquith. It was formed as a multi-party war-time coalition, the measures needed to win the war with the required support from across the political spectrum. At the same time the War Council was renamed the Dardanelles Commission. Accordingly, the establishment of a coalition government and the effective abandonment of party politics was a clear indication of the gravity of the challenges facing the United Kingdom as the war with Germany and its allies continued.

But the war wasn't progressing well for the Ottomans either. British submarine HMS E11, commanded by Lieutenant-Commander Nasmith, had arrived at the Dardanelles to join the submarine campaign in the Sea of Marmara. E11 passed through the Straits on the night of 18 May and went on to sink two transports, one laden with ammunition, forced another to run aground, sunk a gunboat and several other smaller craft. Upon reaching Constantinople E11 searched for larger prey hoping to sink SMS Goeben or the Breslau. Nasmith settled for another transport. The Ottoman city, knowing that an enemy vessel was in the area, went into panic. E11 ran amok until it was forced to return when it ran out of torpedoes. For this successful tour Nasmith was awarded the Victoria Cross. The Goeben, which had avoided E11's rampage, itself had also been in action. The Russian fleet, which had bombarded the Ottoman fortifications at the mouth of the Bosphorus on 25 April, the same day as the Gallipoli landings, and again on 2 and 3 May, had returned. During an engagement on 10 May, the Goeben was hit three time by the Russian fleet during what became known as the Battle of the Bosphorus.

Russian efforts at the Bosphorus did little to help their Allies at Gallipoli, but the Entente Powers were growing. In May, Italy joined the war on the side of Britain, France and Russia, something the country had been aligning itself with during the immediate pre-war years, for military and economic support. Unknown to Orlo, a secret pact had been negotiated on 26 April 1915 by which Britain and France promised to support Italy annexing the frontier lands in return for entering the war on their side. On 3 May, Italy resigned from the Triple Alliance and later declared war against Austria-Hungary at midnight on 23 May. It wouldn't be until July that Italy declared war on the Ottoman empire. For now, Bulgaria and Romania remained neutral.

* * *

Sunday 9 May 1915

Perfect spring day. Cool breeze, warm sun, everything lovely but the war. The great attack went on for 3 days and, by the end of yesterday evening, was brought to a standstill, with a small advance on the part of our troops, but no real impression made on the Achi Baba position. There is no concealment on anybody's part that the attack has been a failure and that if we are to get on at all, we must have more troops, guns and ammunition. Late last night a long telegram to that effect was sent to Lord Kitchener which will not make very pleasant Sunday reading for him. The effect of it was that in spite of using all our forces we had made no real impression upon the enemy's position, the scientific semi-permanent works of which, protected by machine guns, were too strongly held to be rushed. Turks had 40,000 to our 25,000 rifles, as they have 20,000 to Birdwood's 12,000, and they are able to reinforce from Adrianople and the Asiatic side. The only way to push on is to send more troops and more munitions. "I fear that is a very unpalatable conclusion but I see no way out of it". No doubt the general is anxious and disappointed, and the GS too. Events can only be waited for, but it seems that now we have let ourselves in for it we cannot possibly draw back and troops will have to be sent. The French have already another division on the way with General Gouraud to command the Army Corps. The East Lancashire Territorial Division has now all arrived from Egypt and a wire from Kitchener received last night said that the Lowland Division was being prepared to be sent, but that ships for it must be sent back from here, which will mean some delay.

Now for detail. *Thursday the 6th* was a very blowy day, wind being very cold, and it was quite impossible to see anything of the attack from here. From reports received up to 3 p.m. obvious the advance only getting on very slowly, the Lancs Brigade on left is being entirely held up by a redoubt. General much irritated by a wire from WO saying "ammunition supply for your force not calculated on the basis of a prolonged occupation of Gallipoli peninsula. If, after reinforcements now on their way, enemy cannot be driven back and force, in conjunction with fleet, cannot reduce forts guarding Dardanelles, the question will have to be reconsidered. It is important to push on". General justly annoyed at some member of the Army Council wiring like this, as it is obviously too late to reconsider anything. He sent back a rather cross wire which received a sniffy reply, only latter was tempered by a private message from Fitzgerald to CGS, saying that all Kitchener wanted to know was the approximate expenditure and would keep us supplied.

The result of the day was that progress was much below our hopes. The Hood Battalion RND suffered heavily, Asquith and Wedgwood being wounded and many officers lost. Information, however, got by Deedes shows that Turks have lost very heavily and are very afraid of ships' guns.

Friday 7th another stationary day on board for me, and still the very cold wind. Attack continued all day with any quantity of firing. The line advanced a little more, but Lancashire Fusiliers Brigade, after getting on 500 yards lay down and would not move. Finally they were ordered to retire to the reserve and their place taken by 87th Brigade. A few bursts of telegrams and intervals of chess with Hony—a very pleasant fellow, Oxford man, who is in Levant consular service, and officially interpreter attached to Operations.

Yesterday, *Saturday 8/5*, a perfect day. The general and all the General Staff spent the day on shore on Hill 114. There were two tremendously hot times. One from 10.30 to 11.30 a.m. when rifle and artillery fire was very heavy. Enemy aeroplane was seen very high up from *Arcadian*, and a few shots fired at it from 3 p.m. Went ashore in the afternoon with Hony, Hodgson, Graves and Maxwell. We sat first under Hill 138 and then under Hill 114. Things were pretty quiet all the time except for a certain amount of artillery fire from French on right, and really there was very little to see. The scene dominated by Achi Baba towering over Krithia and the woods below was peaceful enough. A herd of goats were browsing in the foreground, men were exercising mules, and little bodies of men and wagons went from time to time along the dusty roads. The banks on which we sat smelt sweetly of wild thyme. Every now and again shrapnel burst in the centre, a few shots were fired at our aeroplane, and occasionally the vicious pop-pop-pop of a machine broke out. We came back just after 5, and unfortunately, for at 5.30 a terrific bombardment took place lasting about ¾ of an hour: every available weapon was being used, and the whole line advanced with the bayonet. But these results were, as I have written, failure in spite of a certain advance, especially by Australian brigade in centre.

A word on internal politics

The general strikes me as a weak and too highly strung man. Pollen, walking with me on the *Queen Elizabeth* the other day, told me as much. He came out chiefly to help the general if he could, but found he couldn't do much. Said he was too afraid of Kitchener, and never would run his own show in his own way, a thing he was always trying to buck him up to do. At first the general used to ask his advice about telegrams but this incensed the CGS so it had to be stopped. The CGS' view intelligible, for though Pollen has been a staff officer he is not on the GS and therefore not under CGS, and the position of an ADC aged 50 is something of an anomaly. I fear the general is run by the

CGS, who may be a good soldier but is a stupid man, with no ideas. A good looking man with a ruby complexion, good natured, but fond of his own way. CGS relies almost wholly on Aspinall and Dawnay, leaving old heavy-eyed Bolton out in the cold, which annoys Bolton. Aspinall strikes me also as pretty stupid in certain ways. He takes an extraordinarily long time to explain anything which is not a good indication. I think he is good at organisation, etc., as is Dawnay, who is really intelligent. Colonel [sic: Brigadier-General] Simpson-Baikie has just arrived to be GSO1 temporarily, in place of Colonel Williams. I rather think, as does Bolton, that he will by no means be ignored by the CGS as Colonel Williams was, and that there may be a certain amount of dissension, for I don't fancy Simpson-Baikie thinks much of things as they have gone so far. Fuller is one of the nicest and hardest workers and most efficient men here. He works very quietly and makes no fuss, but he gets more done than all the rest put together, and helps them a great deal more, I think, than they realize. Grant, the other O(b) man, is now ashore as staff officer in I [Intelligence], the hardest work and the best work is done by little Deedes, who knows Turkish thoroughly and whose face is exactly like a Turk's. He has a small face, with a beaky nose and sunken eyes, and great wrinkles on both sides of his mouth. What Colonel Ward does, I don't know. I gather from Keeling there are always violent discussions in Intelligence, Ward, Lloyd and Deedes all proclaiming their own view as to where Turkish regiments are. I back Deedes all the time, who really runs the show.

There is a good deal of friction between Army and Navy over regulation of transports, but that is a Q matter, of which I only hear echoes. Q say the PNTO is very inefficient and never does what he is asked to do.

The rest of today extremely quiet both for me and for

the troops. I actually read some chapters of GKC's "Victorian Age in Literature".[1] What he says about women novelists struck me in particular as good and witty. Received from Harold[2] a pocket Thucydides which I asked him to send me, also letter from mother dated 20th in which she says the WO wrote after I left: "He has been a pillar of strength to us ever since he came and we want to keep him". Very gratifying.

News that 658 were saved out of 2100 on *Lusitania*, and America is enraged.

Today Hony told me of his adventure in Kurdistan which resulted in his killing a Kurdish chief, who with his followers sniped at him from behind rocks. Luckily his followers fled after 5 minutes' shooting. Hony and his Turkish boy were able to get on their horses and evade pursuit. He then had to lie doggo for a month in the village of the Nestorian archbishop. Finally he decided to leave, though an escort was at first refused him. But after he left the escort followed quickly, only, typically, one of the escorts was a near relation of the killed man, who sent word to the clan. Luckily for Hony, who only knew this later, the other zaptiehs[3] were up to the dodge and pushed on quickly.

Monday 10 May 1915

Wire from Kitchener in answer to our doleful one. Chiefly asking questions. Evidently disappointed that ships' guns can't do more, and surprised that we have not more rifles. Says he is naturally anxious about situation and is pushing out ammunition via Marseilles.

Poor Dawnay up 2½ hours last night owing to repeated

1 Gilbert Keith Chesterton, author.

2 Harold Beresford Butler.

3 Turkish policeman.

appeals by the French for British troops to support them in view of impending attack, though reports from our people said that nothing was doing and all quiet. We were firm in spite of a personal appeal from d'Amade and of course nothing happened.

These words may perhaps be modified in view of d'Amade's letter of today. Undoubtedly his division has suffered very heavily and is right to ask for his line to be reduced.

A long wire sent to Kitchener today explaining situation more fully: nature of ground, numbers, etc. Casualties up to 5th are about 494 officers and 12,200 [other ranks], for next 3 days about 3,000. Many of the earlier cases are slight and will soon return. General said "Fully realise your anxiety but I have confidence in ultimate result though progress will be slower than I hoped... Regarding future operations only sound procedure is to hammer away until enemy gets demoralised and in this, Admiral [de Robeck] agrees. Meanwhile grand attacks are impracticable and we must make small advances during night and dig in during day till we get Achi Baba when hope to be able to make progress without this trench method, but Achi Baba is really a fortress. If 2 fresh divisions can be spared, organised as a corps, I could push on from this end and from Kaba Tepe with good prospects of success, otherwise I am afraid it will degenerate into trench warfare with resultant slowness. Chief anxiety comes from French who murder sleep by crying for help all night long, however, the new commander will probably alter this. Everyone in good spirits and full of confidence".

During last night 15th and 16th Battalions, 4th Australian Infantry Brigade, earned 3 Turkish trenches but were subsequently turned out, only our artillery got well among Turks and did great execution "Turks lying so thick on the ground as to form a fair obstacle".

King's Messenger bag arrived with lots for me including sketching apparatus and gaiters from Mother as birthday present. Delightful letters from everybody. With reference to d'Amade, Dawnay thinks his real fear, which he (Dawnay) did not realise last night, was for the moral of his troops owing to losses of officers, which very likely is the case. Anyhow, a pat on the back has been sent to him in a letter tonight.

Internal politics

Dawnay agrees that CGS is a good fellow but has no brains. Rather surprised me by saying that Aspinall ought to have been made GSO1 and that he was a very able fellow and had just the right kind of training for this kind of job, and that Aspinall felt Baikie's intrusion very sorely. Dawnay's testimony is not one to be set lightly aside as he is a business man; all the same Aspinall does not really convince me on purely general grounds of out of the way ability. We shall see, but I think a little leavening of the Braithwaite hump by Baikie won't be a bad thing.

Tuesday 11 May 1915

Another stagnant day. Weather turned overcast and much colder. A fellow came on board with a note to me from Colonel Williams asking me to see he got lunch and a bath. Turned out to be Neave... at my Tutors. Later on, a subaltern RE turned up, and he was Sutton... with whom I boxed and played cricket. Both had lunch with Hodgson and me. Sutton had come home from South America to serve and Neave a captain in the Essex [Regiment]. He had been one of the V Beach people and told me it was the most frightful affair. As soon as they got near the land in tows they saw it was a disaster. Heaps of dead and sunk boats on the shore, and wounded kicking about in the water at the edge. From the last lighter to the land was sea in which you had to wade up to the waist and then 20 yards of rock which was absolutely swept by fire. About 6 attempts were made to land, and 8 out of every 10 men killed each time. The regimental view is that Operations covered themselves with shame in attempting to land on that beach, and that even afterwards there was no organisation. On the 2nd night things were so bad that another man had to go up and down the lines of our troops with revolvers to keep the men in their lines. If they had given, they would have been swept into the sea. He says Captain Unwin, commanding the *River Clyde*, deserved the Victoria Cross several times over, repeatedly hoisting in wounded out of the water under heavy fire. It becomes fairly obvious as one gets bits of information here and there that none but British regulars could have stood what the 29th Division had to stand, and that the plan of landing, if it could be now devised over again *would be very different.*[4] Even now, the troops at the front complain of want of organisation, and that, I daresay, is partly due to the unfortunate fact of our being on board ship. Neave said the Turks' hidden machine guns were the devil: impossible to locate them, and that the New Zealand brigade, in their last advance, ran right over some of them without finding them. Says the troops are well fed, which is a good thing. Turks, on the other hand, according to accounts from prisoners, are badly fed.

Chief excitement of today the fact that, in view of the persistent news of 2 German submarines having been heard of coming from south, all ships are to move from this anchorage. At one time it was proposed that General and a minimum of staff should dig in on the cliffs here and

4 Orlo later added after this point: 'This is not true. There would have been improvements'.

the rest go back to Tenedos; later, I am glad to say—as I should have gone in to the cliffs, it was decided *Arcadian* should go with all staff to Tenedos, where presumably some of it or all of it will camp on shore. Everything seems a bit vague, and it is rather a tiresome position. It certainly adds one more element to the originality of this expedition.

Wednesday 12 May 1915

Still off Cape Helles but going to move soon, I believe. Wire from Kitchener this morning saying shortly he is sending us Lowland division with brigade of 5″ howitzers and 1 or 2 brigades field guns.

Quiet and uneventful day. Towards sunset, *Arcadian* left for Tenedos where anchored at about 7. Not to disembark at present.

Read report written by Major Striedinger ASC on landing at W Beach. Showed ammunition supply very difficult and that if troops *had* been able to advance position would have been desperate. As it was with troops only ¼ mile from beach many men whose rifles would have been useful in firing line had to be used to carry ammunition. Criticizes fact that shell fire had no effect on barbed wire on beach which caused heavy losses, and that much more useful than ships' guns would have been a battery of machine guns on armoured pinnace. As there was no shell fire transports should have come in much closer. As it was, considerable delay in landing reinforcements. The night of 25th very precarious. Troops, whose nerves were shaken, fired away a tremendous amount of ammunition but held on. Moral [is] to land at once all the infantry you possibly can with all water and ammunition they can carry, then a few guns and finally all possible pack transport.

Thursday 13 May 1915

Beautiful day. News from Hunter-Weston he had pushed on 600 yards on the left by sending double company of Gurkhas along cliffs by night: the position consolidated later in the day.

Bad news. In the fog last night a Turkish torpedo boat came down and torpedoed the *Goliath*; all but 200 were saved. A good feat for them. All our destroyers were away. *Goliath's* people thought it was one of our ships and hailed it.

The general and a few others went over to the peninsula in a fleet sweeper. Too many shells were falling on and about W Beach. Several horses were killed, some tents knocked down, and Greek labourers panic stricken. But they can't get away so they must dig in as they do at Anzac.

In the afternoon the staff crowded ashore en masse. Tenedos an extremely picturesque island, with steep knobs of hills and quite fertile valleys which grow vines, corn and profusion of wild flowers. A good many fig trees and birds singing. The town extremely picturesque. The little houses, covered with red tiles, all cluster together in narrow streets, which slope up from 2 beaches. Between the 2 beaches stands an old stone fort with tower, gateway and gun holes all complete. The main beach forms a little harbour in which were a cluster of sailing boats and, in front of the fort gate, a wide empty space with two trees, chiefly used for drying nets. Powell and I walked through some of the winding streets, which had gutters down the middle, among friendly glances of inhabitants the younger females of whom were not bad looking, and so out into the country where we were very glad to stretch our legs. We found our way past fields and a house or two to the prisoners of war camp, presided over by Major Salmon who had about 40 prisoners (wounded) and 20 marines.

The camp [is] on a grassy slope with charming view over the island. Stayed talking there a bit and great preparations were made to give us tea, but it was just ready as we had to go back to catch the boat. However, we had some giaourti which was very refreshing.

We both rather envied the attractions of camping there in such jolly weather. We had not long returned to the ship when the decision was arrived at that GHQ should camp on shore, not only because of submarines but also because we are in such bad communication with telegraph on this ship. Rather consternation on the part of Q and Churchill, for we are not yet properly equipped for camping yet and there is no transport in the island.

A wire came from the admiral saying he had a satisfactory but very confidential wire from Admiralty to show which foreshadowed the reorganisation of his squadron.

? Italy coming in.[5]

Friday 14 May 1915

This day was comic in some respects for, after breakfast orders were given that all officers' kits and servants were to go ashore immediately in a lighter towed by a fleet sweeper. Colonel Beadon and Major Striedinger have been out since dawn reconnoitring for a camp, and one having been decided on. So there was a tremendous packing up and rushing to and fro, and people in charge of messes took a good deal of trouble to get up their canteens and stores.

"I" office was entirely packed up. The embarkation of kit, stores, tents and escort took quite 2 hours, and it was discouraging to hear that the whole available transport of the

5 Orlo put a question mark before this statement, showing he was unsure. Separate correspondence from the Admiralty that day to de Robeck discusses reorganising the fleet to accommodate a British-French-Italian fleet. In little over a week Italy declared war against Austria-Hungary.

island consisted of 9 mules and 3 donkeys, which would have to move all the stuff dumped on the quay about a mile inland. Work was all mildly disorganised for the day, which was very warm, but towards tea time it began to be realised we should not get ashore for the night, and this was definitely fixed soon after, orders being given for officers' servants and a minimum of kit to return to the ship, but not before an urgent telegram in cipher had been sent to the Base Alexandria to send urgently latrine screens and toilet paper. A party including Maxwell, Churchill and escort slept ashore, having erected tents. Many of us meanwhile were left without servants or even washing articles. My man returned and brought my hand bag, however. After dinner, the admiral arrived and had a long private talk with Sir Ian. I went to bed at 11 p.m., but before I got to sleep, Fuller came and told me we were not going ashore at Tenedos after all.

Saturday 15 May 1915

Accordingly, our kits all came back, the camp was all struck, Churchill and co. returned, and about lunch time we sailed to Cape Helles again where we spent the afternoon. About 6 p.m. up anchored again and arrived at Imbros, where anchored again in company with *Lord Nelson*, *Jauréguiberry*, and a few others. So now we have only Samothrace left to visit. At present it is quite uncertain if we are going to camp or not, and not a soul knows. We don't dare unpack our kit. The whole thing is quite a comedy.

Persistent rumours already that (a) Bulgaria, (b) Romania, (c) Italy, (d) Holland are coming in. No news, but a very private wire from Kitchener this morning asking on behalf of War Council how many men we want, assuming that troops were available, to bring our expedition to successful conclusion.

Sunday 16 May 1915

A beautiful day but spent in absolute stagnation off Imbros. We were practically cut off from telegrams and there was nothing on earth to do. Apparently all hope of camping is off for the present: Tenedos was supposed to be unsuitable because near to nobody, troops or Admiral, and so close to the mainland as to be dangerous if Germans knew where we were. So there we are, threatened with death from cirrhosis of the liver. Keeling and I walking on deck compared notes as to what we saw of internal politics. Both of us, not being soldiers, are made recipients of the others' grievances, and there are a great many of them—one result of being on board ship so long. Pollen has a down on the CGS and Operations, and showed quite unnecessary heat this evening when his suggestion about tips for the stewards was not so very cordially received by Aspinall (before dinner he had once more told me his sorrows, saying that this 8 weeks had been both extremely boring and extremely disagreeable), the AG has a down on the CGS because he is always being left behind, Q is worried to death over camps and difficulties of water communication, and I quarrels all day with itself; all have different ideas as to the value of information, and Deedes and Lloyd both think Ward a stodgy old cuss who knows nothing, and Ward gets annoyed when the CGS sends for Deedes and not for him, the head of the branch.

Only other excitement today was that Greek islanders turned up in a boat with Australian uniforms in their possession. They were at once put under guard as possible spies. They said they had found the uniforms in the sea—an obvious lie. After some discussion, they were threatened violently in Turkish by Hony that they would be shot if ever seen again and allowed to go minus the uniforms and no business done. Wire from K that he was very anxious about number of rifles going out of the country; apparently situation in that respect is rather serious in England. All these reinforcements for us put a very sudden strain on things. The general visited Anzac today and saw General Bridges, commanding Australian Division, who is very seriously wounded. Slight advance on our left by 29th Division.

Monday 17 May 1915

Answer sent to Kitchener's inquiry as to number of troops required. No more space or water on peninsula for more troops. If any other nation came in or Russians landed to divert Turks' attention, could do with present force, if kept up to strength, plus the Army corps already asked for. If situation not so changed, then an additional Army corps would be necessary, and would have to be kept on Tenedos, Imbros and Lemnos.

In afternoon went ashore with Keeling and clambered about the rocky hills of Imbros which are very rough going. Only a few little bits of the island cultivated and the ensemble even in bright sun is rather desolate. When we got back to the beach, found Bertier, Maxwell and Braithwaite, and pulled with them back to the ship in the dinghy which against the head wind and choppy sea was hard exercise for which very grateful. Saw a striped swallow tail on the island, only with white instead of yellow ground colour—a very beautiful butterfly.

Tuesday 18 May 1915

Uneventful and windy. The King's Messenger bag arrived with no letter from Alice or Mother, very disappointing. Two ordinary mails arrived later, however, bringing a letter from Alice of April 27, papers, and birthday presents from the girls. We sent out a good many wires today. One portentous one giving our requirements in gun ammunition. Late in the evening a most despondent wire from K in answer to our demand for 2 Army corps: it must have been written in a desperate fit of the blues: the Germans would have rejoiced to read it. It said: "I am sure you fully realise what a disappointment it is to me that my view, that with the support of naval artillery you would quickly be able to dominate the Dardanelles forts, was a miscalculation. The demands for reinforcements and ammunition which we can ill spare from France create a very serious situation. This requires the gravest consideration, as to how long we can support two fields of operations. I am sure I can rely on you to do all that is possible to prevent the possibility of withdrawal, with all its dangers in the East, coming into the field of possible solutions".

This a very unreasonable wire. He and the others had no business to have preconceived views on the easiness of an operation of the difficulty of which they could have no conception. They ought not to have undertaken it unless prepared to support it to the full. It is obvious from the papers how serious the ammunition question is, and unless there was some reason for undertaking this expedition against the ordinary dictates of prudence, I cannot help feeling it was a mistake, even if it turns out well.

However, Sir Ian and the CGS came out strong in their reply. They just patted Kitchener on the back and said "I see nothing in the situation to cause you despondency. Remember you asked me to reply on the assumption that you had troops at your disposal. We make slow but sure progress every day".

Wednesday 19 May 1915

I heard them talking about it at breakfast today and they were quite pityingly patronising about Kitchener, which is a good sign. News today that heavy attack made on Anzac lasting all night from midnight, heavy rifle fire and guns of all sorts from 9.2″ downwards. Enemy suffered very heavy loss and situation well in hand. This the first fruits of the fresh troops the Turks have brought up.

Today very windy. Dawnay gone off to spend a week on W Beach to get some matters straight.

In the afternoon, Monty Mackenzie turned up with Captain Kenny, the Sultan's ADC, in a torpedo boat. He had apparently already had interesting adventures. Coming from Alexandria in the *Franconia*, he landed on W Beach while it was being shelled. Was then sent off to Tenedos in a motor boat towing a lighter with a broken aeroplane, after which they passed the night at Tenedos. Yesterday they set out in the motor boat for Imbros in a heavy swell, and just as they were making the bay the motor broke down, and they were adrift. Kenny very sick and Monty felt pretty bad. By quite good luck they just made an inlet called Purgos, just off the west coast of the island, and rather nervously landed not knowing if island was Turkish or not, if inhabitants were friendly, and seeing many tins of oil on the beach, thought it might be a German submarine depot. They had 3 NCOs of Military Police with them, and they mounted guard all night with loaded revolvers. The inhabitants were very friendly, though Monty says they sent all their women into the interior, fed them and sent a horseman to inform GHQ. Hence their rescue by a torpedo. Monty seemed very well and cheery, and very pleased to be here. He had more kit than I expected, but his tunic was an ordinary soldier's one, far too short, which he had picked up on the quay at Alexandria, and his other tunic of drill was shorter still. He said it was a relic of Tel-el-Kebir rescued from the tailor at Alexandria where he got measured. It is not yet quite known what is going to be done with him. I saw he got a cabin and introduced him to a good many people. He has already told me a good deal about himself. His new novel, "Guy and Pauline", all about Burford and Guy Hazelwood, just finished.[6] If Harpers take it for serial he gets £1500, £500 for book in America, £1000 for book in England for first go off. After the *Comedy of Youth* series is finished he proposes a work in about 30 volumes taking a village in England and a family and tracing them through all the ages up to the present. Proposes to get that done by the time he is 48! Spoke with great admiration of Defoe: says he is well worth a literary study. An idea for me.[7]

Told me the original of Jennie whom Mavro has just married is a certain Christine Maude (Humphreys) of the Alhambra Ballet, with whom Mavro had long been in love. It was their relationship which gave him the study for *Carnival*. Says she is a perfect Cockney and it will be a great mistake to try and make a lady of her.

The attack at Anzac continued today and was repulsed with very heavy loss. Turkish casualties quite 7000. Ours 500.

Thursday 20 May 1915

Very interesting news today. Coalition Cabinet in England. Winston, Haldane, Crewe, Harcourt, and Birrell gone out: Balfour, Bonar Law, Frederick Edwin Smith, Earl of Derby, and Chamberlain come in. Wonder what the results will be. Also, that Fisher has resigned.

Information from WO that beginnings of mutiny in peninsula, and 50,000 Turks hors de combat. *Goeben* hit 3 times on May 11th.

Anzac quiet during the night.

6 Mackenzie dedicated *Guy and Pauline* to Sir Ian Hamilton and GHQ MEF.

7 Orlo later wrote about Defoe in 'Some Great English Novels' (1926).

One or two discussions with Fuller yesterday. It is quaint that when he has a point to make his eyes glitter like a heron's. Usually his face so demure.

Went ashore this afternoon and walked with Monty and others. A very pretty walk along a footpath, luxuriant with wildflowers, up onto a hill from where a lovely view over the valleys out to the sea beyond.

How obsessed novelists are with the number of their circulation. Monty actually suggested that critics ought to take into account, e.g., that he "does" 25,000 to Hugh Walpole's 24,000, in making a critical estimate of the two.

Friday 21 May 1915

Very quiet day on board ship with little to do. Nothing much in the way of operations. Anzac try to arrange an armistice so that French [sic: Orlo would have known this was incorrect and should have written Turks] can bury their dead. Read a letter from Birdie[8] written 28th giving a more private account of the landing, which showed again the magnificent dash of the first rush, the subsequent scattering and heavy counterattacks, the disorganisation due to the landing of battalions in wrong order and rushing them to the front at once, and the consequent very bad moral at night, which Birdwood described as a "nightmare", because the senior officers urged him most strongly to re-embark and he was repeatedly getting messages forecasting "disaster" etc. from commanding officers.

News by wireless that Henderson had joined the coalition cabinet; also that Italian and Austrian embassies in Vienna and Rome respectively had asked us to look after their interests and that Austrian and German consulates had left Rome.

Talked a good deal with Monty during the day. He told

8 Lieutenant-General Birdwood.

me a good many things. (1) His experiences touring in America, which seem to have been frightful. All the time he was suffering from neuritis, and yet was often travelling all night, every day and playing every day. The food was awful, cockroaches abounded and it was very cold. Also he was writing stories at £125 apiece for one of the American magazines. On the day of the dress rehearsal at Toronto he got an abscess in his tooth which swelled up his face enormously. He had to go to a dentist and have this burnt out. Then he had to play with a pad of cotton wool in his mouth and the grease paint burning his burnt face. After the performance he had to sit straight down and write a detective story for the magazine.

(2) Of the life he lived while working with Pelissier. After the performance 6 of them started in a motor for Brighton, stopping for a drink at the Marquis of Granby. They had a special room in the Albion Hotel, where there was champagne, brandy, gin and rum waiting in large quantities, and here drinking all the time they worked till about 7 a.m. Then they might get an hour or two's sleep. Then bathing, more champagne, lunch and drink again, dinner and then back to London to play. Said he had a great row with Pelissier when he wanted to marry his sister because he drank too much; says the son a very jolly child.[9]

(3) In the evening we talked a good deal about his work. Said, as regards criticism, he was so apt to think others were right, and hence it worried him. I ventured to say I didn't think his character stereoscopic enough. He replied with what I think the true answer, that it was due to the amount of self-consciousness still left. That it was young work not yet arrived at objectivity. We talked of what other people had said of his characters, how Arnold Bennett

9 Referring to Compton Mackenzie's nephew.

couldn't stand his work and he couldn't stand being identified with Arnold Bennett's school, how Christopher didn't like his characters, how Cyril had written and, surprisingly, grasped the point of "Sinister Street Part II" after a struggle, how Henry James had encouraged him by writing to Pinker that, with the exception of Wells, he was doing the best work going and adding that "Mackenzie for Mackenzie is better than Wells for Wells." I pleased him by referring to the comedy in his work which so many people don't see. Told him Stella disappointed me in Vol II. Admitted that, but said she was having a rest and would come on again. This led to his telling me various ideas for future novels. Stella to have a volume, another one about the politician who is to save his soul by a scandal, another of the young high churchman who is to seem a George Herbert while secretly raging with discontent, another to Sylvia Scarlett about sex and lesbianism. Also, two by the way plots. (a) Two old American ladies, who, having lived in poverty and puritanism in Iowa, came into money, launch out into a villa at Capri, and all their puritanism turns to fanatical championing of a discredited count. This to be called "Vestal Fires". (b) Of a daughter of a stuffy west Kensington family who goes on stage, becomes beauty girl, and marries young Irish peer, goes with him to lead country life in Ireland where not she, but he, becomes tired and wants to show her off in London. There he becomes ruined and killed, and she goes back to stage as Lady Clairhaven, where success is brief and her prestige soon obscured by claims of youth: goes back to west Kensington, same result. Finally marries a society journalist—her first love—and remains life a stuffed bird of paradise to supply his columns with matter.

Told me also how he liked to work, i.e. long and continuously without going out. To be in a room with other people, especially, as he said, if they were doing other things that rather bored them. He liked to have Faith playing the piano, Mavro doing a jigsaw, and Secker laboriously building bricks. He says he will miss Mavro now, but hopes to get another "devoted slave".

Finished today "The Voyage Out" by Virginia Woolf. No plot, just study of characters thrown together by a steamer trip to Brazil. Very sympathetic in parts. Obviously a desire to touch on all the big subjects—as usual in a first book. Some of the characters good. e.g. St John Hirst, the ugly clever man (? Adrian Stephen), Rachel, and Helen Ambrose, her aunt. A lot of good stuff in her that I hope will be pulled together.

Saturday and Sunday, 22 and 23 May 1915

Nothing much to record. Had walks on shore each day. Liver is getting rather bad and I had to get a dose from the doctor.

Monday 24 May 1915

Armistice at Anzac so went there with Pollen, Monty and others. See account attached. Very warm on shore and panted a good deal going up the steep hills. The Provost Marshall, one Bowler, was very glad to hear I was Uncle Jes' nephew.[10] Practiced before him. Spoke with tremendous admiration of Uncle Jes. Said nobody in New Zealand had been so revered by the people. He introduced me to Godley, who also knew Uncle Jes. N.B.: the story of the conference about armistice was interrupted by voice of New Zealander "Have any of you f--- got my kettle".

11 letters arrived by King's Messenger. Great envy on the part of others.

10 Sir Joshua Strange Williams (see Introduction).

Visit to Anzac

I went yesterday (May 24) to see the Anzac position on the slopes of Sari Bair. It was an appropriate day for an outing, it being Whit Monday, and also there was no danger, as the Turks had asked for and obtained a suspension of hostilities from 7.30 a.m. to 4.30 p.m. to bury their dead, who were lying thick in front of our fire trenches after their big attack of a few nights ago. Birdwood had been very anxious that this should happen as the dead bodies were beginning to smell.

Monty Mackenzie, Pollen, Brodrick, Churchill and I went over in the tiny torpedo boat 044, built somewhere in the 80s, and it took us over an hour getting across. Luckily, it was a fine day and the sea was smooth.

The only thing to be said about the Anzac position is that it is amazing. To imagine it if one had not seen it would be impossible. The first impression from a boat is that of seeing the cave dwellings of a large and prosperous tribe of savages who live on the extremely steep slopes of broken sandy bluffs covered with scrub which go up from a very narrow sandy beach to a height of 300 feet. Off the shore are several ships from which supplies are unloading, in shore are about 6 landing places in the shape of rough piers or stranded lighters. All along, between the bluff and the sea are transverse tiers of wooden boxes rising to about 10 feet which contain stores. These are so arranged to act as traverses from which to shelter from the shrapnel with which the beach is daily shelled. In the sea and on the lighters are crowds of naked men bathing, and everywhere on the beach and up the sandy slopes, the place is in perpetual motion like an ant-heap of khaki ants.

There is just a narrow roadway between the biscuit boxes and the foot of the bluff, and beyond it the dugouts begin at once. These are simply holes in the hill side, with roofs in some cases of sandbags and earth on rough baulks of timber, with mackintosh shuts over the entrance, biscuits and boxes lying about. On the beach and on the lower slopes is the home of headquarters and the administrative departments, all in dugouts, not a tent to be seen, and up the hill, till the sky breaks over the crest, there is nothing but these holes, steep footpaths, green arbutus and sandy declivity.

The position seen from above is a semicircle from the beach with inner lines. The Australian Division holds the right sector, the New Zealand the left. In the centre is a kind of bastion still held by the Turks. But this bird's eye view makes it look much too simple. The firing line is a few yards over the top of a very steep declivity which descends almost precipitously 300 feet into a valley which goes round in a semicircle and on the other side of which rises abruptly a series of lower broken hills…

In front of our firing line is a plateau gradually rising, and the Turkish firing line is from 30 yards to 20 feet away from ours. Our trenches are deep and communication trenches and foot paths run right down the steep slope, which like all the rest is covered with arbutus bushes and a kind of wild rose and pitted with little dugouts, some only just large enough for a man to crawl into. A good road has been made along the bottom of the valley and alongside it are more dugouts, water places, telephone wires, etc., with strapping men everywhere in shirts and breeches, working, cooking or eating. It is almost inconceivable that a whole Army Corps headquarters and all should be holding such a position, the whole exposed to shell fire and with the air of hanging on by its eyelids. And yet as a matter of fact it is an extremely strong position to hold, though a very difficult one to advance from. They have got all their guns up the steep hill, which in itself is a wonderful feat. We toiled

Stores in the Anzac sector (O.C. Williams, IWM).

right up to the top and saw the burial parties at work, a line of flags held by sentries of both sides marking the dividing line. The smell really was appalling. About 3000 Turkish dead were buried by the Turks. After that we went down the hill and ate our lunch outside the dugouts of the headquarters just above the beach. I saw most of the people I had met before at Cairo. At 4 p.m. we left again.

Took several photographs which I hope will do well, but nothing could reproduce the ensemble, together with the activity animating it. All here argue that it is the most amazing thing they ever saw.

Tuesday 25 May 1915

Feeling rather rotten all day. About 12.15 p.m. a German submarine sank the *Triumph* off Kaba Tepe: a bad blow, [but] nearly all crew saved. We have a transport anchored alongside on each side which makes ship very stuffy, and flies disgusting.

Wednesday 26 May 1915

Windy again so could not get ashore. Nothing much to record.

Thursday 27 May 1915

Still blowing. At breakfast heard news that submarine had sunk *Majestic* near W beach; everybody saved including General Fuller and Ashmead Bartlett. News that Italy at war with Austria confirmed by wire from WO.

Walked on deck for half an hour with the general. He rather full of the submarine. Said that in his own heart, he had been at this moment more confident of making a good advance than at any time in the campaign, though he had not said so and till this submarine appeared had hoped in the next 2 or 3 days to get on a good bit. But now, if ships can't bombard and troops can't be fed it would be impossible. Told me that after March 18 he had written to Mrs Winston [Churchill], knowing her husband would see it, saying that under the present exceptional circumstances surely it would not be impossible to surround your battleships with lighters having no cargo but very heavy iron nets, as there was no need for the battleships to move, but protection was the great thing. Also thought some protected pen could have been arranged for supply ships. Told me how some years ago he had taken his courage in both hands and made himself heard on the Committee of Imperial Defence relating what submarines had done in combined manoeuvres at Malta. Afterwards Lord Fisher, whom he described as "a strong and able man, but a thorough rogue who plays for his own hand" came and told him that what he had said would probably have momentous results in deciding between the pro-submarine school and the anti-submarine. It did, and when he was saying goodbye to Fisher in March, Fisher reminded him of it.

Later in the day, as we set off to the *Majestic*, heard that our E11 had done splendidly in [the Sea of] Marmara: sunk one big ship with 6″ guns and heavy ammunition on board, chased another into Rodosto and sunk her at the pier, then gone on to Constantinople and torpedoed another ship there by the Arsenal.

After lunch, had a bit of a row in a boat and then walked for ¾ hour with Powell on shore.

Friday 28 May 1915

Nothing particular. Move to the shore decided and preparations for camp begun. Stayed on ship all day suffering from diarrhoea.

Saturday 29 May 1915

A strong attack made on Anzac at Quinn's Post, where enemy blew up mine and occupied crater and support trenches. They were turned out with bayonet and Turks in the support trenches surrendered. Further their heavy columns marching to support success were caught by our artillery and demoralised, 2nd line throwing bombs at their first line. Their casualties said to be between 1500 and 2000. Ours 300.

In afternoon, strenuous walk on shore with Powell for nearly 4 hours. We pushed right over rocky paths to the divide. It was a lovely day and the view of western end of island was lovely: rich valleys with trees and a fine fertile plain on which several prosperous villages. Coming back we made too bold a circuit and had to hurry, go bang over several rocky hills, stumbling and swearing. Just got back to the new pier with 5 minutes to spare and dry as a bone internally. Dawnay came back from W beach and Bolton goes for 10 days tomorrow. Powell and I shall miss "Bessie" as we call him. He and Powell rag one another all the time, and both being stout and burly are rather a comic pair.

Colonel Williams back for a day or two but returns to command his regiment, the Hants.[11] Simpson-Baikie to succeed Breeks as Brigadier General Royal Artillery, 29th Division.

Sunday 30 May 1915

Scirocco, headachy weather. Did little all day but finish the Boddington Sonnet.

Monday 31 May 1915

Process of packing up and leaving the *Arcadian* whom perhaps we shall never see again. Did not actually get ashore myself till after 5 p.m. GHQ camp is in a pleasant position on the low spit which curves round into Kephalo Point. Soil of the camp sandy covered with stubbly grass and here and there a few patches of corn. Officers' lines 4 rows of tents, and men's lines run out at right angles. A few marquees for offices, and 3 marquees as mess tents. The General has a little camp to himself by the one poor tree. The view of the hills of Imbros beyond the bay from here is very beautiful. On the southern side of the island sand dunes leading down to sandy beach make very nice bathing place. A great rush on first landing to get hold of wood, packing cases, etc. to make tent furniture. I found Ashley had already nabbed a chair and a canvas bucket,

11 Hampshire Regiment.

and told him to keep a good look out for other things. The mess was inaugurated in great style with free drinks. Operations and Intelligence mess together, with Maxwell as chief mess president, and Hony sub president.

Orlo outside his tent at Imbros (Family collection).

King's Messenger bag brought hardly any private letters; probably he left a day earlier. One from Harold for me very interesting on situation in England, and giving reasons for the depression which is evidently reigning in England just now. Said he thought conscription would be needed. The advance on Aubers a costly failure. Great disappointment with our inability to take Achi Baba.

4

'DEFENDERS IN CLOSE SIEGE'

PUSHING ON DURING JUNE

There was more gloom for the Allies during June. Despite the Russian victory in the Carpathian campaign against Austria-Hungary, in May the Germans launched a surprise offensive in support of their ally that cracked the Russian lines in the battle of Gorlice-Tarnów. By June, Russia's shattered armies began a 300-mile retreat in what was probably one of the greatest Central Powers victories. The enormous casualties suffered by the Russians—some estimates put this figure at over a million men—did serious damage to the army as a fighting force. Russia was outclassed in everything except bravery. Any hope of Russian support that Hamilton believed he may have received in Turkey, ended with this battle.

The plans for the next battle of Krithia were rather more realistic in the extent of an objective and more innovative; lessons were learnt from the earlier failures. The objective was limited to an advance of about 800 yards, so the notion of capturing Achi Baba was temporarily abandoned. The first step was to capture the Ottoman trenches; the second was to advance a further 500 yards and dig a new trench line. There was better intelligence of the Ottoman defences and defenders, who were now dug-in in good tactical positions across the Helles front. To shorten the advance across No Man's Land the British had sapped their line forward during a series of night digs that brought the jumping off position to within 250 yards of the Turks, as opposed to the previous 1,750 yards. By this stage Hunter-Weston had been promoted to temporary lieutenant-general and placed in command of VIII Corps (29th Division, Royal Naval Division, 42nd Division and the 29th Indian Infantry Brigade). It would be these battle-weary men that would be called upon once again.

The Third Battle of Krithia started on a sunny but breezy 4 June, beginning at 8.00 a.m. with a bombardment that would conclude at 11.20 a.m., at which point the troops would feint an advance by cheering and showing fixed bayonet, hoping to lure the Ottomans back into their trenches and encourage their artillery to fire to give away their positions. At 11.30 a.m. an intensive bombardment of the Ottoman front line would restart, hopefully catching the Ottomans manning their trenches and with counter-battery fire then suppressing their artillery. At noon the guns would increase their range whilst the first wave of the infantry would go over the top. A second wave would follow up at 12.15 p.m. In support of the infantry four RNAS Rolls Royce armoured cars would advance along the Krithia roads, providing supporting fire from their Maxim machine-guns, and, valiant as it may seem, they would drive up to the Ottoman wire and using grappling hooks literally tow it away.

From left to right the British and French troops were deployed as follows: 29th Indian Brigade would attack along Gully Spur; the 29th Division would attack the other side of Gully Ravine on Fir Tree Spur; the 42nd Division would attack astride Krithia Nullah; 2nd (Naval) Brigade would attack up Achi Baba Nullah and Krithia Spur, and both French divisions would attack along Kereves Spur. Combined, Hamilton had 30,000 men in the assault, supported by additional artillery in the form of six French quick-firing 75mm batteries. Although this was the highest number of men ever allotted to a Helles attack, they were opposed by a much-

strengthened Ottoman line that fielded similar numbers in well prepared positions supported by artillery.

The French, the RND brigade and the 42nd Division made a promising start, but this early success was not to last. During the French advance the formidable Haricot Redoubt was captured, but further advances were halted by the heavily defended, deep and wide Kereves Dere ravine. A counterattack forced the French back, losing the redoubt and the ground that the French had just taken. This dangerously exposed the RND's right flank, into which the Turks poured murderous enfilade fire. When the RND's advance faltered, the next to be impacted were the 42nd Division, which thus far had made some deep advance of up to 1,200 yards, but like dominos, the once coordinated, broad front attack quickly collapsed. The 29th Division and 29th Indian Brigade on the left flank also struggled to make progress. Most of the ground gained had to be relinquished or was lost to Ottoman counterattacks. The British blamed the attack's failure on the French, which was a little unfair considering they were facing some of the most formidable Ottoman strongpoints at Helles.

It was apparent to the high command that attacking on a broad front, unless there was a certainty of success at all points, was probably going to fail. Reinforcements in the shape of 52nd (Lowland) Division, under Major-General Granville Egerton, brought some urgently needed manpower, but without sufficient munitions they had their limitations. On 7 June, as the Third Battle of Krithia was being fought to an unsuccessful closure, Lord Kitchener, the Secretary of State for War, sent a telegram to Hamilton confirming the availability of three New Army 'Kitchener' divisions (10th, 11th and 13th Divisions). Whilst too late to make any difference to the outcome of Third Krithia, this was excellent news for future offensive planning.

Out of failure comes ingenuity and later in June there were some limited successes. Hamilton authorised two attacks: one on the extreme right flank at Kereves Dere, the other on the left at Gully Ravine. These divisional attacks had the limited local objective of biting out a key part of the Ottoman line and holding it against counterattack. 'Bite and hold' was again proving itself to be successful and allowed Hamilton to neutralize key Ottoman redoubts that had contributed to the failure of the recent Krithia attack.

On 21 June, General Gouraud launched a French attack with two divisions, supported by mass artillery, with the objective of Hill 83, on the crest of the Kereves Spur, and the head of Ravine de la Mort. The fighting went on into the night of 22/23 June, which resulted in the French finally capturing the Haricot Redoubt and gaining a footing in the Quadrilateral Redoubt on the top of Hill 83. Fighting then continued until 25 June as the French consolidated their gains. For the first time they had won a position that overlooked the Turks. However, French fortune would end when on 30 June General Gouraud was wounded by a shell. The blast of the explosion hurled him over a two-metre-high wall; both his legs were broken and his right arm damaged, later amputated when gangrene set in. The elderly General Maurice Bailloud took over temporary command of the Corps Expéditionnaire d'Orient until another replacement could be sent.

On 28 June, Lieutenant-General Hunter-Weston launched the attack at Gully Ravine using 29th Division, 29th Indian Brigade and 156th Brigade from Egerton's newly arrived, but inexperienced, 52nd Division. The objective was to capture five lines of trenches on Gully Spur, nearest the sea, and two lines of trenches on Fir Tree Spur, on the slope leading towards Krithia. A concentrated artillery bombardment that comprised mainly British and French field guns, some naval fire and supported by newly arrived trench mortars, began at 10.20 a.m. At 10.45 a.m. the infantry advanced and in two hours had successfully captured all five trenches, a kilometre in depth, along Gully Spur. Unfortunately, the attack made by 156th Brigade on Fir Tree Spur was less successful due to insufficient artillery support, despite their best efforts and enormous loss. The brigade suffered the death of its commander and 1,400 casualties, about half its strength, of which 800 were killed. Hunter-Weston's callous remark that he was 'delighted to hear that the pups have been so well blooded' was not well received by their divisional general. British casualties for Gully Ravine in total were 3,800, and Ottoman casualties were as high as 14,000 by the time the battle had fought itself to a close on 5 July.

The success of Gully Ravine now put the British almost within touching distance of Krithia, barely a kilometre away. Following the June battles there was a naive expectation that the Ottomans would offer little resistance and were low in morale and short of ammunition. This was far from the truth and, although the Ottomans were on the defensive and had suffered devastating casualties, they were a long way from conceding. At this time Orlo was becoming more vocal in his criticisms of Hamilton, especially his failure to stand up to Kitchener. He was not alone and others on the staff were becoming equally disillusioned. Another who was critical of the General was British war correspondent, Ellis Ashmead-Bartlett. Bartlett was a more contentious figure, as highlighted by Orlo. He had some military experience as an officer in the Boer War, but by 1915 was a journalist for the Daily Telegraph and was selected as the Fleet Street representative for the Gallipoli campaign. Supremely self-confident and a colourful writer, he was never one to shy away from adding fictional material to improve a story, but as the campaign progressed, he had also become deeply critical of Hamilton and came into conflict with the censorship arrangements imposed by GHQ. He came to the view that Hamilton and his staff were concealing the truth from the authorities at home. Bartlett returned to London in June after he lost his belongings on the Majestic and went straight into politicking, meeting many of the key political and military figures. Whilst he was away Hamilton had appointed Orlo's friend, Compton Mackenzie, in his place. This would only be temporary as Bartlett was to return later in the month to find his freedom of movement severely curtailed and censorship even stricter.

The overall failure of the Krithia battles highlighted to GHQ that two more Army Corps would not be enough to take the Kilid Bahr Plateau, let alone Achi Baba. Hamilton cabled Kitchener requesting not only more men, but troops to relieve his forces that had been fighting since 25 April. All needed rest after being called upon to attack time after time. Hamilton got his wish, and three new divisions were sent out to Gallipoli. The 13th (Western) Division arrived in early July; the other two, the 10th (Irish) and the 11th (Northern) divisions would arrive towards the end of the month. Kitchener also hinted on sending a fourth and maybe a fifth division which Hamilton readily accepted. This re-energised the staff who got to work on how to use the new men once they had arrived.

* * *

Tuesday 1 June 1915

Up and bathed with Powell at 6.30 which intend to do every day as it is very pleasant. Working practically all day till 6 p.m. when a short walk with Powell. During day Ashley contrived me a table, a boot stand and a pair of standing shelves out of wood he procured. My tent now quite comfortable. Weather very pleasant with warm sun and cool breeze though one could do with just a little less wind. We all go about in shirtsleeves and drill with sun helmets.

News from Intelligence shows clearly that the Russian defeat in Carpathians has induced them to absorb all the troops that were meant for a landing in Turkey. This is a blow to us as it increases the forces available against us. Also no hope of Italy doing anything to help in Asia at present. Meanwhile great preparations going forward for the next big attack in Southern section. This is to take place on June 4, a good date for Etonians: apropos of which there is a proposition to hold a 4th of June dinner on W beach on some date in the near future.

Wednesday 2 June 1915

Much the same as regards myself. Walked by myself at 6 p.m. nearly up to Kephalo and back. A strong wire was sent to Kitchener about gun ammunition, and another very important telegram informing him that owing to Russian defection we were faced with a fresh situation, and that we could certainly not get on without 2 Army Corps more, though even then this estimate was made on supposition of support from Russia. This wire plainly written was rather stupidly transmogrified by [the] general with long literary words. e.g. "am unable to contemplate with soldierly equanimity the massing of the forces I have adumbrated". Why must he use such words. Really Sir Ian does not impress me. He can't say a thing direct, nor bring himself to stand up to Kitchener. For instance, our Base Commandant, General McGrigor, when he came out had a definite promise from the QMG[1] at the WO he should be IGC when that appointment was made. Now Kitchener wires to say that General Wallace was being sent for the job from Egypt, and Sir Ian hasn't the pluck to tell him that a definite promise had been given to McGrigor, but tries to suggest other things against Wallace which quite fail to put Kitchener off.

Thursday 3 June 1915

Kitchener replied asking definitely if with reinforcement asked for Sir Ian was convinced he could "take the Kilid Bahr plateau and so end the Dardanelles operations". Sir Ian has deferred reply till after the action of tomorrow, which is to begin at 11 a.m. with bombardment, with infantry advance at noon. The object is to take enemy's front trenches all along line, and push forward about 500 yards on left and right, consolidating all positions taken; further, of course, if possible.

News in Poldhu[2] that yesterday Germans had attacked London with 20 Zeppelins. Details scanty. Obviously some damage done by fires. German wireless says wharves and docks were bombed.

Today Sir Ian consulted me as to whether I thought Monty would like to step into Ashmead Bartlett's shoes. The whole episode rather amusing. Ashmead Bartlett is a most offensive man whom everyone hates. He was on the *Majestic* when she was torpedoed and lost all his kit, and obtained leave to go [to] Malta to refit. Just before leaving GHQ refused to pass a wire and a letter that he wrote—apparently very gloomy in tone—saying more men,

1 Major-General Sir John Cowans, QMG.

2 Poldhu Wireless Station, Cornwall.

munitions etc. were absolutely necessary. After he had left we wired to Malta telling them to let through none of his messages there. Today, hearing Ashmead Bartlett had left Malta for England, Sir Ian wired to Kitchener all about him, saying that he was a Jeremiah, and suggesting he had better stay at home and that a more cheerful correspondent be sent out. Meanwhile he was appointing Monty to act temporarily and perhaps the Newspaper Proprietor's Association could be approached with a view to retaining him. Monty had said it was just what he would like to do, and didn't mind about money. If he were accepted by the NPA he would get £2000 a year plus expenses. He thinks journalists would never agree to his appointment as representative of newspapers. Sir Ian took a very great interest in the whole matter, which I don't think is a general's business.

There will soon be trouble about the mess—as Maxwell's ideas are a bit too grandiose, and officers are beginning to say that they must live within their field allowances. We have no good Mess Sergeant and things are not strict enough. Our Greek cook is, I should say, a robber and has a violent temper.

Friday 4 June 1915

Fear [I] have slight stomach chill: feeling rather rotten and upset within. Nearly everyone gone to W Beach to see after the big attack. The bombardment has now begun and the guns are booming like anything in the distance. A very idle day luckily for me as I was feeling rather seedy all day.

The staff who been at Helles came back about 8.35 and brought us news that while the centre had got on well about 600 yards, the extreme left and extreme right had failed to advance much. On the left the Gurkhas got on a bit, but the battalion on their right were absolutely held up by barbed wire. On the right the French advanced and took the Haricot[3] but a strong counterattack drove them back and their retirement left the RND in the air. They suffered heavily and had to come back. Some say the French 75s shot into them. A night attack was made along the cliffs at 10 p.m. by the Gurkhas but failed. Altogether, the day which began well was disappointing, chiefly owing to French retirement. French troops not very much good, and that is the truth.

At 11 p.m. Anzac made an attack on the trench beyond Quinn's Post which was successful till 6.30 a.m. when a strong counterattack with heavy bombs drove out men back to their original trench, communication trenches and bomb proofs remaining in their hands.

Saturday 5 June 1915

Tummy a little better. Aspinall and Dawnay busy drafting telegram to answer Kitchener's question of the 3rd. When done Dawnay took it in and said it had been thrown into the basket till the Press telegram was done. "That's the worst of having a journalist in command", he said. To which Aspinall replied: "That's not fair: all journalists are not mountebanks".

Dawnay's view is that it is essential to make an attack upon some new front e.g. Enos, and that the FO must be stirred up to get some other nation to come in. Otherwise even with 2 more Army Corps our progress to the Kilid Bahr plateau would take many weeks.

Sunday 6 June 1915

Further news of the June 4 action. Naval Division report clearly shows that French on their right simply didn't come on. At the hour of advance only 12 men left the trenches.

3 Haricot Redoubt on Kereves Spur.

Twice in the afternoon: RND wished to attack again but French would not advance. As it was the failure of French allowed RND to be enfiladed from a redoubt and lose very heavily. The Collingwood Bn lost 25 officers and 600 men.

The Turks attacked our left heavily today with 2 new divisions and recaptured some trenches. Most of these recaptured again and in the evening 155th Bde (Lowland Division) sent from Mudros to Helles to assist.

Two long wires sent to Kitchener tonight:

(1) gave account of operations of the day, and said that Doran, who had only just come out from England to command 88th Bde had been suspended for incompetence.[4]

(2) The long wire based on Dawnay's appreciation of situation. Points made: That previous estimate of reinforcements required (2 Army Corps) based on expectation of Russian assistance and also of more help from French. The staff and artillery of latter good, but Senegalese, Eurasian and Algerian infantry quite hopeless. Our progress to Kilid Bahr must be slow and with 2 Army Corps would be considerably expedited, unless some sudden change in situation e.g. Bulgarian understanding with Turkey. What is needed above all is a fresh ally to come in on another front of operation. Even Sir Ian was contemplating this if more troops sent, though admiral was against Enos because submarines and open anchorage, and Smyrna and Adramyti too far off. The moral and political effect of fresh ally at any of these places would be felt at once. Birdwood estimates 4 brigades necessary to extend his front sufficiently for serious

4 Aspinall-Oglander said he was 'invalided' (C.F. Aspinall-Oglander, *Military Operations*, Vol. 2, p. 49).

attack towards Maidos. One Army Corps would therefore be allotted to him. The other would be to relieve RND and French in front line.

Hear only 3 British, 4 Native officers and 196 men left of Sikhs. Letter from Marquis saying flies and dust on W Beach were dreadful. We are certainly much better off here. Monty has prepared a despatch. Apparently he had a very funny interview with Maxwell who was green with jealously like a low comedian one of whose speeches has been cut. He talked pompously of how all the press would be against him, and how much harder it was to write for the press than to write books etc. He got no change out of Monty. He is a very silly little man who spends most of his time beautifying his tent and getting the cook to give it a cement floor. A mess committee has now been appointed to control him.

Idle afternoon. In evening tried to sketch Sari Bair from the sandhills, results awful.

At night sent another long telegram to Kitchener saying that not only must we have reinforcements but also reliefs, since the Turkish have fresh troops and ours have been fighting since 25th. Ours at best are better than Turks at best, but all continuously under shell fire and have no rest. Unless reliefs are sent we shall be reduced to position of defenders in close siege, as men undoubtedly getting worn out. "If I have sufficient troops to enable me to avoid calling on the same units too often I have confidence in ultimate attainment of Kilid Bahr. Impossible to forecast time required until I see some limit to numbers enemy can draw on. On June 4 want of fresh reserves just prevented our confirming success and capturing whole position".

Monday 7 June 1915

[no entry]

Tuesday 8 June 1915

Excellent wire from Kitchener. "Cabinet fully realise your difficulties and are determined to support you. We are despatching 3 divisions of new army, one of which will leave about end of week and the other 2 as transport available. The latest ought to reach you not later than the 1st fortnight in July, and the fleet by then will have been reinforced by a good many units less vulnerable than those now with you to submarine attack and give you continuous support. Till then while steadily pressing the enemy no need to take any premature risks".

This news bucked up everybody a good deal. It means that we really are going to see this thing through, and gives us something surer to look forward to in future. Another wire from Kitchener said that Ashmead Bartlett would have to come back unless we could frame a definite complaint against him or there would be difficulty with Newspaper Proprietors Association.

At the end of a message came the news to me that a Zeppelin had been destroyed.

Reply sent re: Ashmead Bartlett. No objection to his returning. Objection was to his going to England. Will Compton Mackenzie be accepted in meantime as a kind of eye witness.

WO replied Ashmead Bartlett was returning and Monty would be accepted as stop gap till he came. Had a walk with Monty in the evening. Among other things told me that his mind was more feminine than masculine, intuitive and emotional rather than masculine: hence the success of his books. His mind rather childish, so that when not working could be quite happy amusing himself like a child. He was apparently a fantastic prodigy as a child. Learnt to read by 1 year 10 months. By 2½ knew all stars. Head of St Pauls told him he could be the greatest scholar since Porson, but after getting his scholarship he just idled, which no doubt was a good thing.

Aspinall tells me he thinks Monty a most delightful person, as he certainly is.

Wednesday 9 June 1915

Loathsome high wind all day which makes tents flap like things demented and brings a thick layer of sand over everything. Pretty busy all day. Besides ciphers helping to get together some stuff for next despatch. Fuller leaving us to be temporary lieutenant colonel and AA&QMG of 29th Division.

Thursday 10 June 1915

Good news of Military Attaché Russia that new Black Sea Expeditionary Force would be ready about beginning of July.

Friday 11 June 1915

[no entry]

Saturday 12 June 1915

[no entry]

Sunday 13 June 1915

Last 3 days uneventful. Strong N.E. wind blowing all the time making tents flap like mad things. My exercise cut off by getting a ganglion on my left ankle due to boot rubbing. Today long telegrams sent to WO in answer to queries as to our position, prospects, future plans etc. with urgent demands for answer. Obviously new Cabinet considering this campaign very seriously, also that someone who has been here (? Bartlett)[5] has been talking to them in rather

5 Orlo wondered whether it was Ashmead-Bartlett.

an alarmist way. One query was weather [sic] we could not cut off Turkish supplies if submarines could do so on sea side. We replied that was what we wanted to do, an advance of 2 miles from Anzac, would dominate Maidos and Boghali and make even sea communication very dangerous, and also destroy usefulness of Ak Bashi Liman. The move forward there is what we intend as soon as more troops come. Suggested that quantity of shallow craft in and near Panderma would make complete stoppage of sea supplies from Asiatic shore very difficult. We did not favour suggestion to go in at Bulair, and Admiral cannot recommend Enos because of its open anchorage, impossibility of maintaining communications and want of small craft.

Monty suffering last 3 days from bad attack of neuritis and influenza and colic. Was very wretched and in great pain, but getting better by this afternoon.

Made another effort to sketch.

Monday 14 June 1915

Wind in the south, but strong and cool. Nothing of much import. Captain Anstey, a gunner, joined the staff. Doesn't look a very lively one. Worked at the despatch.

Tuesday 15 June 1915

Lovely day. Up at 6 and bathed with Powell. Anniversary of my wedding day. Alice's and Betty's birthday. Wish I could be wafted back to England at any rate for the day.

Yesterday Dawnay, who is something of a poet in his leisure hours, showed me what he thought the best of his poems, addressed to a friend of his killed in Flanders. It was very good in many respects, with deep emotion in it. The idea that the friend had at last come to enjoy the permanent vision of truth, instead of the partial glimpse which is all that we enjoy; in the presence of God. Dawnay has a strong spiritual side, and though I don't follow his particular views, it is a characteristic that always distinguishes a man from others. He and I had a walk together after tea, and talked of many things. Apropos of the GS said he had had to be very cunning to get the CGS to make Aspinall GSO1 in Operations, as he deserved, for the CGS, he thought, wanted in his heart of hearts to give it to Hore-Ruthven to whose wife he was devoted. He said Simpson-Baikie was a good man, but irritated the CGS so much, which was obvious. Says Aspinall is very good but doesn't tackle the CGS in the right way. You can do anything with CGS, he said, if you tackle him diplomatically. Dawnay is really the man who ought to be the GSO1. Both Aspinall and CGS are fundamentally stupid, however good staff officers they may be. It is Dawnay who really keep on thinking of things and working out schemes and appreciations in his head. He seems to think highly of Anstey, and would like to get Powell as well when Ruthven comes. I should say that would do for old Bolton. We then talked of a good many ultimate things which was refreshing.

Wednesday 16 June 1915

Storm of wind in the night, heavy rain this morning and much colder. Graves' tent pole broke in the night owing to his cords being too tight. Walked a little with Monty and began his new book "Guy and Pauline" which has arrived in proof.

Thursday 17 June 1915

Sunny again and warmer. Good many wires all day. The sending of the 3 new divisions leads to a lot of wiring. Appreciations and preparations for the big move at Anzac when they do come are progressing. After tea did a little sketch and finished "Guy and Pauline". It is a very touching story and the story of the girl very beautiful. Description of Burford Country excellent. The whole much less diffuse though man still an abstraction of himself. I call it the best he has yet done: there are faults but he is improving his weaknesses.

Friday 18 June 1915

Centenary of Waterloo odd. Aspinall, brevet major, now temporary lieutenant colonel. Bathed again. Jolly day but still windy. *Prince George* going to bombard Asiatic batteries.

Saturday 19 June 1915

During 19th trenches of SWB heavily bombarded and suffered from HE shell. 125th Brigade lost some trenches but fine counterattack of 5th Royal Scots won practically all back.

Sunday 20 June 1915

RND captured trench but bombs forced them to retire; when Turks got into trench again they were enfiladed by machine gun fire from RND trench on right and suffered very heavily. Altogether Turk casualties about 1000. Liman von Sanders confirmed wounded in left leg. Col Skeen, GSO1 ANZAC spending 2 nights here in camp. Another new arrival Captain Milward in Q department. Monty gone for 2 days to stay with Hunter-Weston to write up recent engagement. Turks firing away HE shell like anything. 100 on 8th Corps HQ.

The fact is that the Turks are at present far better supplied with ammunition than we are. Our amount of HE shell is very small and WO state that until its manufacture increases, they cannot increase our proportion. To one of their telegrams we sent the answer that, as they couldn't supply, "we realize it is no good crying for the moon but you must realize till ammunition arrives it is no good crying for the crescent". The Turks also seem to have an unlimited supply of bombs of which we have still only a fair quantity.

Monday 21 June 1915

Some indication of our probable rate of progress given by the fact that, we having pressed for more Japanese bombs [i.e. mortars] and guns, an order has been placed that will not begin to be completed in Japan till 2½ months hence.

Long wire sent yesterday in answer to inquiry as to advisability of diversion in Asia. This was [discouraged] on several grounds. (1) The Asiatic shore of Dardanelles is heavily entrenched. (2) Without a largely increased number of troops we could only hold a bridgehead there which would create little diversion and complicate the already difficult supply question. A diversion by Greece at Smyrna or lower down would be far more useful.

The Greek elections have resulted in a majority of about 60 for Venizelos. But the King's condition is very serious, and Gounaris is taking advantage of this not to meet Parliament till July 20.

The Germans seem pushing on in Galicia, and according to their own reports have penetrated Russian main line NW of Lemberg[6] which is now seriously threatened.

The whole of today since 4.30 a.m. the French have been engaged in… attack. The guns seemed to be firing, with varying intensity, all day long. I woke to them and went to sleep to them. According to reports they did very well. The 2nd Division took the 1st and then the 2nd line of the trenches opposite them which includes the "Haricot" and stuck to them. The 1st Division on the right also took the 1st line but were driven out by a counterattack. Gouraud

6 Lviv.

in a very definite order at 2 p.m. told this division that they could take their time but these trenches had got to be recaptured. The infantry attack did not begin till 7.50 p.m. but was successful according to latest reports. The French battleship *Saint Louis* made good practice on Asiatic Battery.

The day was beautiful. The wind is getting less and the heat increasing. Finished 1st draft of 2nd despatch.

Captain Mitchell, RN, rejoined GHQ.

Tuesday 22 June 1915

Kitchener wires new divisions will arrive July 10, July 18, July 28 respectively: inquires our views as to possibility of employing a 4th division. It is doubtful (1) as to ammunition supply (2) room for more troops. Information 15,000 reservists gone from Constantinople to form a new division, and 9000 militia with reservists to replace casualties. Since July 9 10,000 wounded arrived Constantinople. Monty returned today from the Peninsula where he seems to have enjoyed himself. Walked with Powell to rest camp off K Beach.[7] Great change in the place since we first arrived. A camp for 4000 men set up where the cornfields were, besides a casualty clearing section, field bakery, Base Park RE, Egyptian Works Company etc. Crowds of RND bathing in the sea. The slovenly behaviour of the sentries and the absence of saluting amused and rather depressed Powell.

Wednesday 23 June 1915

Very calm in morning and bathing delightful. We replied to Kitchener's query whether we should like a 4th division by saying yes, even if artillery came with only certain allowance of ammunition and no prospect of more. Said it might just turn the scale.

7 Kephalos Beach (Imbros).

No particular excitement otherwise. After tea walked over to lighthouse with Dawnay talking of many things, friends, the difficulty of getting the right people to dinner, the possibility of asking husbands and wives separately. Then as we sat on the cliff looking out towards Anzac, we talked of the future advance from there. Dawnay said he was convinced that 60,000 men should be pushed in there, some beforehand, the rest from trawlers on the day of the advance. He would set all the men there now digging all day new places for troops, and when the day came collect all the best officers from everywhere. Unfortunately, to his mind, the CGS is not convinced of the feasibility of his plan: he rather inclines to landing near Helles and turning the flank of the Achi Baba trenches. Dawnay thinks that they will find equally strong trenches opposite to them on the flank. Rather dolefully said that when people are persuaded into doing things against their inclination they don't do them wholeheartedly. An appreciation has gone into the general showing the futility of landing more troops at Helles and there we are at this moment. A great deal hangs on the decision where the new troops are to be employed.

Thursday 24 June 1915

King's Messenger late again. Telegram from Kitchener today giving names of 3 new divisional commanders: Mahon 10th, Hammersley 11th, Shaw 13th. Said Mahon would shine particularly in a tight place; Hammersley good but would require watching to see he didn't suffer from strain; Shaw a painstaking and methodical man who knows his work.

Saw by wires that 7th Gloucestershire Regiment coming in which Jenks is a captain.

News by wireless Germans have recaptured Lemberg (German source).

Friday 25 June 1915

Very warm. No particular occurrence. Chanak bombarded, set on fire. Colonel Sykes who was spotting from the balloon says firing very good and fires excellent. Surrey Yeomanry detachment arrived. Met Bonsor (Major in Command) on beach this evening. Walked after tea with Powell.

Saturday 26 June 1915

Distant thunderstorm in morning. Some rain. Wire from Kitchener saying Cabinet had not yet decided to send 4th division but asking if we could do with a 5th division if they could manage ammunition which seemed doubtful. This looks as if anyhow portion of Cabinet anxious to push this matter through. In evening Cuninghame MA at Athens turned up, and said King's illness would delay things a bit, as German party were doing all they knew.

Amery also turned up. He [is] on some special mission at Balkan capitals.

General and CGS went Anzac and were nearly blown to bits by an HE shell.

Walked with Powell. King's Messenger bag at last, many letters.

Sunday 27 June 1915

Lovely day. Nothing much doing all day, but preparations for tomorrow's attack on the left in the air. Bathed twice. The CGS promoted major general.

Monty went over to Helles today and lunched with 8th Corps when General Bailloud to lunch. They apparently had a regular Carlton menu beginning with iced cocktails and ending with '58 brandy. Great contrast with GHQ. Related funny conversation he had with Ashmead Bartlett, who told him that he had been to London and seen everyone, Kitchener, the Committee of Imperial Defence, Asquith etc. and told them exactly what ought to be done i.e. land at Enos. Said he supposed that Monty, like himself, had come up against the "smallness of the military mind". D his conceited eyes. He has already got £1000 down for his book and 20%. I shall do all I can to get it for review. Dawnay will try to get it for the *Spectator*.

Monday 28 June 1915

Very hot day. Sir Ian, CGS, Dawnay off to watch operations on the left. The bombardment began at 9 a.m. and at 11 a.m. the infantry attack was launched.[8] Went up on to the dunes just before 11 and saw the bombardment which was terrific, *Talbot* and 2 destroyers, *Scorpion* and *Wolverine* were making splendid practice on the trenches along the cliff. The troops engaged were 29th Division and 156th Brigade Lowland Division. On the cliff edge the Indian Brigade. The 87th and 156th Brigades went forward at 11 and carried—the 87th 1st two lines of Turkish trenches and the 156th got into nearly all H12[9] only in 2 places Turks remained in possession. The Boomerang trench taken ¼ hour before general bombardment ceased by 50 men who got in without loss. There the 86th Brigade went through the 87th right on to the 3rd line of trenches on the extreme left, into which they got. The whole objective of attack was accomplished with small loss and if consolidation is successful against all counterattacks, and the 2 little bits of H12 are taken it will be a success, as GC [Hamilton] wired to Kitchener, beyond expectation.

Dawnay says attack of 86th Brigade was magnificently timed and carried out, the men going forward in successive lines as on a field day with tin disks on their backs to

8 This was the Battle of Gully Ravine.

9 H12 was the trench line on Fir Tree Spur.

show to artillery, and at perfect even distance. Everybody agreed it was a very good show admirably carried out. 86th Brigade only lately been reorganized, after heavy losses of landing so its success very gratifying. Anzac meanwhile demonstrated along whole line and made right flank attack. Turks on left of 29th Division were quite taken by surprise. 150 prisoners captured chiefly by first rush into the Boomerang.

Long wire sent tonight in answer to inquiry about employment of 5th division. GC said that as 4th and 5th could not come simultaneously, he would adhere to his original plan of pushing on at Anzac with first 3 divisions. The 4th and 5th would reinforce these in case of first non-success; in case of success these 2 would either push through at Helles, or more probably land in Asiatic shore and be expected to push through to Chanak, Turks' forces in Asia being by then reduced to minimum by British advance. This would enable safe base to be set up in Morto Bay secure from future bad weather. To sum up we accept 4th and 5th divisions short of ammunition, though the more we can get now the easier task will be.

Wire from Hunter-Weston tonight for more HE 6″ and 4.5″ for tomorrow. The answer showed our present state with regard to this nature.

Tuesday 29 June 1915

Tummy rather deranged all day. Quiet day with no particular events. The early morning counterattack easily repulsed. Hunter-Weston in his reports puts down the partial failure of 156th Brigade to want of artillery preparation. Says we wanted 8 more howitzers and 600 rounds ammunition. The heavy casualties here due to this cause. New arrivals today. Major Hore-Ruthven VC to be GSO2 O(b) and 2nd Lieutenant Bass... to assist in SS ciphering.

There was supposed to be a general mess meeting after dinner to decide if Intelligence and Operations messes should split up. But when the time came the secessionists refused to put a motion, so it fizzled out. Our cook has given notice, and we have wired to Malta for 2 cooks. We have got a mess sergeant from the Surrey Yeomanry and things are already going better in the mess.

Wednesday 30 June 1915

Everything all over dust owing to violent squalls of wind last night and steady west wind later. Today GS old tent removed and much larger store tent set up in its place. Ruthven taking charge of O(b), and Powell goes to O(a). I am charged with duties of situation for Anzac and general summary, besides draft despatches. French said to have repulsed a counterattack and taken position called the Quadrilateral at 7.30 this morning. What they have actually achieved seems a little doubtful at present (3 p.m.). What they achieved was to capture series of trenches called the Quadrilateral opposite their left-centre and prolong them to south, thus completing gains of 21st. Turks lost very heavily. Our right-centre did some damage with machine gun fire. At 8 p.m. General Gouraud badly wounded by a shell: broken right arm, left leg and dislocated hip. His loss a serious one as he has got the French troops into a far better state since he came. We have wired urging that a 1st class man be sent to replace Bailloud who succeeds him, who is an old man not up to the strain. Today also we have wired to WO (1) saying our IGC was not good and we must have another. (2) that the Director of Works is sacked and Lotbinière put temporarily in his place.

This evening had a very pleasant walk with Deedes talking about news and things. He agrees with me in putting chief confidence in Dawnay and Hunter Bunter, and in thinking the combination Aspinall-Dawnay a strong one and owing to their respective positions not likely to be disturbed by jealousy or friction. Deedes would have a good many people sacked if he could, and enlarged on the waste of ability that there is, in which I agree. He complains very much of the apathy of Colonel Ward who, having no axe of his own to grind, takes very small interest in the various schemes and will not struggle against inertia of subordinates. I asked Deedes, who had been 6 weeks on the Peninsula, how troops viewed things. He said morale in some units had been bad e.g. RND where heavy losses. Naturally men can't understand why we don't get on, and also, unlike men in France, they have no real recreation and rest when in support. They have no canteen and when they are in support they are either sitting all day doing nothing under heavy shell fire or working all night on fatigue parties. Among officers, even generals, there is a great deal of criticism of GHQ and conduct of operations—also of administrative services e.g. water supply, disembarkation difficulties.

Night 10 p.m. attack on J13[10] held by 6th Gurkhas. Lt-Col Bruce wounded and men after throwing all their bombs charged down on enemy using Kukris with great effect for first time. At dawn another attack by ½ battalion, more than half shot down. The events of last few days have brought confidence here much higher. Turks seem to be obviously demoralized and apprehensive. It is easy to draw their fire. Men will not go into trenches in Quinn's Post, unless specially picked and promoted. But they still fight very stubbornly when attacked.

10 A trench on Gully Spur, just inland from Fusilier Bluff.

5

'GHQ GROWS AND GROWS'

PLANNING ANOTHER ADVENTURE

While Hamilton awaited the arrival of the new divisions, his staff continued to plan the forthcoming August offensive. Several ideas were considered. Some favoured a landing on the Asiastic coast, others the Bulair Isthmus, or even renewing the attack at Helles. However, Anzac was chosen to be the focus. Meanwhile, the offensive spirit needed to be maintained: to gain tactical advantage; to assure moral ascendency; and to keep Ottoman eyes fixed upon Helles, rather than Anzac. The unceasing routine of trench raiding, sniping, bombing, and mining continued, whilst those at Helles prepared for another small-scale tactical advance, this one being the sequel to the action of 28 June.

On 12 July, 52nd (Lowland) Division, with the French on the right, attacked along Achi Baba Nullah, with the object of straightening about 2,000 yards on the right-centre to bring it in line with the advances made at Gully Ravine. Two lines of trenches were captured, and retained, despite a series of fierce Ottman counterattacks and retaliatory shellfire. Support in the form of the battle weary RND were sent forward on 13 July to help consolidate the gains, whilst on their right the French had managed to advance their line down to the mouth of the Kereves Dere. After two days' fighting, the result of what became known as the Battle of Achi Baba Nullah was an advance of up to 380 yards but at a cost of thirty per cent British casualties, some 3,100 men.

The French suffered 840; General Joseph Masnou, commanding their 1e Division, was mortally wounded, succumbing to his wounds a few days later. Ottoman casualties were estimated at about 5,000.

Despite the French gains they weren't necessarily in any better position. They not only had to endure the enemy to their front, but due to their position on the extreme right flank of the allied line, they remained exposed to Ottoman artillery fire to their right and rear from the Asiatic coast. General Bailloud, commander of 2e Division, was so disturbed by this, that he demanded that they land a force in Asia to silence the Asiatic batteries. Whilst this was considered, it would have to be part of a future operation as current resources were already allocated to the August offensive. In the meantime, the suppression of fire from those batteries would have to be handled by counter battery fire from artillery on Helles, supported by naval Monitors. French morale was down; they could give no more.

Calls for more ammunition continued throughout July, in particular hand grenades which the Allies were lacking. This led to soldiers improvising their own grenades from the tins containing the soldiers' ration of jam, hence the name 'Jam-tin' bombs. They were simple to make and consisted of filling an empty tin with bits of metal and even stones into which an explosive charge and a fused detonator were placed. As an interim measure they helped supplement the meagre supply of official grenades that those on Gallipoli received. News later in the month that Kitchener and the Dardanelles Committee were going to give Gallipoli preference over the Western Front was well received by Hamilton and his staff. Finally, it looked like the MEF might get what they wanted in terms of men, ammunition and artillery.

Planning for the forthcoming offensive continued throughout July with knowledge of not only the three new

Kitchener divisions, but also confirmation from Kitchener that he was sending the two additional divisions that he alluded to in June, the territorial 53rd (Welsh) Division and 54th (East Anglian) Division. Hamilton was also informed that 2nd Mounted Division, which was stationed in Egypt, was available should he need it. Even with this injection of six new divisions, there were doubts amongst some of the planning staff that the offensive would achieve its objectives, and maybe at best only secure Suvla as a base for future operations. It was becoming clear to GHQ that this offensive had to succeed, failure was not an option.

By this stage the first of Kitchener's divisions, the 13th (Western) Division, had arrived. The division came into existence because of Army Order No. 324, issued on 21 August 1914, which authorised the formation of the six new 'Kitchener' Divisions. They were formed of volunteers who answered Kitchener's call to arms in 1914. After a few months in camp where they were uniformed, equipped and hurriedly trained, the first of their transports left port on 13 June and sailed to Alexandria. By 4 July, all units had moved to Mudros where they prepared for landing at Gallipoli. Between 6–16 July the divisional infantry landed on Helles and relieved 29th Division. The division's first taste of action was on 23 July when the Ottomans attacked their trenches near Gully Ravine, but they were driven off with ease, a good start for the division.

This was partly due to good British intelligence which had received reports of an impending attack, so all front-line units were on high alert. Intelligence was also aware of a potential chemical attack, possibly asphyxiating gas or liquid fire. Whilst there were no reports of poison gas being used at Gallipoli, at Anzac there was a report that the Ottomans had fired an inflammatory shell into a trench, but the fires were easily extinguished. Similarly, the French reported that some type of liquid was sprayed into their trenches that the Ottomans unsuccessfully tried to ignite with grenades. Following the use of chlorine gas by the Germans on the Western Front, the Dardanelles Committee in London, as well as senior commanders of the MEF, were alarmed by the possibility of Ottoman chemical attacks and repeatedly debated whether they should pre-empt this move by initiating the use of gas. This not only raised ethical and moral concerns, but also those of prestige related to the British reputation in the Middle East and the Indo-Muslim world. Precautions were made by issuing soldiers with protective masks, but for now Hamilton was adamant not to use gas. If the Ottomans did use it first, then he would be more relaxed to its use as a retaliatory weapon.

On 17 July, Lieutenant-General Hunter-Weston fell ill, reportedly from exhaustion, and a few days later was evacuated sick. With Hunter-Weston gone the tempo of leadership changed. His replacement was the experienced General Francis Davies who had been commanding the regular 8th Division on the Western Front since late 1914. Whilst waiting for Davies to arrive, temporary command of VIII Corps went to Lieutenant-General Hon. Sir Frederick Stopford, who had arrived ahead of his IX Corps. With Stopford ashore, plans were well under way for the August offensive. But would this break the deadlock?

Meanwhile, allied submarine operations continued and saw HMS E14 conducting three patrols in the Sea of Marmara. E14 first completed the passage of the Dardanelles and entered the Sea of Marmara on 27 April, remaining there until 18 May. A second patrol was made from 10 June to 3 July. To enter the Sea of Marmara was quite a feat of daring. First the submarine needed to dive under the enemy minefields and steel-wire anti-submarine cables. Despite great navigational difficulties from strong currents and a

10-fathom deep stratum of fresh water that often made it very hard to control the boat, they had to avoid shore batteries and continual hostile patrols. E14 succeeded in sinking torpedo gunboat Paykisevkei, the Nour el Bahr, a Turkish minelayer, and the former White Star liner Guj Djemal, carrying over 6,000 troops and a battery of artillery bound for Gallipoli. With her supplies running low, E14 was ordered to return and, fighting off several Turkish attacks, rejoined the fleet on 18 May. Its commander, Edward Courtney Boyle, was awarded the VC, his two officers the DSC and the members of his crew the DSM. A third patrol of 24 days took place from 21 July to 12 August 1915, by which time Submarine E14 with Boyle and his crew had spent a total of seventy days in the inland sea, quite a feat considering submarine warfare was still in its infancy.

In total the British claimed that a battleship, an old coastal defence ship, a destroyer, five gunboats, 11 transports, 44 steamers and 148 smaller vessels were sunk by submarines in the Dardanelles for the loss of one Australian, three British and four French submarines. The German official history suggests a lower number; the difference may be partly explained by some ships being beached and later repaired and refloated. There is no doubt that presence of allied submarines caused the Ottomans to regularly reroute troops bound for Gallipoli by land, and largely paralysed all shipping in the Sea.

* * *

Thursday 1 July 1915

Strong westerly wind and much dust. My morning's work increased by doing of "summary of situation" wire for Anzac and Proemial[1] telegrams. Day quiet on all fronts but in evening 10th Gurkhas driven by heavy bomb attack on J12[2], but recaptured by Inniskillings in morning and held. Bathed with Val[3] in evening.

Friday 2 July 1915

In night of 1st/2nd heavy bomb attack on part of J13. 10th Gurkhas driven out but recaptured by Inniskillings. Nothing much to record.

Saturday 3 July 1915

All quiet. In evening walked with Ruthven over to K Beach to see Colonel Hawker who is now Camp Commandant there. A most cheery hearty man, who took us to his camp: bubbling over with conversation. He has a jolly pitch with his dining table under a big fig tree which gives complete shade, and there are no flies. A French intelligence officer dining with Deedes said Turkish casualties at least 125,000, and morale bad: especially afraid of our artillery. Said that 1000 troops had lately mutinied at Chanak, and that 12 officers with their hands and feet nailed to boards had been taken to Constantinople to terrorise others. [Submarine] *E14* returned after 24 days in Straits. Torpedoed big steamer in Panderma and 10 sailing vessels with granite blocks, grain, food and petrol. Aspinall and Dawnay now hatch plans all day for the coming big

1 'Proemial' was the telegraphic address of the Secretary of State for War, Lord Kitchener.

2 A trench on Gully Spur.

3 2nd Lieutenant Braithwaite.

push with the 3 new divisions[4] which are daily being embarked from England.

Sunday 4 July 1915

Beautiful day, very hot. Quiet on all fronts. Scheme is on here if possible to make Mitylene into a rest camp for 1 or 2 divisions, a move useful and necessary in itself and likely to deceive the Turks into thinking we contemplate landing at Aivali where they are showing considerable activity, clearing out Greeks, fortifying etc. Walked with Deedes again in evening.

Monday 5 July 1915

Another lovely day. Owing to fact that a destroyer had gone to fetch the King's Messenger bag today it arrived thus early and gave us much pleasure. Better news of Alice made me very happy.

Today the Turks started heavy bombardment at 4 a.m., the heaviest yet experienced, from Asia and peninsula on beaches and our line. Preliminary to attack all along line. Enemy infantry driven back with very heavy loss. In RND section about 50 Turks got into our trench but were immediately hurled out again, 300 killed. Another attack on right of 29th Division wiped out by our rifle and machine gun fire, also attacks on left of 29th reportedly with heavy loss. Turks added heavily to their losses and failed completely. They dropped 1000 shells on beaches and 4000 elsewhere, besides heavy bombardment at Anzac.

News from Kitchener today just decided [to] send 2 more Territorial divisions[5] to follow 10, 11, and 13 of New Army. Very good news.

4 10th (Irish), 11th (Northern), and 13th (Western) Divisions.

5 53rd (Welsh) and 54th (East Anglian) Divisions.

Tuesday 6 July 1915

Nothing active doing but very heavy day of cipher telegrams. DAG telegrams very tiresome and long. Today wired to Kitchener asking permission to land a division at Mitylene without asking leave of Greek Government and justifying it by precedent of Lemnos and fact that 2 naval guns and a searchlight already landed there. Took walk with Powell in evening and bathed. Wonderful evening sunset. The cliffs of Peninsula bright rose colour.

In the evening there came for Sir Ian from General Bailloud a very disturbed and disturbing kind of letter saying that the situation was very bad, French morale poor, guns from Asia dreadful, losses fearful and that we *must* land in Asia to silence the Asiatic batteries.

Our most serious shortage just now is of bombs and hand grenades. All units and formations are crying out for them and the DDOS sends frantic wires to Egypt, Malta and the Base asking for an increased supply. Only yesterday a party of Dublin Fusiliers who seized a knoll had to leave it when all their bombs were exhausted.

13th Division HQ and 38th Infantry Brigade have arrived [at] Mudros.

Stopford, Commander of 9th Army Corps is at Alexandria.

11th Division sailing daily from England.

Wednesday 7 July 1915

All quiet, nothing to report.

Thursday 8 July 1915

All quiet again. In evening rode with Powell and Val on yeomanry horses from 5.30 to 7. The country very bad for riding, but it was very enjoyable. Rubbed some skin off myself.

Friday and Saturday 9/10 July 1915

All quiet. Feeling stiff and not very well inside.

Sunday 11 July 1915

Still feeling rather rotten. News from WO that all German South West Africa had surrendered to Botha. Monty came back day before yesterday, but had suffered rather from neuritis at Tenedos. All yesterday was in bed with feverish influenza but is better today.

Monday 12 July 1915

Still seedy. Attack by 52nd Division and French carried 2 lines opposite them.[6] Quite a success.

Details not yet to hand, but quite a substantial advance.

The sun is very hot, and the high breeze prevents our tent being opened properly, as papers all blow about. One longs sometimes for proper shade. By Jove how bored I do get with this life and this work, especially when I don't feel well. However coming operations may liven things up next month.

Read "The Good Soldier" by Hueffer. A perfectly odious book and devilishly clever. Only a disgusting mind could have written it and only a clever man inspired by H. James.

Keeling back from Athens. Glyn from War Office came to stay a few days and report on us.[7] King's Messenger brought lots of letters, including news that Hugh Cass killed out here.

6 Battle of Achi Baba Nullah.

7 On Glyn, Hamilton wrote: 'Glyn has been sent out as a sort of emissary, but whether by K. or by the Intelligence or by the Admiralty neither Braithwaite nor I are quite able to understand' (I.S.M. Hamilton, *Gallipoli Diaries*, vol. 2, p. 15).

Tuesday 13 July 1915

Feeling a bit better. From tea time onwards the cipher telegram situation became very congested owing to a large number of long telegrams having to be sent.

(1) to WO asked for a lot more ships and civilians from shipping companies to run transport arrangements for army.

(2) to Kitchener asking, that if by chance things had come to a standstill in France, we should have preferential claim to guns and High Explosive and giving amounts needed.

The French continued their attack this afternoon and made good progress right up to Kereves Dere, the RND also went in and, though reports [are] obscure, it seems that at one point the Turks got well on the run and were mowed down in the open by our artillery. The French and English seem to have taken at least 200 prisoners each.

Wednesday 14 July 1915

Nothing

Thursday 15 July 1915

Very hot. Monty off to Mitylene on SS work.

Friday 16 July 1915

Again very hot.

Saturday 17 July 1915

Same. Tents fearful. After tea walked out and slept on the sand on bathing beach. News that Winston is coming next week to confer on behalf of Cabinet. Preparations in O(a) for the big move going forward very busily. Trying to bring 2nd despatch further up to date.

Today the GC [Hamilton] and Aspinall visited Gully Beach and front trenches on our left. The general was in J13 while shells actually burst on the parapet in front of him. His coming back was perilous. He left Gully Beach in a rowing boat to go on to his destroyer and the Turks began shelling the rowing boat, dropping shells within 30 yards. The destroyer kept going further out and once when she stopped a shell hit her, luckily doing little damage and only wounding one man. The destroyer whipped off and shouted to the general's boat to row to Helles which it did under shell fire. He was an hour in the boat.

Intelligence received points to a big Turkish attack impending by land and sea with 100,000 new troops, gas, inflammable liquid and under the eyes of 145 Turkish Ulemas.[8] Preparations being made accordingly without interfering with those for our general attack.

Apropos of Winston. GC wired to Kitchener today "I had hoped we were too far off for visitors but you know you can count on my loyalty to you in all circumstances".

Wednesday 21 July 1915

There has been little to record lately. Life is very monotonous. The only element of variety is the strength with which the wind blows: when it is high as it was yesterday and is today the amount of dust swallowed upsets my stomach. The news this morning is that Winston Churchill finds he cannot leave England. So much for that.

From intelligence received it seems to be thought very probable that the Turks are going to make a big attack on June 23rd.[9] Anyhow preparations have been made to meet it and we very much hope they will come on.

I have had walks with Dawnay and Deedes in the last day or two. Dawnay is not very optimistic even about the

8 'Ulemā are a body of Muslim scholars recognised as having specialist knowledge of Islamic sacred law and theology.

9 Sic: 23 July.

result of success in our next big push. Seems to think the best we could hope for would be to get a strong position across the peninsula and build a safe base at Suvla Bay. Deedes seemed to think the best to be hoped for was that we should have 3 more divisions to throw into Asia and then reach Chanak before the winter.

Another thing I have talked to Deedes and Dawnay about is the GC. I find that my ideas are quite correct, that he really does nothing at all, never has a scheme, has a shallow, at times obstinate mind, no grasp of detail. His first despatch, so praised in London, was almost wholly written by his staff. This plan of the 2nd big push, not only was not thought out by the general, but was Dawnay's idea which, supported by Dawnay's arguments, induced him to give up his own idea of still plugging at Achi Baba, simply as Dawnay says that the DM [*Daily Mail*] might come out with the poster 'ACHI BABA.'

He doesn't for a moment realize how serious and extraordinary the situation is here. If this next attack fails, it means, in all probability, thorough and complete failure. This campaign is practically run by Dawnay and Aspinall, 1 a dugout captain and the other a captain in the Munster Fusiliers. I wonder how many people realize that. It is also run to some extent by Hunter-Weston and Skeen, Birdwood's GSO1.

Thursday 22 July 1915

Tummy still poorly. Lunched with Pollen at general's mess. Maitland and Churchill there and de Laborde came in: quite a pleasant time. Nothing occurred today and no signs of impending attack. Sent an urgent wire today saying that situation regarding 18 pounder ammunition was again becoming serious. Also non despatch of new keys for 10 pounder fuzes had created disturbing situation. Reserve 10 pounder dangerously low owing to 5760 rounds arriving short of 5496 fuzes.

Wire from Kitchener giving gist of Bailloud's letter to Millerand as to his position and 'suggestion' of landing on Asiatic shore, asking for our remarks as there was committee of Cabinet on Dardanelles on Saturday. Our wire sent late last night referred to what we had said before, that this could not be done without abandoning present place of operations, as no boats available: Landing in Asia might be necessary later, but meanwhile battery on De Tott's and monitor off Rabbit Island should be able to deal with Asiatic guns.

Hankey is coming out instead of Winston to discuss some matters with General.

Details of landings etc. for the push at Anzac early next month are being carefully worked out, and plan for naval cooperation getting cut and dried.

Friday 23 July 1915

Not much to record. E.P.[10] tents with double flies being put up for all officers: we shall have ours tomorrow and be able at last to take our hats off in the office. At 3 p.m. Turks attacked northern trenches with men left J11-13. Our front trenches bombarded and small force of Turks dashed for our sapheads. Two of our machine guns opened fire and the survivors retired. 40 dead Turks lying in front of our trenches, probably more from shrapnel behind. Regiment engaged were N. Staffs of 13 Division, Kitchener's Army. Our casualties: 2 officers and 28, mostly wounded.

At Anzac Turks fired inflammatory shell from noiseless gun. It burst making holes 1 ft diameter and setting alight to ground 8 ft diameter, easily extinguished. Last night

10 European (or English) Privates' tent (a rectangular tent used by the Indian Army).

Turks threw some liquid into French trenches and then tried to ignite with bombs but failed.

Saturday 24 July 1915

Our E.P. tents up. *Such* a relief to be able to take off one's helmet and be cool in the office. This was quite a day of extra comforts for me as my man had made me a wonderful office chair with wood picked up off the beach, and in the evening lo! my long lost bed and camp armchair arrived having left England on May 4. So I slept royally. After tea rode over alone to IXth Army Corp HQ to deliver a letter and back over the dunes, very pleasant.

Captain Moberly arrived to be GSO2 O(b) and Ruthven goes to O(a). Moberley was in 29th Division and was wounded. Seems a nice man. Thus GHQ grows and grows. No news. The Russians seem [to be] having a very hard struggle round Warsaw.

Wednesday 28 July 1915

Nothing of any particular importance to report for last few days. Had a ride with Val on one of CGS's horses on 25th; made me a bit sore again. Our front extraordinarily quiet and preparations for more pushing on. General Hunter Weston has gone home sick to England, and today we hear from Kitchener that Davies, commander of 8th Division, is coming out at top speed. Keeling returned with the King's Messenger day before yesterday.

My draft of the 2nd dispatch won to my surprise extremely high praise from Aspinall, and from CGS. It has gone to the general with no alterations. It will be interesting to see how he alters it. I thought it very dull in comparison with the 1st dispatch (not a word of which I wrote). News in week's papers not particularly cheering. French's dispatch giving details of the gruesome fighting [at the] end of April and May. Russia very hard pressed, and strike of Welsh coal miners which led to a proclamation under the Munitions Act.

Thursday 29 July 1915

Chief event of today was a wire from Secretary of State to the effect that they were anxious to do everything possible to enable Sir Ian to bring to a successful termination the operation he had conducted with so much ability, and saying that he was to say at once if he wanted any more troops, ammunition or guns, that all the troops in Egypt were at his disposal: as regards ammunition told him that they were stopping supplies to France in order to supply us and that operations in the Dardanelles were of the greatest importance in the short time before bad weather supervenes. This of course is a wire of different tenor from the answer sent to our wire on 13th July asking for preferential treatment as regards guns and ammunition, for our requests were then definitely refused on ground that they could not wholly cease to supply France. We also were never given to understand that troops in Egypt were unreservedly at our disposal. We should have liked this information earlier, but wired in reply referring to our wire of 13th saying that was what we wanted especially all possible HE. A special ship is being sent to Marseilles to get any more that is sent. We have also wired to Egypt for his views about sending 2nd Mounted Brigade dismounted.

This is apparently the first fruits of Glyn's return to England.

Friday 30 July 1915

Good wire this morning, that on 24th Turks were heavily routed at Nasiriyah leaving guns etc. behind them, that road was now open to Bagdad and pursuit being pushed vigorously. Hurrah. Excellent news in every way. Active operations on southern front [i.e. Helles] to commence on August 4.[11]

We initiated the playing of stump cricket with a tennis ball after tea in our mess with excellent results.

Saturday 31 July 1915

Very calm day and very hot in consequence. Egypt are going to send us 4000 men of 2nd Mounted Division. He [General Maxwell] is rather disturbed at prospects of taking so many white men from Egypt.

The WO are sending us a lot of ammunition, including all they can possible scrape up anywhere with 2 batteries 4.5″ howitzers to meet our ship sent to Marseilles, which will get back to us between Aug 11-14 and enable us to be a bit more prodigal in forthcoming operations.

The 8th Corps attacks on Aug 4 and 5 are to be on the G.H.F. trenches which make the re-entrant in our line.

Dined with the general last night who was very cordial. Told him Alice had met Lady Hamilton and gone over Endell St. Hospital.[12] Berthier came in and said Colonel Girodon, chief of French staff, had come back very well, and ready to check Bailloud's inquisitiveness. Said relations between Simpson-Baikie and French Artillery very cordial. French lending us 2 Dumézils with 100 rounds each and Street (GSO1 8th Corps) says this is in return for 4 dozen pots of jam. This kind of thing is *not* known to the highest authorities.

11 It actually commenced on 6 August.

12 The Military Hospital, Endell Street, London, was founded in 1915 and staffed entirely by women.

6

'THE SECOND PHASE OF OUR CAMPAIGN'

THE AUGUST OFFENSIVE

The summer months at Gallipoli were to bring little respite from the campaign's horrors. The beaches were narrow, cramped and continually swept by shell fire. The oppressive heat during the day wearied the men and sapped their energy. Water was scarce and rations were monotonous. Worst of all were the flies. Great swarms covered the battlefield and bred off putrefying corpses and excrement. When eating, it became impossible not to consume anything without a mouthful of flies. Not surprisingly, dysentery became rife and casualties from sickness grew to an extent that more soldiers were being evacuated sick than those with wounds from enemy action. Orlo referred to it as the 'Gallipoli Gallop'. Many of those that had survived earlier battles had been weakened by disease, even new drafts would fall ill within days of arriving. It would be these weary troops that were needed to launch the next major offensive.

As planning progressed for the Anzac offensive, a problem arose: how to accommodate the new divisions and then manoeuvre them in battle when the Anzac area was already congested. Supply was also a concern for the MEF, which was in no fit state to support a long-drawn-out operation. Anzac had a small and congested beachhead where movement was difficult, not only due to its size and difficult terrain, but also because its beaches were exposed to enemy fire and the mercy of the weather. With autumn approaching and with the risk of the campaign extending into winter, the need for a safe harbour became paramount. The August plan was widened to include a new landing at Suvla Bay, which was suitable as a harbour and future base for subsequent operations.

The plan, which went through several iterations, was not revolutionary in its objective but was imaginative in the series of complex stages to reach that goal. The bold and daring plan was essentially a flanking manoeuvre. This consisted of a major night breakout through the lightly defended maze of gullies and ridges to the north of Anzac, and then a sweeping move to the east to facilitate the dawn capture of the Sari Bair heights, crowned by the summits of Hill 971, Hill Q and Chunuk Bair. If successful, a follow-on advance would be made to push the Ottomans off Second Ridge, to finally capture Baby 700, Battleship Hill and 400 Plateau, before taking Third Ridge. The Suvla landing was limited to securing an immediate support base for the offensive. Any advance across the peninsula would be secondary to these operations. The weakness of the plan, however, was its over complexity and reliance on the completion of each step, critical to the success of the overall offensive. The whole idea relied upon a rapid advance and use of initiative, things that had been lacking so often in the execution of the campaign so far.

The offensive began on 6 August with several diversionary actions designed to mask the true intentions of the objective. These comprised a feint attack at Helles, planned to draw Ottoman attention and reserves to the south, and a similar attack against Lone Pine. Whilst the British feint at Helles failed in its intent, the Australian assault at Lone Pine was a success. Not only was Lone Pine taken, but the Ottomans had brought up their reserves to help in its recapture. After 3 days and 4 nights of ferocious fighting the Australians had held onto their gains. While the battle of Lone Pine raged, further attacks at The Nek, Pope's Hill and Quinn's Post, together with an earlier attack against German Officers' Trench, were disasters.

By early morning, 7 August, the attacks inside the Anzac perimetre had come to an end. They had all been in vain and provided no assistance to the New Zealanders, who at that very moment began their own assault on Chunuk Bair. Throughout the previous six hours, columns of already exhausted men had advanced into the dark, fought their way through lightly defended outposts and into the tortuous scrub-covered mountainous terrain to the north of Anzac. For the Australians and Indians their objectives were Hill 971 and Hill Q, and the New Zealanders were to tackle the heights of Chunuk Bair. The left column, that of the Australians and Indians, soon found themselves in difficulties. Disorientated during the night movement, they had become hopelessly lost. Meanwhile, the right column, the New Zealanders, pressed on as planned up Rhododendron Spur towards their objective. Behind schedule, by the time the sun rose they were 500 metres shy of the summit. Unsure of what lay ahead, they made a costly mistake and halted. This action sealed the fates for those they were supposed to be supporting at The Nek, Pope's Hill and Quinn's Post. It also gave the Ottomans time to reinforce the hill, which until then was largely undefended. Despite intervention by Major-General Godley, who ordered an immediate attack, any hope of capturing Chunuk Bair that day had gone. It would be at dawn on 8 August that the New Zealanders, supported by the British, finally captured the summit.

Hill Q was captured by the Gurkhas on 9 August after desperate hand-to-hand fighting, but then, tragically, a salvo of allied shells slammed onto the summit. As quickly as the hill was captured, it was lost. A few hundred yards away, the New Zealanders had miraculously held onto Chunuk Bair despite almost 48 hours of constant counter-attack. Finally, on the night of 9 August, they were relieved, the British taking over their positions. It was a tentative hold at best. Occupying the reverse slope, they were vulnerable to surprise attack. Just before dawn, 10 August, the Ottomans launched a massive counterattack that consisted of multiple waves of troops cascading over the summit of Chunuk Bair. Surprised by the ferocity of this bayonet attack the two British battalions were overrun in minutes. Few who stood their ground, survived. Chunuk Bair was lost. It was only the steadfastness of New Zealand machine gunners lower down the slopes, and support from the artillery and Royal Navy, that prevented a complete collapse of the line. That said, the counterattack was costly, resulting in some 9,000 Ottoman casualties in eight hours; but the action was decisive. Never again during the campaign would the Allies stand upon Sari Bair.

Meanwhile, IX Corps, under the command of Lieutenant-General Sir Frederick Stopford, had landed successfully at Suvla Bay, across beaches code-named A, B and C. This new amphibious landing took the Ottomans by surprise but, despite facing initial light opposition, the British failed to exploit this and secure the ring of hills that surrounds the Suvla plain, from the village of Anafarta Sagir in the south to Ejelmer Bay in the north. Only after their capture would Suvla Bay be truly secure. The landing at Suvla was mismanaged from the outset and the situation quickly reached the same stalemate that prevailed on the Anzac and Helles fronts. It was at Suvla that Hamilton, disheartened by the lack of progress, intervened. He sent Aspinall to Suvla to discover first-hand what was happening as clear reports

A common character in Orlo's diary, General Sir Ian Hamilton was both praised and criticised by GHQ's staff. An unknown photographer snapped him exiting a tent (Stephen Chambers collection).

from the shores were not forthcoming. The reality ashore was not good. Stopford was reported to be in excellent spirits, wholly satisfied that he had IX Corps ashore, but was almost dismissal of having not reached the high ground. By the time Hamilton, Braithwaite and Dawnay arrived on the afternoon of 8 August, almost twenty-four hours after the landing, it was too late. The Ottomans had been reinforced and there would be no opportunity now to take the hills. Hamilton wrote in his diary: 'My heart has grown tough amidst the struggles of the Peninsula but the misery of this scene well nigh broke it ... Words are of no use.'

Even with the newly landed reinforcements of 53rd (Welsh) and 54th (East Anglian) Divisions the tide of battle could not be turned. Territorials straight off the boat from the 53rd Division were hurriedly thrown piecemeal into a renewed attack on Scimitar Hill, but with little effect. Aspinall and Anstey, who were at Suvla that morning, could do little more than observe yet another failed attack. On 12 August a brigade from 54th Division attempted a daylight advance across the exposed plains of Suvla towards the foot-hills of Kavak Tepe, but this too failed. There were serious concerns in IX Corps that the 54th Division was a danger and might bolt at any minute. Moreover, there was a loss of morale in the 53rd Division which, under the shelling, was getting so shaky that local commanders thought the troops could break and seriously jeopardise the line. It was not a good start for the Territorials.

Hamilton cabled Lord Kitchener on 14 August, reporting that the IX Corps generals were unfit for command:

> *'The result of my visit to the IX Corps, from which I have just returned, has bitterly disappointed me. There is nothing for it but to allow time to rest and reorganize unless I force Stopford and his divisional generals to undertake a general action for which, in their present frame of mind, they have no heart. In fact, they are not fit for it. I am exceedingly reluctantly obliged to give them time to rest and reorganize their troops.'*

Kitchener replied:

> *'If you should deem it necessary to replace Stopford, Mahon and Hammersley, have you any competent generals to take their place? From your report I think Stopford should come home. This is a young man's war, and we must have commanding officers that will take full advantage of opportunities which occur but seldom. If, therefore, any generals fail, do not hesitate to act promptly. Any generals I have available I will send you.'*

Change was quick. Hamilton dismissed Stopford, replacing him with Lieutenant-General Sir Julian Byng who was serving in France. Also transferred from the Western Front were Generals Frederick Stanley Maude and Edward Fanshawe, who took over command of the 13th and 11th Divisions respectively. Until their arrival, IX Corps was temporarily commanded by Major-General Henry de Beauvoir de Lisle, commander of the 29th Division. Hamilton intended to retain Mahon in command of the 10th Division, but Mahon was infuriated that de Lisle, whom he disliked, was appointed above him and quit, saying: 'I respectfully decline to waive my seniority and to serve under the officer you name. Please let me know to whom I am to hand over the Division'. On 17 August the commander of 53rd Division, Major-General Lindley, voluntarily resigned, on the grounds that his division had gone to pieces and that he did not feel it in himself to pull it together. Hamilton, who had now acknowledged the failure of the August offensive, cabled Kitchener on 17 August to inform him that his coup had so far failed. The offensive, the largest British attack of the war so far, had failed with an estimated 25,000 British and 20,000 Ottoman casualties.

But Hamilton had not given up. To improve the Suvla situation he saw hope in the experience and leadership of de Lisle and his 29th Division, which would be moved up from Helles to support IX Corps. Supported by 2nd (Mounted) Division (minus their horses) who had landed during the night of 17 August, he would attack again. A lot rested upon de Lisle's shoulders. He was not liked by many and had a reputation for a brute force approach. Moreover, at Suvla he was in strange surroundings and in command of a disorganised and exhausted Army Corps, with officers and men with whom he was unfamiliar. Casualties had been heavy. Morale was low, and the beachhead was exposed. De Lisle's immediate task was to organise the corps so that it was able to renew the battle. The MEF faced the problem of mounting casualties through combat and disease and no hope of any early reinforcements. This understrength force was struggling to defend the large expanses of north Anzac and Suvla they had recently taken. The plan's objective was therefore to improve the local tactical situation by capturing the W Hills, Scimitar Hill and Hill 60, with a view to shortening the defensive line. If the next attack failed, GHQ recognised that they may have to relinquish Suvla altogether.

The attack commenced at 3.00 p.m. on 21 August. Its start time was specifically chosen on the basis that the setting sun would allow the infantry to advance with the sun at their backs, thus aiding the artillery whilst also blinding the defenders with the glare. Unfortunately for de Lisle a midday haze had developed over Suvla that masked the Ottoman positions. It was no surprise that the British bombardment was ineffective, exacerbated by the limited supply of munitions and knowledge of the enemy positions. The bombardment achieved little and at worse resulted in alerting the Turks of the pending attack; a heavy retaliatory bombardment pulverised the British trenches, packed with troops waiting for zero hour. The 11th Division's attack against the W Hills became confused, lost direction, faltered and came to an abrupt stop in front of the Ottoman positions. Further attempts were made during the evening to renew the attack, but these also failed. The 29th Division in the meantime had attacked Scimitar Hill; despite obtaining a foothold on the hill, they were forced to withdraw. The 2nd (Mounted) Division, de Lisle's reserve, were then thrown into the battle, but they too were forced to withdraw after briefly recapturing Scimitar Hill.

Generals Byng, Maude and Fanshawe arrived to take over their new commands on 24 August. Byng, the general that Hamilton had originally requested back in June for the Suvla operation, had arrived too late. Aspinall remarked: 'the experienced pilot has arrived but the ship is already on the rocks.' The last battle in August was on Hill 60, which formed an important junction between Suvla and Anzac. Here bitter fighting raged until 29 August, when most of the hill was taken by a composite force of British, Irish, Indian, New Zealand and Australian troops. British historian Robert Rhodes James was caustic: 'For connoisseurs of military futility, valour, incompetence and determination, the attacks on Hill 60 are in a class of their own.' Although most of Hill 60 was eventually captured, the composite force couldn't completely evict the Ottomans, who clung on until the end of the campaign.

The August offensive was undoubtedly flawed. Both Suvla and Anzac relied on at least one of the offensives breaking through, but both fell well short of the mark. There was genuine anger after this latest failure as high expectations were dashed, and opportunities were seen to have been frivolously thrown away. This was certainly felt amongst staff in GHQ as Orlo described in his diary. The MEF was no nearer to its strategic objective than they were during the April landings. Like everything before it, the August offensive had battered itself to a stalemate. Hamilton's coup de main had failed, and without more reinforcements nothing more could be done. Would the Dardanelles Committee continue supporting Hamilton? Politically, was there any alternative?

* * *

Sunday 1 August 1915

Last night Australians captured small network of trenches on Anzac's right opposite Tasmania Post. Bombardment and 4 mines fired. 12 killed, 75 wounded, at least 75 dead Turks and position improved thereby.

Nothing much to record except that while I was bathing at 6.30 who should come along beach but Marquis who had come over to spend night with me. Very glad to see him. He looked very well and was very cheery. Dined him in the mess and got him empty tent. After dinner able to have good long talk with him. Very interesting to gather the views of one who was nearer the front, though his knowledge was only partial, and his hearsay from visits on the beach. He said there was a good deal of depression or rather anxiety about, for people realize how short time was before the bad weather. Said the two really bad things were medical organization and engineering. The latter, according to him, was often worse than useless, and many places could have been made shell proof that were not e.g. rest camps and signal dugout where a shell today killed 6 men and wounded several others. He had little good to say of naval transport arrangements or of Army Ordnance: Expressed strong dislike of Lowland Division. Said he loathed the whole thing indescribably. RND pretty tired.

I only realized from him that Lord Rochdale was George Kemp. Some weeks ago he, being in command of a Manchester Territorial Force Regiment and temporary brigadier general, claimed his right as a peer to go back to Parliament. Marquis met him on the *Aragon* at Mudros and said he burst out to him in an overwrought state that he had done this, because he thought the position was pretty bad and he conceived it to be his mission to go home and tell the truth. Two days ago we got a wire from Kitchener asking why he went home and saying he was talking wildly. GC [Hamilton] replied that he had tried to stop him but did not know he had the power. Kitchener replied no peer or MP had the right to leave the forces, and that Rochdale had been ordered back at once.

The uncertainty of war illustrated well tonight. Urgent wire from Anzac saying water pumping engine had broken down, wells rapidly failing and water boat not arrived. Position very serious and such large water fatigues necessary that unloading of hay and forage had to be stopped.

Monday 2 August 1915

Water position at Anzac still serious and Anzac says unless it can be improved partial withdrawal must be considered. Meanwhile owing to report of Turks having concentrated 5 divisions at Keshan against possible Italian landing at Enos, the attack by the 8th Corps arranged for 4th and 5th has been postponed 48 hours.

Tuesday 3 August 1915

Nothing to record. Made acquaintance of Captain Vitale, Italian liaison officer. Talked of d'Annunzio etc.

Wednesday 4 August 1915

Very calm hot day with southerly wind. After tea, having asked Val to get me a horse he provided me with his own cob. This steed proved rather mettlesome, and no sooner was it just outside camp than it began prancing and bucking. It reared and I slipped off, but rather foolishly got on again. Then after more bucking the steed bolted and finally began to go straight for the barbed wire fence round the camp. I failed to pull him round and fell off just short of the wire. My back was a good deal bruised and I was carried into my tent in a stretcher after some excitement; rushings up of ADCs and the general himself. The horse burst through the wire and was soon caught. My back very stiff and painful to move.

Thursday 5 August 1915

In bed all day till dinner when got up and sat in chair. No bones broken and stiffness gradually wearing off. Very pleasant and restful. Read *Troilus and Cressida* and *Titus Andronicus*.

Friday 6 August 1915

Got up after breakfast, though still stiff and to the office feeling really much the better for my day's rest. Slept during the afternoon so as to be ready to take night duty tonight. Had to move very gingerly all day, and laughing extremely painful—in fact, just like "every picture tells a story".

Today and tonight the second phase of our campaign really began with a series of operations main and subsidiary in which nearly all our forces engaged.

A. Attacks by 29th Div today and 42nd tomorrow on Turkish trenches in centre of southern line. 4 p.m.

B. Attack on Lone Pine work (Anzac right) to distract enemy.

C. Main attack on Anzac left, coupled with assaults in centre. The objective to move NZ and 13th divisions round over low hills north of Hill 305 [Hill 971], clear the outposts and take 305 and Chunuk Bair by assault, thence coming south-west to help in attack on Baby 700.

D. Landing of 11th Division at night under Hammersley at Suvla Bay and New Beach, to be followed by dawn by 2 brigades of 10th Division. These to secure Suvla Bay as base and to press on to 2 low hills [Yilghin Burnu and Ismail Oglu Tepe] on left of Anzac where guns commanded Chunuk Bair.

A. The assault of 29th Division was partially successful but the trenches gained were recaptured during night.

B. Quite successful and no counterattack during night.

C. This began up to time and though it went slower than hoped, went very well. The brigade under Russell rushed its outposts, cleared the low hills during night and by 9 a.m. Gurkhas reported about to assault Hill 305. At the same time attacks on Quinn's and Courtney's Posts had failed, but the New Zealanders held the Nek, and were about to assault Baby 700.[1] 500 prisoners taken.

D. Practically no news all night, but apparently troops landed without much opposition as cable was connected with Imbros by 2 a.m. About 9.15 intercepted wire from 11th Division to 31st Brigade coming from Mitylene implied that all was well and that while 32nd and 34th brigades went for Yilghin Bair the 31st to go for Ismail Oglu, these the low hills on Anzac left.

There was a good deal of outcry during the night from Anzac about evacuation of wounded. Casualty Clearing Stations not turned up, second troop ship wanted, and beach full of wounded and under shell fire. Obviously arrangements not carried out well.

It was a quaint night. Very different to that of the first landing. We kept the office open all night and I sat up till 4. Dawnay, Aspinall, Barttelot, Monty and Lloyd were up the same time. We were all prepared for a lot of work and very little tuned up. Wires were few, and sometimes when a large one came it turned out to be an ordinary routine code wire. One opened by Aspinall actually began "Bamboozled". We had cocoa and biscuits and chocolate, and stood about, Monty gave an excellent imitation of Ward and altogether it was about as unlike the popular image of what goes on in a General Staff during attacks which are vital as could be imagined. Private message came to me from WO that Warsaw had been evacuated.

1 This is incorrect, but indicates how inaccurate was the picture at GHQ.

Saturday 7 August 1915

Fighting all day. Anzac troops pushed up and took Chunuk Bair and got near Hill 305. 11th Division consolidated, landed 10th Division and pushed to E and Yilghin Burnu. French had one success in south and 8th Corps took F12 and G12 trenches. Very different time to days on *Queen Elizabeth*. Here GHQ lived its normal life only a trifle more electric, the map in Aspinall's tent being spread out and stuck with flags to mark positions. Results of aeroplane reconnaissance coming in at intervals over telephone. Still difficulty of clearing of wounded and supply of water.

Sunday 8 August 1915

General pushing on from Suvla, but not as far as wanted. Apsinall wiring at 5.30 said he was convinced golden opportunities were being lost as 9th Corps were resting. Ginger of sorts was applied. Also 53rd Division were sent to Suvla. Some slackness with the navy at lunch time; no horses and mules landed and question of supply becoming serious. This was improved later. Also 2 hospital ships not having arrived at Anzac, situation as to wounded was critical.

News after dinner from Anzac that hoped to take 971 at dawn. Troops very done but in excellent spirits and all fought magnificently.

News today that *E11* sunk Turkish battleship yesterday of *Torgud Reis* type. *E14* sunk gunboat and 1 large empty transport, and both together shelled troops marching along road to Maidos causing much delay and heavy loss.

Apsinall returned tonight. Gather from him the 9th Corps have wasted 24 hours: "combination of new troops and old generals not a good one". Apparently being tired with their exertion on 7th, they just sat down and did nothing all day, old Stopford by way of saying you could not attack strongly entrenched positions without artillery, without going to see if there were any strongly entrenched positions. Every hour after the first surprise was of vital importance; and everybody here is very much annoyed. Sir Ian gave peremptory order to get on.

Monday 9 August 1915

Anzac's dawn attack was unsuccessful and the Turks counterattacked heavily in the night, but the troops held their positions. No news of 9th Corps. 8th Corps were counterattacked last night but drove enemy back.

During the day CGS [and] Dawnay were at Suvla all day, also [the] general. They did not seem very satisfied when they returned. One battalion had actually got on to Tekke Tepe in morning but driven back again owing to no support. The 9th Corps did not manage to do much all day; there was fighting on left Kiretch Tepe and on right. Turks counterattacked, but were taken on the flank by 4th SWB and mauled. The 53rd Division went over but old Stopford failed to put them in in force and they did nothing. Cox nearly got on to 971 but failed again. No general of 9th Corps comes in for any praise but Shaw of the 13th Division who are at Anzac. Wire sent home tonight admitted disappointment and said "As no man puts new wine into old bottles so the combination of old generals and new troops seems unsuitable, except in case of 13th Division". There have been heavy casualties at Anzac but the Turks there have lost very heavily indeed. 630 prisoners, 9 machine guns, 1 Nordenfeldt, heaps of bombs. Life at GHQ very quiet all day.

Tuesday 10 August 1915

News that at 5.30 this morning Turks regained Chunuk Bair, though their attack at first repulsed by 2 battalions:

2 more battalions now sent up 54th Division, 6 battalions being sent over from here. Operations today made no particular progress. It was found impossible to make another attack on Chunuk Bair before reorganization. The right centre of 9th Corps (53rd Division) attacked but was counterattacked from Baka Baba, and though the counterattack was dispersed by 34th Brigade no progress was made. The 10th Division all day was held up on Kiretch Tepe Sirt all day. Aspinall and Anstey went over, and though they were still dissatisfied Anstey thought they had got a better grasp of the situation by the evening. 6 battalions of 54th Division were landed at Suvla yesterday and 6 spent night here. After tea standing by the map Dawnay said to me "Well, cipher, there's only one word I think and that is *échoué*.[2] The crushing thing is that all the staff arrangements which were very difficult, worked, and one wonders if anything more could have been done. What is going to happen now, I really don't know". But that was perhaps an undue excess of pessimism. We sent home a very long cipher cable tonight giving a report of the operations up to date, and speaking properly in terms of the very highest praise of all that had been done at Anzac, and admitting disappointment with the 10th and 11th divisions, but still breathing confidence that we should do the job.

As for me, it was a strange contrast that after lunch Vitale came to my tent and held forth in Italian to me on the beauties of the decadent French poet Samain whom he admires very much. He confessed that he was a bit of a poet himself and a *soldato sbagliato*[3], that he had the *anima artistica*[4] and did not feel at home in the ordinary crowd. A very interesting conversation which went on to

2 Translation: 'failed'.

3 Translation: 'failed soldier'.

4 Translation: 'artistic soul.'

English literature. I advised him of some novelists and gave him my book on the essay. All the while 12 miles off the 53rd Division were fighting.

Wednesday 11 August 1915

Quiet day nothing much to report. The 9th Corps trying to pull itself together and no attacks made there or at Anzac. The CGS went over, also Dawnay: A night march was projected for tonight by 54th Division with attack on Kavak Tepe at dawn but was countermanded I presume, on the spot.

Thursday 12 August 1915

Again nothing doing. Telegraphic orders were given for attack tomorrow on Kavak Tepe, but on 9th Corps saying they couldn't get water up, operation was telegraphically countermanded and CGS went off at once with Dawnay to Suvla and Anzac. Everyone here pretty down on the 9th Corps, though perhaps we expect too much of them. The most tremendous pity that there are no regular troops with them. As it is they have no self-reliance and then COs don't seem to have any dash.

Aspinall moaned to me this afternoon that Sir Ian had given him a second dispatch which he wanted to go home today. Aspinall said it was no more like my dispatch than a cat was like a pot of jam. He had only brought it up to May 8 (!) and had made out of it the most appalling *Daily Mail* article, which would have made him the laughing stock of everybody. Aspinall had taken it to the CGS who had stopped it, but the situation is made delicate by the fact that Sir Ian thinks it a "gem".

The 10th Division captured a trench 75 east of bench-mark on Kiretch Tepe. The 53rd Division tried to advance on the Kuchuk Anafarta Ova, but met with resistance and failed to do so. A later report said the engagement was bigger than at first supposed and brigades were considerably disorganized. The transports were shelled at Suvla yesterday and the *Swiftsure* was hit, 18 casualties.

Friday 13 August 1915

Attack on right of 9th Corps and left of Anzac fixed for the 15th in which 54th Division to take place and 100 Gurkha scouts who are promised 70 rupees for every Turk rifle. GOC 9th Corps anxious not to move 54th from his centre yet sent following wire this morning:

"GOC 53rd Division reports division exhausted and quite incapable of defence. This makes position in my centre most serious in case of attack. Turks show distinct signs of offensive along our front which is a long one. I have no troops except 54th Division to replace 53rd who are only a danger and may bolt at any moment. Feel it my duty to inform GC at once".

This wire was answered at 4 p.m. by a wire telling Stopford to publish a stringent order to this division that cowardice was punishable by death and not to mince matters. Reminded him he had power under the circumstances he described to confirm and carry out the extreme penalty. At the same time he was to hearten them up by telling them replacements were on the way.

A wire also arrived from Anzac at 3:30 p.m. to say that scarcity of water had produced a very critical situation. Birdwood said he could not undertake any general attack with the least hope of success; but would assist Stopford's advance by advancing a brigade and helping with all available guns on his left.

Sir Ian and CGS went over to Suvla at 4 p.m. to see 9th Corps and confer with Admiral.

After tea went to bathe with Vitale, who to my great

pleasure overflowed to me in Italian all the time. He told me something of himself, i.e. that he had a *viva simpatia*[5] for a Russian girl in Cairo, that he had been a widower for 14 years and had a daughter aged 14, and that subsequently he had been engaged to an English girl, only her mother had subsequently managed to break it off. He also confessed to me he thought Colonel Ward was showing him a certain *freddezza*[6], which that old stick probably has for he is bored to death with having Vitale on his hands. Nobody seems looking after Vitale properly, which is a great pity. His position is a not very satisfactory one since he has no instructions himself and nobody has any instructions about him. If only Ward were a man of the world with tact and consideration all would be well, but he is just the worst kind of wooden Englishman to deal with foreigners. I shall see what I can do unofficially. Robin Buxton turned up tonight as liaison officer in Intelligence.

Saturday 14 August 1915

Last night Sir Ian sent home a wire saying: "I am bitterly disappointed as the result of a visit to the 9th Corps. There is obviously nothing to do but to let the divisions rest and reorganize. Stopford and his commanders have no heart for a general attack. We shall never have such a chance again, but the only thing now is to go slow till we can come on again". I fear this will upset Kitchener a good deal, who has absurdly preconceived notions of the rapidity with which we ought to push on to the Marmara shore before trenches have been dug everywhere.

Talking to Powell this morning I asked him what he thought was the real cause of the failure to push on to that ridge at first. (1) He said the chief cause was confusion after

5 Translation: 'deep sympathy'.

6 Translation: 'coldness'.

landing at night, difficulty of getting water and rations, and not knowing where transport was. (2) If the 53rd and 54th Divisions had been any good we might still have taken the ridge, but things were only a danger. (3) Better commander might have done more, and certainly 2 regular divisions would have. (4) The scheme, though well-conceived, was probably too extensive for the troops which were at our disposal. So there it is; we must still hope to get the Anafarta ridge, but the Turks will have lots of time to fortify it, and the beaches are meanwhile under fire.

Two telegrams came from Kitchener today, the first asking if we had any competent generals to replace Stopford, Hammersley and Mahon if it was desirable to do so, and saying that he thought Stopford ought to be sent home. "This is a young man's war and we want generals who will take advantage of opportunities". Why the devil didn't he make that reflection before? We answered saying that we would like to put de Lisle in Stopford's place. A second wire from Kitchener said we could have Peyton (GOC 2nd Mounted Division) as Corps Commander if we liked, and that he had asked General French for a Corps Commander and 2 divisional commanders suggesting Byng, Horne and Kavanagh, and ended "I hope you have relieved Stopford already". We replied we preferred de Lisle for 9th Corps as he had local experience, and asked for Corps Staff if Byng came for 53rd and 54th Divisions. Transport *Royal George* sunk by submarine between Alexandria and Mudros, some 500 out of 1300 reinforcements saved.

Bathed with Vitale, Buxton and Pitcairn.

My efforts on behalf of Vitale bore some fruit today. Aspinall gave him an account of the situation and it was arranged in Intelligence that he should go about with the liaison people. He read me some Carducci and d'Annunzio today.

Sunday 15 August 1915

After breakfast wires were sent to Stopford and de Lisle to the effect that de Lisle was to take over today, and Mahon was requested to waive his seniority. So that's that. Mahon refused to waive it, so he goes home too. I gather Ruthven thinks he has not had quite a fair chance. Brigadier-General Hill succeeds him temporarily. Several wires from Kitchener arrived later. He has asked French for a corps commander and 2 divisional commanders: Byng is being sent as the one, Maude and Fanshawe as the others. They embark at Taranto next Thursday; so Hammersley is definitely superseded. Kitchener wishes Byng to take the 9th Corps, so de Lisle won't get any more than a division. There will be no other Corps formed at present.

Today the 10th Division made a little progress on Kiretch Tepe. The 87th Brigade go to Suvla tomorrow, and the date of the next push depends on de Lisle's appreciation of situation. Anzac are quite firmly fixed in their new line and the water situation is getting easier.

Bathed with Buxton after a short walk, and began reading "One of our conquerors", liking it better than before.

Glyn turned up again today, giving, I gather, a very depressing account of general European situation, saying that Germans were now going to march down through Servia [i.e. Serbia], when Bulgaria would join them and then would enter Turkey.

Meanwhile neither Anglo French nor Italians can get on, and Italians are threatened with disaster in Tripoli. Obviously the most pessimistic view, but we have got to be prepared for a bad summer if we weather the crisis, we shall do. Glyn also said Russia on the verge of revolution.

Monday 16 August 1915

Nothing much to record.

The Granard incident. Lord Granard, who is colonel of an Irish Pioneer Regiment in 10th Division wrote to general, saying he should feel he had violated his oath as Privy Counsellor if he had not written "to the King and some of my other colleagues" his views on things out here which were "not in accord with present policy", and he let the general know in case he should prefer to have him no longer under his command, in which case he would go back to a position in France. The truth was, as Ruthven who was at Suvla today said, he was in a blue funk, and had been at de Lisle 3 times trying to get sent home for having written to the King. Our reply was (1) a wire in the morning to say that all Lord Granard's letters were to be censored. (2) a letter saying "All Privy Counsellors, privates, generals, colonels are bound by military obligations in face of the enemy. Obligation of all soldiers is to fight together. Military discipline is not lightly to be set aside. We will leave it there, subject to any action which the King or Lord Kitchener may command or order". The whole correspondence was sent home in cipher and Granard is the laughing stock of the GS.

Tonight very long cipher sent home, 6½ typewritten pages giving a resumé of operations since August 6 and an appreciation of the situation. Matters were not minced. The want of energy of 9th Corps leaders, inexperience of troops and broken readiness of 53rd Division were plainly stated. The position at present was clearly given; with the fact that we are now inferior in numbers to the Turks (45,000 drafts, 50,000 new) and we must have large reinforcements to get on. Our coup has failed with heavy loss, but it was within an ace of being a big success. Our new Operations mess started at lunch and bids fair to be successful and more comfortable.

Tuesday 17 August 1915

No particular incident. Began work on another despatch. After tea and on way to bathe with Dawnay had a talk with him and had his views on the situation. He seems really down-hearted about it all and says his sleep is suffering through thinking what can now be done. He said he didn't see what they could possibly do at home now, and would like to be at the meeting of the Defence Committee today. Didn't see how in view of the immense political consequences they could now let this thing go. At the same time position here was extremely grave. He confessed he really didn't see what we could do or know what was going to happen. He supposed if anyone on the staff had been really great he would have insisted as soon as we got back to Alexandria that the thing couldn't be done. He remarked that it came very hard on Aspinall, who had done so well and saved the situation often. I incline to agree to this about Aspinall. He may have no large ideas and not much foresight, but in matters of organization and arrangement he has been extremely good—a first class staff officer.

Two of our seaplanes did magnificent thing today. Rising from mother ship near Bulair with a 14-inch torpedo fastened between their floats they flew across peninsula and to Ak Bashi Liman where they dropped down on to sea and discharged their torpedo at ships, blowing up a tug and a 6,000 ton transport, and flew away under heavy fire. The prospects of this form of attack developing are rather terrifying.

Wednesday 18 August 1915

Not much to record. General, CGS and Dawnay went over to see 9th Corps and Anzac with a view to arranging about next attack of 9th Corps. In the evening was present while Aspinall, CGS and Dawnay were discussing the plan by the map. The idea is for Anzac's left to advance a little on Rhododendron Spur and for 9th Corps with 10,000 men, 11th Division, 87th Brigade to advance on Ismail Oglu Tepe and the ridge running south-west from Anafarta Sagir. The reserve will be 10th Division, Peyton's 5000 men of 2nd Mounted Division who will push in on the left of the attack. The extreme left will be held by 53rd and 54th divisions. Dawnay seemed a little doubtful if 9th Corps had a clear idea in their heads of what they wanted to do.

A more hopeful wire was sent home today saying that 9th Corps was showing quite a new spirit under de Lisle. Peyton taking over 10th Division temporarily and his Mounted Division to be attached. Lindley at his own request relieved of command 53rd Division, not feeling himself able to bring them up to scratch. Lawrence takes his place. Sitwell relieved of his brigade command "as he cannot be made to move".

Bag arrived. Interesting letter from Gregg dated August 6 giving summary of views from Russia, showing what a very bad blow the Germans had given them.

Thursday 19 August 1915

Sudden drop in temperature with high wind; dust very unpleasant but otherwise rather invigorating. Took a walk after tea to the point and back. Nothing to record. The other 2 brigades of 29th Division going round to Suvla tonight to take part in forthcoming operations. De Lisle's scheme thought to be a bit too ambitious and wire sent to that effect. Wire from PM today could not answer our long wire of Monday in Kitchener's absence but as he returned tonight hoped to send a prompt answer.

Accident in the aerodrome in which a Captain Collitt[7] was killed. Keeling off to Athens for 5 days.

7 Sic: Flight-Commander Collet.

Dawnay wants a holiday badly and so does Aspinall. Sat by Dawnay at dinner and we took our mind off things by pleasant discourse of books, Gilbert and Sullivan, etc.

News from "I" that Bulgaria shows signs of coming to terms, hence scheme for blowing up bridge at Uzun Kopru[8] postponed for a day or two. Hankey left for England.

Friday 20 August 1915

Little to record. The general in the morning congratulated me on my draft of second despatch and asked me to lunch. Lunched with him very pleasantly. Talked of Anatole France and novelists. Bathed with Buxton and Vitale.

Saturday 21 August 1915

Answer to our telegram of Monday arrived from Proemial to the effect that at this stage in the campaign a decisive success was necessary if possible. Hoped we should do our best without incurring undue risk or heavy losses without corresponding advantage to carry our operations to successful conclusion. Meanwhile in conjunction with the French a serious offensive was being organised in France, in view of which we could expect no large divisional units. But a number of scattered units and drafts were being sent here and to Egypt, to the latter Terriers[9] from Malta and Gibraltar, garrison battalions and Scottish horse, to us mainly drafts, and 3 fortress companies, in all some 12,000 men. Ended by saying that if our present operations fail, the defensive would be necessary for a considerable time.

This about sets the limit to what it is possible for us to achieve: i.e. at the very best, to secure Anafarta Ridge and Chunuk Bair, at the reasonable best to secure Anafarta Ridge only. Or so it seems at first sight. Must talk with

8 Uzunköprü

9 Territorials

Dawnay. Meanwhile much depends upon result of today's operations by 9th Corps which begin at 2.30.

A Turkish officer deserted to 11th Division yesterday and gave some valuable information.

Read cursorily this morning Aspinall's appreciation of the situation which was fully agreed to by CGS and General. In that, after admitting the failure of our aims, he went on to consider the question of the future. Pointing out that on our present front in north there were less than 2 ½ men per yard, he recommended that unless the attack today were really a howling success, we should retire to a line we could really hold strongly; i.e. evacuate Suvla Bay entirely and if possible hold a line Anzac–Ismail Oglu Tepe–Yilghin–Lala Baba. This would mean considerable reduction of front, since line IOT [Ismail Oglu Tepe] to Lala Baba need only be lightly held. In spite of difficulties of beaches and gunfire Anzac would thus receive large reinforcement with which we ought to be able to take Sari Bair.

At the worst, if we failed to take Sari Bair and to hold the line above, we could reduce front still further by withdrawing to Damakjelik Bair. This would expose Anzac to more shelling but would be practicable. If this is approved 9th Corps should have orders not to advance a foot beyond line required; i.e. W Hills. This was therefore the objective of today's advance. 11th Division on right and 29th on left were to advance and make W Hills and get astride the low ridge running South West from Anafarta Sagir. 10th Division and 2nd Mounted Division in Corps reserve.

Up to bedtime reports were not decisive. The Anzac brigade under Cox advanced satisfactorily to Kavak Kuyu and joined right of 11th Division. 11th Division took southern portion of Hetman Chair trenches.[10] 29th got

10 Battle of Hill 60.

on to lower slopes of the ridge but had to retire owing to enfilade artillery. Ruthven wounded, shrapnel thigh.

After lunch today read Dante and Shakespeare with Vitale. He made me read the Francesca Canto.

Sunday 22 August 1915

Position this morning much the same. Have not made foot of W Hills, though some advance by 29th and 34th Brigade. The move to reduce the line decided on, and important conference on subject at 9th Corps HQ today.

No wire to Kitchener yet (11 a.m.).

Dawnay, talking to NA[11] this morning, expressed his view, that even the line through Damakjelik Bair would be untenable through the winter, owing to length of line, number of troops required to hold it and probable wastage. He says 20,000 a month. By the end of today all the troops who attacked yesterday were back in their original positions. The 87th and 86th brigades and some of the Yeomanry have lost heavily.

(Read Shakespeare with Vitale after lunch. Bathed with him and to my great sorrow lost my signet ring, I presume in the sea which was a little rough.)

The result of the conference today will be another very long wire. Doubtful if it goes tonight.

9 p.m.: Kitchener has just wired telling us to wire operation orders given to Stopford.

Monday 23 August 1915

Mahon, having eaten humble pie, is returning to command 10th Division. Byng, Maude and Fanshawe arrived on a destroyer today. Maude is going to command 13th Division, Shaw having gone sick, and Fanshawe

11 Captain Mitchell, RN.

succeeds Hammersley in 11th Corps.[12] Hammersley going to be Deputy IGC. Dawnay was packed off to Suvla today and the long appreciation telegram he had written was redrafted by Aspinall this morning and despatched in cipher this afternoon. It detailed the failure of the 21st, estimating casualties at about 6000. Continued to say that as reinforcements could not be sent the only thing was to remain strictly on the defensive. Total casualties including sick since August 6 [are] 40,000, leaving total British force 85,000 fighting strength and French 15,000. Sick casualties becoming abnormal owing to strain and want of rest. In north therefore only 50,000 to hold line 23,000 yards. Average net wastage allowing for normal reinforcement 15%. Anzac, 29th Division, 42nd Division badly in need of rest.

Inevitable that within next fortnight shall have to relinquish Suvla or Anzac, and must envisage possibility of still further reducing in near future. Suvla Bay has advantages but offers no facilities for further reduction of line, whereas the Anzac line does. Hence probably Suvla must be given up, though on account of its advantages and moral effect you may count on my not relinquishing it one day earlier before I need. I do not wish to paint a gloomy picture. It is a mere question of arithmetic and measurement. On this basis fighting strength by middle of December will only be 60,000. A certain percentage must be resting off peninsula and balance will only suffice to hold Helles and original Anzac line.

Aspinall explained tonight how failure of attack on 21st wholly due to bad company leading in 11th Division. The 32nd Brigade instead of going for a communication trench got shoved off to left. They shoved the 86th Brigade off to the wrong hill from which they got enfiladed, and the 87th

12 Sic: 11th Division.

when they reached their objective were enfiladed too. All due to this. If 32nd Brigade had gone on straight there were no Turks to hold them. Then 34th Div[13] got bombed out of trench by Turks saying "Don't fire; we're the Sikhs".

Anzac's advance on the left however was quite a substantial affair, and they shot down at least 1500 of enemy.

Reuter reports today Italy declared war on Turkey and will lead to very important developments in Balkans. Also that in recent sea fight Russians had sunk German battle cruiser *Moltke* (sister of *Goeben*), 3 other cruisers and 6 destroyers. Also Venizelos had taken Greek premiership.

Tuesday 24 August 1915

In the afternoon small thunderstorm and sweet rain which cleared the air beautifully and laid the dust. Walked after tea to point and ran part of way back along beach. Dawnay rather seedy with bad tummy. Fear sickness rather on increase in whole force. Generals Byng, Fanshawe and Maude arrived, and later left for their commands. Byng says at least by March Germans (French too) will no longer be able to replace casualties. Also that a committee is now sitting in England on the situation as regards men, of whom 4 are already decided for conscription and 2 (Austen[14] and Crewe) are ready to be convinced by figures. Keeling back from Athens, but ordered by FO to Nish.

Wednesday 25 August 1915

Quiet morning. Thanks to Keeling took a half holiday and at 2.30 started out for a trudge with coat slung on my back. Walked over to K Beach and up Panagia Road to the spring beyond the divide. One or two showers but a lovely cloudy afternoon. Colours on the hill sides wonder-

13 Sic: 34th Brigade.

14 Austen Chamberlain.

ful. From the divide splendid view of Samothrace, which, after drinking from spring and eating some chocolate, I appreciated smoking. So back by 6.15, very hot and much the better. Made some cocoa and had a hot bath and felt another man. Sorry to find Dawnay had been seedy all day and Powell going to bed early with castor oil. This evening came a wire from Kitchener to say "in view of your MF 578[15] please consult on the spot with Birdwood and other Corps Commanders and wire me result of deliberations. I am sadly disappointed that troops have not done better and that with drafts and reinforcements amounting from August 6 to 47,000 you do not contemplate holding positions". This put up backs rather, and we sent dignified protest to effect: "you cannot suppose so important a wire as my 578 would be sent without deep consideration and sense of personal responsibility from which no amount of conferences with subordinate commanders could free me. However in this instance I had already consulted all subordinate commanders and had personally examined ground which I visit constantly. Do not understand your allusion to 47,000 drafts from August 6, no such number has been advised. Shall give up no ground an hour earlier than necessary, but feel bound to warn you what might have to be done if present sickness rate continues and cadres are not kept up". Various information as to stores and strengths was called for by WO and as Kitchener wanted result of deliberation by Friday morning, it appears that the Cabinet will sit on situation tomorrow.

Hear it was British submarine that sank the *Moltke* in the Baltic.

Vitale told me he thought Italy's declaration of war on Turkey might stir things up in Balkans, by exciting jealousy

15 Hamilton's telegram to Kitchener on 23 August 1915, mentioned above.

of Greece. He also expressed very strongly to me his conviction that this war would produce a new and really united Italy with a common national sentiment reaching down to all classes and not only touching the cultivated.

Two French aviators and one machine lost in the sea.

Dreadful casualties among officers of 7th, 8th, 9th KRRC and 8th Rifle Brigade to be read in papers.[16] So many Etonians. Dick Durnford and Radcliffe killed, Prior and Sheepshanks wounded .... Out here Ainger wounded.[17]

Forgot to note earlier. The CGS has got a friend of his, Lieutenant Colonel R. Taylor, out here, ostensibly to be a brigadier. But now wires home to WO in Sir Ian's name that a BGGS is wanted and says Taylor acting as such pending sanction. This puts Aspinall's nose quite out of joint, and is hard luck on him. But as he is a jealous fellow I can't help being amused. I heard him express himself on the subject two nights ago as being "absolutely contemptible". I can't myself see any particularly need for him, still believe he is a good man (No! later). But it is one of those amusing incidents of local politics that have been wanting lately.[18]

Anstey, back from being GSO2 at Suvla, at mess full of the shortcomings of the 9th Corps. Men wander about doing nothing, won't dig or do a hands turn of work, report Turks where there are none, get hopelessly confused in attack etc., etc. chiefly due to lack of officers and NCOs.

Thursday 26 August 1915

Quiet day. Writing letters for mail. After tea a walk with Deedes at which I mooted idea of forming a kind of general staff of a few friends for some kind of political work after the war. He fell in very readily. My idea to get together a

16 During the German attack at Hooge, Belgium, 30 June 1915.

17 Ainger was killed on 21 August 1915.

18 Orlo marked this 'omit'.

few fellows like him and Dawnay and other men of our own age and try to work for some common aim in various ways, some doing active work, others intelligence, some organization, some writing, each using his capabilities in the most suitable way, with frequent meetings and as much informal talk as possible.[19]

Dawnay off to Athens for a week's leave and Keeling with him to take up his duties at Nish.

Wire came from Kitchener to soothe us down a bit after our dignified protest, saying that as the Cabinet had to make such an important decision tomorrow, several heads might bring out points one might miss but no intention of etc. etc. Said he was having statement of the 47,000 drafts etc. sent by telegram. We replied explaining our position again, referring him to former wire in which he said we must expect no more reinforcements and adopt defensive and saying that it was simply a question of arithmetic and measurement. Glad to hear Younghusband's Indian Brigade returning from Aden to Egypt. Estimate what we are to have from Egypt are 7 TF battalions and Scottish Horse. Byng, we said, was infecting all around him with his energy and cheeriness and had grasped situation very quickly. Birdwood going to make tactical advance to secure important feature tomorrow. Shall hang on to our ground as long as we can. All points in MF 578 were settled after 2 hours close conference with Corps Commanders.

Heavy thunderstorms round about. Heavy rain and high wind all night in camp.

Friday 27 August 1915

High wind still blowing. Scudding clouds all over sky, and fresh autumnal feeling in the air such as one might get at Rhoscolyn at this time. Put on a vest and serge uniform.

19 Orlo marked this 'omit'.

Bathed after tea with Val. Before dinner Vitale read me some D'Annunzio, and we talked Italian.

At 5 p.m. Anzac made an advance to capture whole of Hill 60 on Kaiajik Aghala. They had a very stiff fight, but by bed time had captured a good deal of it.

The WO wire this morning analysing the 47,000 reinforcements showed that some 10,000 belonged to 9th Corps (54th Division) and had been already reckoned by us—and some 4,000 drafts also reckoned. But, as we said in our reply, that left about 29,000 new troops altogether to arrive in next 6 weeks, which improved situation, though our British units were 55,000 rifles below establishment and in 6 weeks would further decrease 20%. We asked if the Mahomeddan battalions in Younghusband's brigade could not be exchanged for Hindu regiments from France as unsafe to use Mahomeddans here. 7 battalions Territorials coming and Highland Brigade.

Kitchener wired asking our views as to ultimate prospect of attaining objective of turning out Turks and what force likely to be required. Required this for information only and could not alter decision to send no fresh divisional units at present.

Saturday 28 August 1915

Suffering from mild diarrhoea. Jolly day. Wire from Bucharest reporting that Rumanian MA convinced Allies would make no real progress till … landings Saros and Kum Kale.

Turks lost very heavily since 6th.

Bulgarians decided to join central powers and would attack Serbia after important initial movement of 250,000 to 300,000 Austro Germans. Greece would preserve benevolent neutrality. This must come soon if at all.

Rather feeble all day. Walked after tea with Aspinall with whom discussed both general's and CGS's character. Aspinall said it was a pity CGS was a weak man too, though a very nice man to work with. When CGS made up his mind to appoint Taylor because he was his friend he came to Aspinall in his tent and told him that he and Dawnay were not in the least to suppose that it implied any dissatisfaction with them and that they should continue to run operations as before, while Taylor, as BG, was to supervise O(b) and I(b), about which he doesn't know very much.[20]

Anzac still fighting for that hill on Kaiajik Aghala.

Sunday 29 August 1915

Still unsafe inside though seemed to be better. Played chess with Hony during office hours in morning and with Vitale after tea. Very quiet day. Began reading Prescott's *Conquest of Mexico* with much interest.

Monday 30 August 1915

Still got the Gallipoli gallop. Recommended by Doc to stay in bed, have only milk and take bismuth and Dover's powder which I'm doing. Day passed quietly. Beautiful weather. Vitale came and sat with me a good deal talking and playing chess.

Tuesday 31 August 1915

King's Messenger came in in the morning. Very still hot day. Excellent news from Alice. Tummy seemed better but after tea seemed to go back again, so stayed lying down.

20 Orlo marked this 'omit'.

7

'WIRES, WIRES, WIRES'

SEPTEMBER'S STRATEGIC QUESTIONS

With the failure of the August offensive, the stark reality of the situation at Gallipoli began to sink in. While large expanses of ground had been taken at huge cost at Anzac and Suvla, the tactically important high ground remained in Ottoman hands. Even Achi Baba, the first day objective at Helles, remained a hill too far for Hamilton's force. The MEF's fighting strength and physical ability was dwindling by the day, and morale was declining. Not only was there little hope of further reinforcements, but the Ottomans had continued to grow stronger in manpower and the supply of munitions, both of which flowed steadily to the Gallipoli Peninsula in ever increasing numbers: it was reckoned that by this stage they had 315,000 men available compared to the MEF's 150,000.

On 2 September Kitchener informed Hamilton that General Maurice Sarrail would be bringing out four new French divisions and would require both the French divisions at Helles to support him. To replace the two French divisions Kitchener would make available the 27th and 28th Divisions, both regular divisions that were on the Western Front. Hamilton was overjoyed and full of optimism about this, but some of his staff officers, like Orlo and Dawnay, were less convinced. Deploying the French on the Asiatic side of the Dardanelles was discussed; if nothing else, it was a tangible political asset for possible future bargaining.

Any decision, however, would need to be agreed with the French, especially as Sarrail would be operating independently of Hamilton. Sarrail, backed by General Bailloud, was in favour of landing his force on the Asiasic coast, with a possible advance to take Chanak, but General Joseph Joffre, his commander-in-chief, was doubtful of its wisdom. Joffre thought the risk was too great should the operation go wrong, and more troops, munitions and drafts would be needed, none of which he could spare from the Western Front. If the scheme did proceed, this strategic change could make Anzac and Suvla less relevant. That said, no one at GHQ was willing to relinquish these blood-soaked sectors and give a moral victory to the Ottomans. Talk continued in GHQ with regards to what reinforcements were needed to not only hold the post August gains, but how to exploit them.

The political scene was also changing. In London, the focus was again back on the Western Front, where Britain had come under pressure from France to mount a joint Franco-British offensive (the Third Battle of Artois 1915; the Battle of Loos) in France. Until the outcome of the offensive was known, Hamilton learnt that no new French or British troops would be sent to Gallipoli. From bad to worse, Hamilton then learnt that there was a new commitment to Salonika (Thessaloniki), in north-eastern Greece. Bulgaria, which had remained neutral thus far, sided with the Central Powers in September 1915, which threatened the Greeks. The Greeks, fearing an attack by Bulgaria, made a plea to the Allies for military support, which was granted. To aid Greece, Kitchener agreed to the sending of an Anglo-French army to Salonika under the command of Sarrail, which immediately robbed Hamilton of the 10th (Irish) Division from Suvla and French 2e Division from Helles. The loss of two divisions was a major blow to any future operations.

If this wasn't bad enough, anti-Dardanelles feelings

were growing back in London, thanks in no small part to war correspondent Ellis Ashmead-Bartlett, who continued to be scathing of how the campaign was being run. This feeling was only strengthened when Stopford arrived home following his earlier dismissal. On 10 September, Dawnay was sent to London by Hamilton with the task to report truthfully on the situation following the failure of the August offensive, and to help make a case for reinforcements for a future offensive. Dawnay, who had influential political and military connections in London, spent the rest of the month meeting with various members of the Cabinet, Prime Minister Asquith, Winston Churchill, Kitchener, and even the King. Dawnay undoubtedly had loyalties to Hamilton, but there was also the national good to consider.

At Gallipoli, September brought little respite from the hot and dry weather. Water was still in short supply: wells had long since run dry or were poisoned, which meant much of the soldiers' drinking water had to be transported from distant places, including Egypt. Their diet still largely consisted of tinned salted bully beef, Maconochies stew, dry biscuits, cheese, bacon and apricot jam, none of which helped quench the thirst. Neither Helles, Anzac nor Suvla were spacious battlefields, and the men were confined to trenches or cramped in reserve areas where sanitary conditions were far from ideal. Along with the monotonous food, lack of sleep, lice, and plagues of flies, Gallipoli was one large graveyard with many of the corpses, both friend and foe, lying partially or completely unburied from the previous battles. It was not surprising that sickness was rife amongst the weak and emaciated soldiers who garrisoned Gallipoli. In some divisions the ravages of sickness had reduced the fighting strength more than had bullets of the enemy, with dysentery, jaundice and septic sores still rampant amongst the men.

From September onwards the fronts settled down to the boredom of trench warfare; sniping, patrolling, carrying parties, trench improvements and salvage duties day and night. Offensive operations were confined to small-scale mining and bombing attacks, which both sides used to gain tactical advantages over each other. Above the trenches the air war being waged by the Royal Naval Air Service (RNAS) and a French army air squadron brought another dimension to the war at Gallipoli. Both forces, working largely independently of one another, became innovators in the use of airpower, using aircraft in the tactical roles of reconnaissance, close air support, and bombing. On 16 September, Orlo describes the beginning of German/Ottoman aerial bomb and dart attacks, the first of which targeted the tented GHQ area on Imbros. The RNAS had two aerodromes on Imbros, including an airship station, so, along with GHQ and numerous tented camps and piers, Imbros became a natural target to attack.

* * *

Monday 1 September 1915

Grey and windy. Jolly but for the dust. Lay down all day with only milk: doctor gave me more bismuth and Dover's powder. Also some jelly. Seems a pleasant fellow called Clements: glad to buy a tin of my tobacco as he wouldn't let me give it [to] him. Said the bread here was very bad, too much water, too sour and too spongy. Quite enough to cause diarrhoea. Stayed quiet all day and did no work. Vitale came in later and discussed Shakespeare and played chess with me.

Tuesday 2 September 1915

Still staying abed but decidedly better. Had jelly today, also to have rice for lunch and soft boiled egg for dinner.

Hear from Hony that a wire to Secretary of State last night by way of giving the appreciation that was recently asked for. Have not seen the wire myself, but even Hony thought it fatuous, for though beginning by stating all the difficulties ended up we are all in a winning spirit ... etc. etc. Also hear this morning arrived very secret wire from Kitchener saying (1) that Sarrail was bringing out 3 new French divisions to act independently: thus confirming our suspicions (2) that he was consulting General French as to sending us the 27th and 28th Divisions. Also Dawnay is going home with the King's Messenger today to lay situation before them.

For the latter news I am devoutly glad. I saw Dawnay this morning for a few minutes in my tent and asked him a few questions. He said: yes, he was going home. During his voyage to Athens and back it had been strongly borne in on him that somebody must go who really *knew*. When he got back he fought hard for this, saying Aspinall must go and was then told he was to go. His instructions are ridiculous. "To answer all questions truthfully but in no way pessimistically". Said it was a big job, for one had really a chance of doing something big for the nation's good, but had to balance that against loyalty to his chief. A really strong man, he said, would perhaps go home and get them both stellenbosched (i.e. Sir Ian and CGS). I said to him plainly I thought at this time the nation's good was much more important than the reputation of Sir Ian.

Asked him what kind of telegram went home last night, and he replied hopeless. He and Aspinall tried over and over again to get a proper version of things sent but it was useless.

I asked "what view then does the blessed man himself take of things?" He replied "Oh, Mr Micawber's exactly".[1]

So again, for I don't know the how manieth time the shallow optimism of an obstinate man, who thinks it unsoldierly to tell unpleasant truths and who is no strategist, has made it impossible for the staff which contains 3 pretty clear sighted men to give a logical and accurate view of the situation.[2]

Dawnay continued that in his view the original strategical aim of this expedition had disappeared, because it could not possibly be attained. This view is not shared by Aspinall, if we get the desired reinforcements. Also he has no desire to give up Anzac unless we hold Asiatic shore. I doubt if Sir Ian would evacuate Anzac anyhow. But they, the GC and CGS wouldn't see it, so it made it very difficult to appreciate for them the future situation as regards the additional troops coming, if they failed to appreciate the present. He thought that if the French made good on the Asiatic side, so that the Allies really held the mouth of the Straits strongly with heavy guns etc. on both sides, we should have gained a real political asset. We could hold a kind of Torres Vedras[3] with no more than normal wastage and have something solid to bargain with. But this of course made our northern wing useless, but that they *won't* see. The aim with which it began is gone and it is only a waste and a danger to hold it. It is here that I hope Dawnay will open the eyes of people at home, so that our winter campaign may be conducted on a proper strategical basis. There are of course objections of evacuating Suvla

1 Wilkins Micawber was a character in Charles Dickens' *David Copperfield*, known for his optimism, famously saying 'something will turn up'.

2 Orlo marked this 'omit'

3 The Lines of Torres Vedras were lines of forts built, under the direction of the Duke of Wellington, to defend Lisbon during the Peninsula War.

and Anzac before any compensation is gained. It will give the Turks a moral advantage and might cause an outcry not only in England but in Australia and New Zealand. But we ought to be strong enough to do it, if necessary.

Have now seen wire sent home on situation. It rehearsed the difficulties etc. and our inferiority in numbers, but said plainly the thing to do was to make another attempt in the north to get astride the Kaba Tepe—Maidos line. To do this not only do we want drafts to amount of 63,000 but 50,000 new formations and 20% reinforcements always ready in Egypt. Pressed the importance of increased submarine activity to make Turkish supply question very difficult.

In answer to Kitchener's wire about French troops under Sarrail we sent a curt reply saying it was noted, and might he consult with Admiral on the question. An independent Sarrail, I gather, not very favourably looked on; and we can't spare much in the way of transport.

My health improved as day went on. Saw Dawnay again. R. Buxton to see me and Vitale to chess.

Friday 3 September 1915

Up and to the office; better, but must keep to light diet...

Talked to Aspinall about things today. He, I found, was much disappointed at not going to England himself because he thought he was going and has had no holiday, and because he thought Dawnay over pessimistic. He ascribes it to the General's getting the impression that he was the more pessimistic of the two, his being the last appreciation sent in, which had wiped out of the General's mind the memory of a far more pessimistic appreciation presented earlier by Dawnay.

Aspinall showed me his appreciation and his draft telegram to be sent on September 1. His points are that our attack on 6th had been complete failure, troops very tired and want rest, also moral declining while that of Turks rising. Our old troops worn out and new troops catching spirit by infection.

He then goes on to formulate the position to be laid before WO. (1) that 8th Corps only needs drafts and even then periodical rests can be carried out. (2) In north only one line of defence. Anzac can afford no troops a rest, having even no Corps reserve, and 9th Corps, having 1 division [and] 5000 rifles in reserve, hopes to rest 2000 at a time. Wastage of 20% per month. But in 6 weeks' time with reinforcements will bring force up to 55,000. We still want all numbers before asked for +20% reinforcements ready in Egypt.

If these come our only chance to make another attempt to get across peninsula from Kaba Tepe to Maidos, though this time it will [be] far harder and with these reinforcements even we cannot be absolutely confident of success. On the other hand attempts elsewhere impossible either for naval reasons or strength of force required.

Aspinall's appreciation not so far off what was sent than Dawnay's, but differs in stating definitely that we cannot guarantee success and stating very clearly the fact of our failure.

A wire went to Kitchener this afternoon about Sarrail's force etc. It said: we are delighted to hear of this new force, our relations with French have always been so good that I am sure we shall maintain cordial relations with Sarrail even under equivocal conditions of independence of command. 2 divisions will be necessary to relieve French troops already on peninsula, and should be very glad to have the 2 regular divisions who should have full complement of artillery. The French field artillery with its very abundant supply of ammunition will be a great loss, and it would be to advantage of both sides if they could be left at Helles till

French had established themselves in Asia. We take it for granted French will land on Asiatic shore of Dardanelles as action further south would have little effect on the general situation. Yet even in that case they wouldn't probably at first weaken Turks in front of us, as they would not at first be as serious a threat to his vitals as we. Aspinall wanted to put "a no more serious threat to his vitals than we".

Aspinall told me that a friend of Dawnay's had written saying that the King had spoken to him very bitterly about the Dardanelles and the heavy losses, and he said "The worst of it is I can't trust Hamilton; he is always so absurdly optimistic".

My getting up caused a relapse and went to bed less well than when I got up.

Saturday 4 September 1915

On my back all day, improving a bit. Quiet day nothing doing.

Sunday 5 September 1915

Better, but still keeping very quiet. At 10.30 or so Marquis, who has come for 3 or 4 days to the rest camp on K Beach, turned up and spent the rest of the day with me, having lunch and tea at the mess. I went to the mess for dinner having some soup, an egg and arrowroot. Otherwise I lived on milk and biscuits, my store from home coming in very handy. Am getting rather there. Marquis seemed well, but still afflicted with remains of a cold and inside not properly right. He seems very fed up with working under Taylor and wants to change if possible. He must be a most exasperating man to work with. Not much news otherwise from Marquis who, I think, enjoyed his day. We talked about many things. After he had gone Vitale tuned up and talked Italian till after 10.30, about national characteristics, Germans, English etc. etc. A very nice man indeed. Says it is a great relief to find someone free from prejudice to talk to.

Pollen came in and asked me to go to Athens with him on the *Imogene* on Thursday. Should like it exceedingly, and hope to get leave.

Monday 6 September 1915

Much better. Diarrhoea practically gone but stayed very quiet all day and went to mess for dinner, soup and 2 eggs. Read St Paul's epistle to Corinthians. Talk and chess with Vitale in the evening.

Tuesday 7 September 1915

Up and to the office as usual. Seem quite recovered. Marquis turned up in the morning and we had a very jolly day together. We made a scratch lunch in my tent off cake and biscuits, and then sauntered over to K Beach, and a little way up the Panaghia road where we went up the side of hill and sat down for 2 hours under the shadow of a big boulder. A most perfect afternoon, warm, still and wonderfully clear. The colours and the view alike magnificent. We enjoyed ourselves immensely idling there, had tea off shortbread, chocolate and water, and so sauntered back to GHQ. Marquis dined at the mess and then left to go back to Helles tomorrow. It has been extremely jolly to see something of him, and I think the 3 days have done him a lot of good.

Wednesday 8 September 1915

The voyage to Athens confirmed and welcome news that *Imogene* sailing today. Borrowed complete mufti from Graves including shirt and squash hat. Quiet day with nothing to record. After tea walked over to the new aerodrome by the salt lake. Beautiful evening and splendid view from hill above aerodrome.

Thursday 9 September 1915

Imogene arrived after breakfast and I got news that she was going off immediately to Mudros to coal before her voyage instead of waiting till evening as usual. So, on Mitchell's advice, having got leave I hastily threw my things into a bag and bustled on board by noon, so as to snatch a little longer holiday. Otherwise I should have left early tomorrow morning in a destroyer with the King's Messenger. As it was, my enterprise was fully repaid. It was a heavenly day. We got under weigh just before one, and after an excellent lunch with Captain Potts, I sat on deck while we steamed to Mudros in a state of utter contentment, occasionally somnolent, occasionally re-reading "Howard's End" and with the satisfaction of having excellent letters from home. We made Mudros about 6 and dropped our hook near the *Europa* at 6.30. The sun was setting gorgeously behind the hills, and there was a fine array of ships in the harbour, which was full of life; the island had thrown up tents like mushrooms since I last saw in April. Soon afterwards Birch, whose acquaintance I made on the *Queen Elizabeth* and who is now doing mail officer on the depot ship *Europa*, came aboard with mail and asked me to dine on the *Europa*. Off I went at 8 and had a very jolly evening in the wardroom which was very full. Birch had another guest, one Strange, Lieutenant RNVR, who runs the Mitylene trawlers. Birch, I discover, is a King's man who lives half in Cambridge, half in London, doing journalism and occasional acting. He knows A.D. Knox, Maynard Keynes and Stephen Gaselee well. Keynes, he says, has been settling the whole economies of the Allies since the war began, being the one practical economist in England.

I played a good deal on the piano too, which gave me a lot of pleasure and seemed to find considerable favour with the audience. Began with Chopin and ended with the Country Girl and Gilbert the Filbert. Sat on talking and only got back to *Imogene* at midnight. Memo: to rope Birch in for the Savile if possible.

Friday 10 September 1915

Aroused earliest by bumping etc. preliminary to moving over to the coal ship. Saw a lovely sunrise through the port hole. Lay on in bed reading and up leisurely. Breakfast 9.25. Coaling began late so fancy we shall be late starting which will curtail my time in Athens a bit. But I don't much mind, being in a too contented frame of mind. At about 12.30 Curling who like me came for the voyage and the King's Messenger Lancelot Lowther came on board and we set off for Athens. Voyaged all day with a following wind. Lowther is a perfectly classic bore, and got up to look exactly like his brother. Curling cheery but stupid. Before dinner tried to put a few ideas before him as he invited it by lauding out in the usual way about socialism.

Saturday 11 September 1915

Rather a roll all night which made sleep less sound than it might have been. Up on deck in pyjamas at 6 and had a cup of tea. Saw the sunrise and the temple of Athena on Cape Sounion. The voyage up coast to Athens quite lovely. The morning was beautiful and the hills came out with jolly shadows. The view of Athens from Phalerum pleased me immensely, for a good deal of the city is not seen but the Parthenon standing on the Acropolis and Lycabettus, and around Hymettus, Pentelicon, Parnes and Aigalious, with Aegina and Salamina on the other side. It gave me a great thrill. So did going up to the Acropolis later with

Monty. In fact from the point of view of supply my imaginative material for a reconstruction of Periclean Athens I was in every way satisfied by my short visit.

We got in at 8.45, rowed ashore and were motored up to the Embassy in the Cuninghame's motor, dropping bags at the Grande Bretagne on the way. Sir F. Elliot asked us to dine with him that evening at Kiphisia—accepted. Walked down Stadium Street and then who should greet me but Alexander Pallis—a great coincidence. Asked me to lunch with him; accepted. Then made a few purchases and went to see Monty at the Angleterre, whom found in bed. Sat talking with him an hour hearing wonderful stories of his doings. Saw his body servant, a good looking youth in Evzone costume, who accompanies him everywhere. Then went to lunch at Grande Bretagne with Alex with whom much talk and a good lunch. He is in charge of all the refugees in Macedonia. Does not think much of British diplomacy. Monty to tea at 4.30 and drive in 2 horse carrozza with Evzone on the box to the Acropolis, where wandered and photographed. Words useless to describe it. So back and had an ice at Café Oraia. Then caught the odd train which starts in the middle of a street for Kiphisia luckily meeting Rendel of the Embassy on the train. Found him sympathetic and musical. Journey took nearly an hour. Dinner en famille Sir F and Lady Elliot, Miss Elliot, the King's Messenger (Lowther), Curling, Rendel and self. Lady Elliott an idiot of the first water who talks nonsense: hear she ruins his career. Miss E. silly minx: did well for Curling. Dinner good and as I sat next to Sir F. was spared much struggling either with the minx or the idiot. At 10 p.m. we all had to catch a train back.

At 11.30 with Curling to Café Panhellinique where Monty joined us at 12. Large ugly café with feeble band. We drank bad beer. Gradually old friends of Monty's, mostly petty officers of Naval mission joined us, and about 1.30 les dames began to arrive. Wretched lot. Monty and Curling went to talk with 2, and I joined them, finding also a very intelligent American war correspondent called Hibben. The 2 tarts were so ugly, common and stupid I really couldn't find anything to say to them (Monty seemed to enjoy playing the fool with Jeanne, whom (idiot!) he talks of "using"). Her companion was truly hideous of Spanish blood. Monty and Curling saw them home and I walked back to hotel with Hibben, of whom I would have liked to see more, only the society of the silly tarts in that café was so oppressive that we had never started talking properly. Got into bed at 2.30.

Sunday 12 September 1915

Up at 9 a.m. breakfasted comfortably. Hear we had to leave at 12. Let everybody else make arrangements which they did very badly for getting to Phalerum and took a little walk half way up Lycabettus. Motored with Potts to Phalerum. Monty and the King's Messenger, J.H. Ward, in another car, Curling had gone on with baggage. All aboard before 2 p.m. and so off with excellent lunch. Ward a great improvement on Lowther. The day unfortunately grey. Feeling exceedingly well and having enjoyed myself tremendously. Quiet voyage out. Monty seasick. Played auction bridge after dinner and lost 5/6.

Good story by Ward. Two sailors in hospital talking about friends who were wounded.

Nurse: Where were they wounded?

Sailor: In the arse.

Nurse: Rectum

Sailor: Wrecked 'em? Damn near killed 'em![4]

4 Orlo marked this 'omit'.

Monday 13 September 1915

Sea calmed down and voyage continued most prosperously. Monty improved and was able to do a very hearty lunch at Mudros where we stayed from 12.30–2 p.m. Arrived Imbros after dark and anchored in harbour at 9.25, wind having risen. Did not go ashore but played bridge again, winning 6 pence on the whole.

Tuesday 14 September 1915

Breakfast on *Imogene* at 7 a.m. and ashore by 8.15 a.m. Back to work. Cold grey day and not very inviting: found parcel from Harrods and letters etc. awaiting me besides new mail in King's Messenger bag. Nothing of excitement had happened since I left.

Important secret wire from Kitchener saying he had just returned from France where he had been settling up certain questions (Our MF630 sent on September 12) we had recently asked, and where there had been confusion owing to French Government having come to a decision without consulting military advisors. After conference with Millerand, Sarrail and Joffre it had been decided that the 4 new French divisions could not leave till the result of coming offensive was clear. This should be known by beginning of October, and if indecisive, 2 British divisions would embark at Marseilles to be closely followed by 4 new French divisions, the whole to have arrived here by mid-November. Millerand and Sarrail were strongly in favour of French landing and acting independently on Asiatic shore. Joffre was doubtful of the wisdom of this, as such a course if not immediately successful might lead to demands for further troops, drafts, munitions etc., which with due regard to the safety of France could not be forthcoming. Also Joffre mistrusted Sarrail's leadership especially as the plans he (Sarrail) had prepared were worthless.

Joffre's staff were very carefully working out scheme for landing in Asia and the results did not seem very promising. Millerand therefore wished Sir Ian to wire his views on this subject for his private information. For the present, therefore, we can only rely on the reinforcements coming that have already been notified to us.

Walked after tea with Aspinall who said news contained in above telegram was rather staggering, as it showed that the large reinforcements of British troops asked for were not coming. So that neither we nor the French would be strong enough to make a push. Asked to dinner with General: other guests were Vitale and the King's Messenger, Ward. The General seemed rather bored and distrait. Heavy rain in the night which made one's clothes damp in the morning.

Wednesday 15 September 1915

Uneventful day. After tea had a solitary ride on a yeomanry steed, very first since the accident. Very pleasant and no mishap, though my seat very bad on yeomanry saddle. Monty and Ward dined at O mess. Monty in great pain with bad sciatica and looked wretched.

Thursday 16 September 1915

While dressing this morning, was delayed by the excitement of a hostile aeroplane attack. The 1st came about 7.30 while I was seated in the rear, and dropped 4 bombs wide. The second came about 8 and dropped 4 bombs near the signal tent. Six men were wounded and holes made in a good many tents. It was found that they also dropped a lot of darts. The noise of falling bombs quite unpleasant to hear, rather as if the aeroplane was falling on one's head. A considerable amount of fire was opened from the ships, also rifles and machine guns. The guns were a bit slow opening fire which gave rise to the note from the ADMS Colonel Keble: "Yes, I am afraid our father and our mother must have been in bed together at the time". Our new airship which went up yesterday is a very pretty sight. She is torpedo shaped, and the bag painted to look like aluminium with 4 short planes, 2 on each side. She goes along with beautiful ease, steers like an aeroplane and makes less noise.

Rest of the day uneventful. Weather rather cold and grey. Took solitary walk after tea and ran along sea shore where also did some Muller exercises for the benefit of my body. Worked during the day at 3rd despatch.

After dark the wind blew up to half a gale and continued all night. Dust very bad.

Friday 17 September 1915

Wind still blowing half a gale and everything smothered in dust. Quiet day but very tiresome. Have caught the cold started by Powell and handed on to Hony. Throat like sandpaper. After lunch sent our cipher wire answering Kitchener's enquiry about French landing on Asiatic coast. The following is the gist of it:—

Though have consistently opposed Asiatic landing, the situation is now clearing up and conditions are altering. Formerly Turks had from 10,000 to 12,000 men on Asiatic shore and large reserves ready to cross at any moment. Now Anatolia and Syria have been drained and the Turks have nearly 4 times as long a front to defend and are more threatened by us. If we can be strong enough to maintain pressure on the whole Turkish line it is unlikely they would have large numbers to oppose a surprise French landing on Asiatic shore. Even with a complete understanding with Bulgaria which would set free all the Thracian troops, at most they would have 5 divisions available, probably scattered at first, and only 2 Nizam.[5] Coast probably not heavily entrenched below Yukyeri Bay.[6] If French bring good troops and succeed in keeping destination secret, good chance of their advancing on Chanak and defeating troops sent against them. The degree of success would depend on whether entrenched positions Kum Kale—Eren Keui could be turned by good road from Yukyeri through Ezine to Chanak. Once Eren Keui reached Turks between Kum Kale and Eren Keui would have to retire leaving Kum Kale in our hands as a base. If Turks endeavoured to make a bridgehead of the Chanak promontory they would require a large force and, once they were cut off on north, supply would become difficult. French occupation of Chanak would not be equivalent to victory, but at any rate, it would cut the supply line from Chanak to Ak Bashi Liman, make the Narrows useless, Nagara net could be cut, 15″ Howitzers could batter Kilid Bahr, allied fleet could enter Marmara. If French failed to take Chanak, at least Turks would have used up last reserves and happy termination, if postponed, would be in sight. At worst clear road would be open to bridgehead where French would draw considerable Turkish forces.

All other schemes beset with difficulties. If armies separated disadvantage of independent commands might be an advantage. If I [Hamilton] gave up Helles it would be very unpopular as Achi Baba so strong and French dead keen to go Asia. If French come to Suvla, independent command would be ludicrous with troops fighting side by side. If that course were taken I should ask allied governments to decide which general had most daring brains and experience (Golly!) and if choice fell on Frenchman

5 Nizam were regular army forces.

6 On the Asiatic coast, south of Kum Kale, roughly opposite Tenedos Island.

would serve under him loyally. Xeros plan certain to be strongly opposed, reinforcements always handy, distances from base and strain on fleet.

Talking to Vitale this evening told me of a very confidential report for Cadorna which he had just seen. Apparently Cadorna much concerned with German victories in Russia and thinks it certain they will be able to detach large forces. Particularly concerned over German and Austrian immense strength of heavy artillery. Italy, like others, deficient in it, and though man for man better than present Austrian troops, artillery has kept him from reaching Laibach.[7] Immense efforts being made to collect heavy artillery, and by February or March will be so provided as to make a really serious advance. Meanwhile must be content with limited offensive, objectives Gorizia and Tolmino.

Saturday 18 September 1915

Lovely calm day but feeling rather wretched and stuffy with cold coming on. At 7.30 just as we were going to sit down to dinner an aeroplane came over and dropped 3 bombs near airship shed. We all went out of mess tent and lay down as moon was shining full on the white tents. Just we had finished dinner another Taube turned up and dropped 3 more bombs about the same place. The O mess scattered like good 'uns. There was another scare about 9 but this time it was one of our own aeroplanes, so false alarm. Sykes says we bombed Turks at 7 places today, certainly doing damage at some of them.

Sunday 19 September 1915

Lovely day. Cold in head a bit heavy but salt and water

7 Ljubljana (Laibach) Castle. During the First World War, it was used as a quarantine station for Italian prisoners of war.

treatment doing it much good. Quiet day with no particular events. Walked and talked with Vitale after tea. Beautiful moonlight night. At dinner time our airship went out for a trial night trip. She is a fine sight by moonlight. Also two of our aeroplanes went up. This a little disconcerting as when a Boche plane comes, as it did, one is lulled into security. The Boche plane dropped 2 bombs somewhere near the airship shed and then made off. 2 machine guns opened fire on her. To bed quietly but about 2 a gale descended on us as suddenly as a cyclone out of a perfectly clear sky and then it was perfectly bloody. Our tent ropes had been slacked because of heavy dew, and I had to get up to tighten them. Then the door flaps wouldn't keep taut, and the bulging of the tent sides upset everything on my table etc., finally two pegs holding the flies came out and I had to go out with a maul and hammer them in. The dust swept in in clouds all over everything. My language perfectly appalling.

Monday 20 September 1915

Half a gale still blowing this morning and jolly cold. Nevertheless, and in spite of cold, felt better; using enormous number of hankies. Fatigue parties are digging shelter trenches against air raids. Quiet day with no events. Rode with Barttelot over to our new camp and back. Very pleasant and had 2 jolly canters. Met Samson and Marix on our way back, Marix on a mule. Samson thinks the airship will certainly be hit one day. No aeroplane attack tonight, only some of our own out at midnight.

Tuesday 21 September 1915

Jolly fresh day. Heard Germans had occupied Vilna. News from Sofia that Bulgarian mobilisation would begin in 2 days, but our minister still thought no attack would be

Unexploded bomb dropped by an enemy aircraft near GHQ, Imbros (O.C. Williams, IWM).

made on Serbia except with simultaneous Austro-German attack. WO telegram says Bulgarians decided *not* to join Teutonic powers.

Walk with Mitchell after tea and inspected the airship in its shed. The lieutenant who showed us over says our airships are not so good as the Zepps [Zeppelins] as we can't make the proper fabric. *Imogene* came in with letters. All much interested in details of air raid on London on September 8.

Wednesday 22 September 1915

Was just beginning No. 2 Muller exercise when machine gun fire announced hostile aeroplane. Got into trench in coat and pyjamas. Just about to begin again when 2 more came. Into trenches again. Each dropped 4 bombs but wide of the camp. Brisk fire opened on them but they were very high. So to my bath. All rather late for breakfast in consequence. One bomb about 100 yards away from General's camp failed to explode. Photographed it after breakfast. Later in morning it was exploded by rifle fire causing all O(a) to get under their tables, and Hony, as usual, to poke himself into the safe.

Wires from Sofia show that Bulgarians are mobilizing to take advantage of German advance on Serbia, but it appears that no such advance has occurred. The Bulgaro-Turkish agreement for cession of Dedeagatch railway completed, and it seems as if mobilisation had been engineered by German solely, at present, as a political move, to embroil Serbia with Bulgaria. Our Minister at Sofia points out seriousness of situation owing to Serbia's refusal to listen to allies and determination to yield only to force. He says if she would make concessions to Bulgaria now it would cut ground from under the feet of pro-German war party in Bulgaria.

Quiet day, walked in the evening. North-easterly wind freshened to a jolly cold gale which continued all night. Much dust.

Thursday 23 September 1915

Very cold wind and dust continued, but all the same the air in itself magnificent, like champagne. Took a walk after tea to K beach and looked at the road and quay and pier there. Very difficult to imagine what that landing place was like when I first set foot ashore, and the Sheltie[8] always went aground on the rocky bottom.

Friday 24 September 1915

The same weather, chilly and exhilarating and fine with north-easterly wind. Keeps aeroplanes off. News from Athens this morning that in reply to Bulgarian mobilisation King of Greece has consented to general mobilisation as measure of precaution not committing country to participation in general war. To take effect from midnight tonight. 20 classes called up to present themselves within 48 hours.

8 A launch boat used by GHQ to move between beaches.

In the evening further wire from Sofia saying it was understood allies contemplated sending allied force to occupy "uncontested" zone in Macedonia. O'Beirne urged very seriously that it should be made perfectly plain to Bulgaria that this would be held for the purpose of *giving it to her* unless her action made such a course impossible to the allies. If this were not done, the sending of a force would only precipitate a rupture. If this be so, it remains to be seen what view Bulgaria takes of such an argument.

Also sent a wire to Kitchener in answer to his inquiry about evacuating Suvla. "We have no intention of evacuating Suvla unless Balkans change situation. We are stronger now—new troops improving and old troops resting. To give it up would be great moral victory for Turks. Also experience shows that if we give up Suvla it means restricting ourselves to old Anzac Cove, where enough stores could not be landed, whereas on new Anzac beach [ie. North Beach] we can land more stores than at Suvla. Also Turks would probably make landing at Anzac Cove impossible if we gave up Suvla".

Began trying an article for Blackwood's on our beginning of this expedition.

Saturday 25 September 1915

Lovely day. Nothing particular to record personally.

Situation grows more exciting. Urgent wire from General Bailloud just after lunch saying he had received orders from French Minister of War to prepare a division for immediate departure and asking us to relieve his 2nd Division as soon as possible. This the first we had heard of it. Sent a wire to Proemial asking for confirmation and pointing out serious difficulty of doing this without getting regular division with full artillery.

Sunday 26 September 1915

The explanation of above came this morning early in very important wire from Kitchener. "In view of Bulgarian mobilisation Greece has asked allies to send force to Salonica to support Serbia if attacked by Bulgaria and at same time by Germans from north. France and GB have agreed to find the force, 150,000 men, and prompt action is required. Though no intention of withdrawing from Dardanelles operations, it is evident that some troops must be drawn from Dardanelles. Understand from your staff officer it would be easy for you to withdraw from Suvla to Kaiajik Aghala front, and Dardanelles Committee had already considered this advisable in view of marshy country and approaching winter. Hence my previous wire about Suvla. Offensive all along line in France has commenced. Infantry attacking today (25th).[9] Great results anticipated which may greatly modify your situation. Until a result is reached French and British reinforcements for Dardanelles operations must be in abeyance. Also yeomanry on their way to you must be diverted and mounted from Egypt. Force required from you is 2 divisions, preferably 10th and 11th, and French will detach a brigade and a division. Wire at once how you propose to meet these requirements. Dardanelles Committee had considered withdrawal from Suvla advisable but had not seen your wire of 24th. 15″ howitzer is required at Belgrade as soon as possible".

That was *something* to start the day on and no mistake. Meanwhile it is a perfectly heavenly day and I am off to Panaghia with Vitale.

Wire from Sofia says Bulgarian mobilisation proceeding with some difficulty. Also that Turk-Bulg. agreement about Dedeagatch does not come into force till October 8.

9 The Battle of Loos.

Members of Operations Section, General Staff, GHQ, at Imbros (Family collection).

Back, left to right: Lieutenant Henry Hony (interpreter), Major Bertrand Moberly (GSO2), Captain Francis Mitchell RN (liaison between army and navy staffs), Lieutenant-Colonel Cecil Aspinall (GSO1), Captain Henry Peyton (GSO3, Intelligence Section), Captain Edgar Anstey (GSO2).

Front, left to right: Major Sir Walter Barttelot (GSO3), Major Guy Dawnay (GSO2), Captain Orlo Williams (cipher).

Inwardness of this is that Turks are waiting to see if Bulgaria is really coming in. If Serbia makes a concession now, and Bulgaria can be kept in state of indecision, Turks will probably wriggle out of agreement and there will be conflict.

9.30 p.m.: It was an absolutely perfect day for an expedition to Panaghia, still, warm and fresh. The colour on the hills and valleys magnificent, the atmosphere very clean and the views exquisite. We hired horses outside K camp which I used when I felt inclined. At Panaghia had a most excellent lunch at Christon's, when we met Laborde[10] and a Major somebody. But a cloud was thrown over the day by the state of Vitale's health. In the morning we had not gone more than 10 minutes when he clutched my arm and complained that his legs were failing him. We stopped a bit and went on. Then it came on again and we sat down and it passed off. He complained of numbness in the hands and arms too. At the outside of the camp we hired the horses and he rode mainly the whole way, but walked the last part quite heartily only felt it again just as we reached the inn. He was rather gloomy all the afternoon, and told me on the way back that he had been very ill in Africa and that one doctor in Naples on his return had told him he might be suffering from premature arteriosclerosis. When we reached the sentry at K camp we got off, but Vitale immediately almost fell down and I had to assist him to the wall to sit on. After a bit he got again and I took him to the hospital at the camp, found Colonel McKenzie[11] the O.C., talked to him, a very nice man and got him to see Vitale. Vitale got off his horse quite well and told him all his symptoms. McKenzie asked him to stay a couple of days anyhow to remain under observation. So I went back alone and gave orders for his servant to pack and go over with all his things. It is very sad, for it looks to me exactly like the beginning of that hopeless malady which struck down Willy Lee.

Not much news when I returned to camp. WO telegram tells of good Russian recovery both outside Vilna[12] and in the south where Mackensen has been driven out of Pinsk. Wire also said Germans claimed that British attack at La Bassee had broken down under artillery fire. A report

10 Lieutenant De Laborde.

11 Mackenzie

12 Vilnuis, Lithuania. He is referring here to the Vilno-Dvinsk offensive.

from the French battleship *Suffren* says that French have broken through on a front of 51 kilometres. If this should *only* prove true.

Sent off long wire in answer to Kitchener's. Gist of it was that objections to abandoning Suvla very great now we had landed there large amount of stores and supplies and also because of great moral effect. GC [Hamilton] says would prefer to take risk of holding same front with fewer men, and later, if necessary, preparing gradually to evacuate. Said he could spare 10th and 53rd or, with more difficulty, 10th and 11th. Could also spare one French *brigade* and total of 4½ British brigades of Field Artillery. Conference of GOCs tomorrow.

Monday 27 September 1915

Jolly still day. Good news in *en clair*[13] wire from Kitchener. British have had considerable success south of La Bassee, captured 1700 prisoners and 8 guns. Also minor successes further north. French have advanced at Arras and in Champagne have made considerable advance on front of 20 miles, capturing very large number of prisoners. Hurrah. Further details not yet arrived.

Cipher wire from Kitchener rather mystifying in answer to our wire asking for confirmation of Bailloud's: "Fact is Greek Government cannot make up its mind to allow our landing at Salonica. No action can be taken for present. French authorities had already been told that their order was premature".

Later clean and press telegrams say allies have captured 20,000 prisoners, 15,000 unwounded in 2 days' fighting. French advance in Champagne, Germans abandoned large quantity stores including 24 field guns. British penetrated in some cases 4000 yards. In Champagne French

13 Un-ciphered.

gained whole of German 1st system and forced them back on to 2nd line. Meanwhile Russians have retaken Vileyka east of Vilna, and at Lutsk have taken 4000 prisoners.

One aeroplane over this morning dropped 4 bombs, 3 near aeroplanes. No damage.

Quiet day. Went over to see Vitale after tea, found him lying in bed and evidently pretty gloomy. However, I saw the doctor later who said that, though he would probably have a stroke sooner or later, there was no reason why he shouldn't come back now to his duties here and carry on quite alright, of which I am glad.

At 11.30 p.m. one aeroplane dropped 2 bombs on aerodrome.

Tuesday 28 September 1915

Lovely day again. Good news from France are maintained though point to no overwhelming success. Kitchener says things are going well and that we have 23,000 prisoners and 40 guns. French reports claim more guns. In Champagne they are now up against German 2nd line of defence.

Another aeroplane this morning at 10.30 a.m. dropped bombs on aerodrome, wounding 2 men, one a Turk prisoner.

Wire from Kitchener says he agrees with us about Suvla for present, at same time does not like the ground we are holding. Greeks won't agree to landing any but small parties in plain clothes at Salonica, which Kitchener tells them is disguising soldiers and wrong. Still, preparations should be made. Thinks Byng and Malcolm ought to go to Salonica with any staff we can spare, which will be replaced. The French Government had behaved in very extraordinary manner in telling Bailloud to detach a division. "I have told them they can have a brigade and will ask you if you can spare a second brigade. Send your views on that subject".

We replied saying very glad to hear his views about Suvla, and Byng and Birdwood emphatic for retaining it, and Byng urged to improve position by closed defences during winter. Concentrating 10th Division at Mudros. Can only spare one French brigade.

French rather tiresome all day. Wire from Admiral saying French admiral had orders to transport cavalry at once from Alexandria to Salonica. We told him they were premature for the present, but Serbian business obviously getting warmer. Walked with Buxton to see Vitale. The new cipher officer, Berry arrived—a maths teacher at Cambridge aged 50. Had spent 1½ days in C2 and that was all he knew about ciphers.[14] Seems a decent kind of fellow, not quite.

Bertier to be awarded DSO tomorrow, Pelliot and [de] Laborde the MC. So had buzz in mess on the strength of it. False aeroplane alarm after dinner.

Wednesday 29 September 1915

3 important wires arrived in the night. One from Bailloud saying that military attaché Athens wired that Venizelos had changed his mind and asked for as many troops, French and British, to be sent to Salonica immediately.

(2) from Kitchener asking when 10th Division would be concentrated Mudros, and when French would reach there.

(3) from Kitchener saying that Malcolm, General A.B. Hamilton and an assistant and Colonel Blakeney—as well as 3 officers from Bailloud's staff—would be detailed to proceed Salonica to make scheme for disembarkation and quartering, Blakeney to make special report on railway requirements from Egypt to make line efficient.

14 C2 was the Parliamentary and Legal; Printing and Stationary Section within the Department of the Secretary, War Office.

'Three cheers for the Liasion Officer.' Medal ceremony, 29 September 1915. The family album records—from left to right—Hamilton, Pollen, Braithwaite, Maitland, Aspinall and Woodward (Family collection).

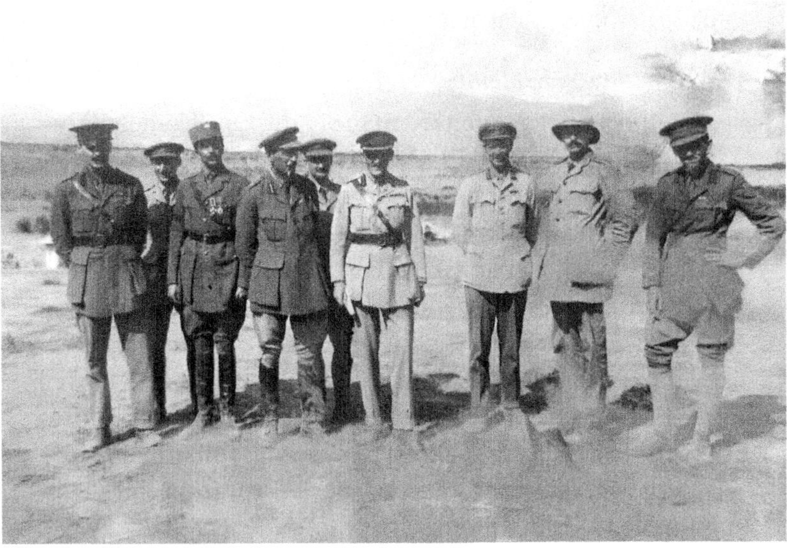

Members of GHQ, likely following the medal ceremony on 29 September (Aspinall-Oglander papers, Isle of Wight record office).

Left to right: Powell, Hony, Bertier de Sauvigny (the French liaison officer to GHQ), Major-General Braithwaite, Moberley, Aspinall, Barttelot, Orlo and Braithwaite Jr ('Val').

Very busy morning quite like old times sending telegrams without ceasing, all about this move of 10th Division etc.

In fact a day of ceaseless wiring to and fro all over the place in connection with the Salonica business, Kitchener, Bailloud, Vice Admiral, Maxwell and the corps all coming in for some.

After dinner Bailloud having received our instructions to send a brigade to Mudros, gaily wires he has orders from his WO to embark a whole division and take command of it himself. This he proposes to do handing over command of French sector at Helles to General Brulard and the remaining division: Bless the man and the French Government!

Wires from Sofia give impression Bulgarians are mobilising against Rumania, and that Bulgaria and Germany will present joint note to Rumania, who is *not* mobilising, demanding free passage of munitions and that Rumania will acquiesce.

Thursday 30 September 1915

Wires, wires, wires all the morning about the move to Salonica. Kitchener says position with French will become strained unless we let them take 2 brigades, and asks if we can manage this if he leaves us 53rd Division. We reply we can just manage and refer to last night's wire. They make rather preposterous demands for staff officers including Tyrrell, whom we refuse. A cipher officer to be detailed in readiness. Tried to get sent temporarily myself till another from England came, but was told couldn't be spared. Probably Bass will go. Don't really want to leave this GHQ but would have found short change amusing. Byng's taking command is now uncertain, if British force is to be diminished. Organisation of transport for 10th Division a difficulty. Also said we could spare no howitzer batteries. As it is the loss of French artillery will be a very serious thing for us, especially as we are now being starved for ammunition for the benefit of France. N.B. Up to now the British forces have never had *anything like* enough ammunition.

News from France quite satisfactory. The progress north of Loos seems very good and advance to Champagne maintained, but apparently French launched imprudent cavalry attack at Souain which was broken by enemy's fire. Very desperate fighting in Russia.

In Mesopotamia at Kut el Amara we have Turks on the run again towards Bagdad. Went to see Vitale. Said he had had slight return of symptoms and was put on a stricter diet and no smoking. At 11.30 order came from Kitchener that 10th Division was to sail for Salonica as soon as possible to keep parallel with French division. Also Kitchener wired saying that Bailloud reported French position at Helles could be held by 1 division. In that case could we spare 53rd.

8

'OUR HOPES HAVE BEEN DASHED'

GHQ GETS AN OVERHAUL

Bulgaria's entry to the war, and the invasion of Serbia by the Central Powers, changed the dynamics in the Balkans and altered British and French strategy. No longer, reasoned London and Paris, did reinforcing Gallipoli make sense when its resources could be better employed at Salonika.

The Salonika campaign, which fills many lines in Orlo's diary, got off to a bad start. Greek premier, Eleftherios Venizelos, was at constant odds with the country's monarch, King Constantine of Greece. Venizelos argued that Greece had an obligation under the Serbo-Greek Treaty 1913 to assist her neighbour. Constantine was not interested in aiding Serbia and wanted to maintain benevolent neutrality in the War, but he did agree to mobilization as a precautionary measure. Both the Allies and Central Powers tussled with incentives for Greece to change its neutral stance, but all to no avail. Constantine was not acting out of high-minded opposition to war but through pro-German sympathies; he had undergone military training in Germany and his wife, Queen Sophie, was German Kaiser Wilhelm II's sister. Venizelos, by contrast, was pro-Allied and saw a way for Greece to aid Serbia without direct military action. As such, he allowed the disembarkation of Anglo-French troops at Salonika. Constantine and his Royalists were furious. The ongoing dispute between Venizelos and Constantine paralysed Greek politics and left the British and French forces in Salonika in a difficult position. Would they be able to march north to aid Serbia, bringing the Greek army with them? Or would they have to defend themselves from their former hosts? When Constantine dismissed Venizelos as premier, appointing Alexandros Zaimis in his place, it didn't alter the situation. Greece remained neutral but reluctantly allowed the Anglo-French force to continue their disembarkation.

In London, as well as Gallipoli becoming less of a strategic priority, there was also growing criticism of Hamilton's leadership of the MEF. Some of this was influenced by a damning letter, originally written for the Prime Minister by Ellis Ashmead-Bartlett but re-written by Australian journalist Keith Murdoch (after the original was confiscated at Marseilles), which was highly critical of the campaign, and which eventually founds its way to the Cabinet. As much as Murdoch's words rattled the Cabinet, he was not as influential in this regard as one of GHQ's own, Orlo's friend, Guy Dawnay. Captain Dawnay had returned to Gallipoli on 11 October after almost a month away, during which he had mixed in all the right circles in London. The King, for instance, was increasingly concerned about the Gallipoli casualty lists and furious with Hamilton for what he saw as his mismanagement of the entire campaign. The general opinion was Hamilton was less of a Commander-in-Chief and more a spectator of his subordinates' shortcomings. Increasingly out of tune with events, Hamilton remained hopelessly optimistic which did not help the situation and only seeded more frustration inside GHQ.

During the first week in October a coming change had been felt within GHQ. Rumours criticising its staff had spread within the War Office and culminated in a cable from Kitchener asking Hamilton if he wanted to replace

Braithwaite with a new CGS. Hamilton declined this lifeline. On 11 October, less than a week after the 10th (Irish) Division began departing for Salonika, Kitchener cabled Hamilton again, this time to ask how many casualties might be expected if Suvla were evacuated? Fearing the worst, Hamilton estimated at least 50 percent of his force and 60 percent of its artillery. The question enraged Hamilton, who noted in his diary: 'If they do this they make the Dardanelles into the bloodiest tragedy of the world! Even if we were to escape without a scratch, they would stamp our enterprise as the bloodiest of all tragedies!' Kitchener was far from happy either, and in a personal telegram to Hamilton, recalled both Hamilton and Braithwaite to London, leaving Lieutenant-General Birdwood in temporary command of the MEF. In time, Birdwood would be permanently replaced by Lieutenant-General Sir Charles Monro, who would journey out with his own CGS, Major-General Arthur Lynden-Bell. Monro was instructed by Kitchener to report back on the reasons for the Gallipoli deadlock as soon as possible.

Monro arrived on 28 October. At once he impressed the GHQ staff with his decisive, personable, and professional approach. Two days later he visited all three Gallipoli sectors and concluded that there was no realistic chance of capturing the Peninsula. He reported:

'The position occupied by our troops presented a military situation unique in history. The mere fringe of the coastline had been secured. The beaches and piers upon which they depended for all requirements in personnel and material were exposed to registered and observed Artillery fire. Our entrenchments were dominated almost throughout by the Turks. The possible Artillery positions were insufficient and defective. The Force, in short, held a line possessing every possible military defect. The position was without depth, the communications were insecure and dependent on the

weather. No means existed for the concealment and deployment of fresh troops destined for the offensive, whilst the Turks enjoyed full powers of observation, abundant Artillery positions, and they had been given the time to supplement the natural advantages which the position presented by all the devices at the disposal of the Field Engineer.'

After further commenting on the problems posed by disease, shortage of competent officers, the Ottomans' ability to hold their positions with a reduced force while deploying in other theatres and, above all, with the lack of any hope of a successful advance, Monro's solution was direct and to the point.

'Since we could not hope to achieve any purpose by remaining on the Peninsula, the appalling cost to the nation involved in consequence of embarking on an overseas expedition with no base available for the rapid transit of stores, supplies and personnel, made it urgent that we should divert the troops locked up on the Peninsula to a more useful theatre. Since therefore I could see no military advantage in our continued occupation of positions on the Peninsula, I telegraphed to your Lordship that in my opinion the evacuation of the Peninsula should be taken in hand.'

It was not so much now a question of whether another British offensive was possible but rather if they could hold off the next major Ottoman attack. By the middle of October the Allied force on Gallipoli had dropped to 114,000 troops against the war establishment of some 200,000. In addition, hundreds of sick were being evacuated every week without replacements. Severely depleted or not, evacuating fourteen divisions from Helles, Anzac and Suvla in winter was going to be an extraordinarily difficult challenge to achieve without heavy casualties. Churchill, on learning of the suggestion, jibed at Monro: 'He came, he saw, he capitulated.' These were strong and unwarranted words from a man who had once stated that it was impossible to secure the Dardanelles. Reluctant to accept Monro's advice, Kitchener decided to see Gallipoli for himself. He sailed in early November.

* * *

Friday 1 October 1915

Wiring all the morning about the move of 10th Division etc. We replied strongly regarding the 53rd Division saying that to leave Helles to be defended by one French division, either colonials or natives, plus 13,300 worn out territorials and RND was too grave a risk to run. We were therefore sending the 89th Brigade there tonight and could not spare 53rd Division. Remarked that Bailloud's present opinion a strong contrast to his previous strong disinclination to stay where he was even with 2 divisions. Fact is he is dying to get away. We were able to quote very neatly to Kitchener a passage from Bailloud's written report to us, recommending that in view of the move of 1 French division, the front held by the CEO should be reduced and a strong reserve established behind allies' first line to be ready for all eventualities. England obviously very hard up for artillery for this Salonica force and we certainly can't spare any. Our sick rate very heavy just now too. Hony struck down this morning with hepatic colic, in great pain and had to have morphine. Now very groggy and sorry for himself, poor thing. Rest of day pretty quiet. Very jolly walk after lunch by myself.

Query from Kitchener about when leading troops of 10th Division would leave. We told IGC he must get off troops parallel with French, and this overrides equipment question. We wired Bailloud catching him out in his double game.

Saturday 2 October 1915

Wire from Vice Admiral early that Dartige wires 1st convoy with 4000 men would arrive Salonica a.m. today; 2nd with 8000 arrive tomorrow. Wired IGC at 7.30 a.m. that he must get off something, even one battalion at once. Bailloud wired that owing to his having to wait for instructions he was unable to pay proposed visit this morning: rather funny. At 9.15 a.m., heard through French admiral that Greek Government emphatically forbid landing of troops at or netting of Salonica. What next!

Perhaps the truest indication of one's present state of mind is that waking up to a perfectly divine morning, when the sea is a jewel and the wind ambrosial and the mountains tinted so delicately, all one thinks is "another bloody day!"

Report as to Greeks confirmed by wire from IGC addressed Proemial, repeated us saying he heard from Navy Greeks had refused landing of troops.

At 12 hear from Vice Admiral French transports leaving Salonica.

Quiet day, and walked with Powell after tea. Vitale appeared in camp and sent by CGS on board *Cornwallis* for a few days.

Sunday 3 October 1915

The weather seems to get more and more magnificent now. Today is like midsummer with a faint southerly breeze, but without the baking feeling of midsummer. Not much news in morning. The French Minister at Athens was apparently the man who stopped French disembarkation at Salonica without reference elsewhere. Seemed to apprehend serious incidents might occur. However wire from Athens this morning from Elliot says Greek Minister of Communications is going there today to arrange matters with Brigadier-General Hamilton, and that western side of port has been set aside for allies.

Bass was sent off post haste this morning with cipher to Mudros en route for Salonica. He was overjoyed and we were left with Berry who seems to be the slowest cipherist ever imagined.

In morning, Bailloud and Girodon came over for a conference.

In evening very interesting telegram came from Athens to say situation during last few days had been complicated by a deep-rooted apprehension on the part of the whole nation including Venizelos, that allied troops, once in Macedonia, would be used to support Bulgarian pretensions at the expense of Greece. "Only yesterday French minister and I were authorized to state that allies considered their offers to Bulgaria to have lapsed through her own conduct. Italian Minister gave same assurance. Venizelos thereupon reassured". At height of crisis news came of arrival of Brigadier-General Hamilton at Salonica of which Elliot had had no warning. The official account gave him out to be Sir Ian, and he was said to have arrived with 25 workmen who started barring the port with wire netting and to have stated his intention to commandeer the railway from Salonica to the Bulgarian frontier. Explanations were given, but in his irritation Venizelos almost refused to allow any landing. Now, however, though he has made an official protest to preserve appearance of neutrality and protect Greek transports from attack by German submarines, he is ready to allow troops to land. The King is also greatly reassured, and has stated that he will support Serbia if attacked by Bulgaria, and has not stated that he will not support her if she takes offensive-defensive action. He insists however that anything should be avoided which would bring Greece into direct conflict with Germany. Venizelos insists that if troops land Greek sovereignty should be respected, local authorities left alone and troops sent up country as soon as possible.

News from Bulgaria shows that mobilization is not popular and not going very well. Also minister at Bucharest pooh poohs idea that munitions will be allowed free passage, as that submission to German Bulgarian demands would be tame.

Monday 4 October 1915

Another wonderful morning.

A good deal of wiring early. Heard from admiral that Admiralty wires that unless allies have been invited to land by Greek Government no move of troops was to take place till further orders. Also heard from Liaison Officer French that Sarrail was to take command at Salonica. A lot of other wires home and to IGC, etc. about the 10th Division and its move. All seems still very uncertain. News came later that French were leaving tonight and we wired that 10th Division should begin to leave as soon as Admiral considered it safe. We also sent a strongly worded wire to WO about inadequacy of hospital accommodation and impossibility of evacuating wounded. Also told them of high sick rate in 9th Corps.

In evening a very secret wire came from Kitchener with preliminary instructions that nobody was to see it besides General and he was to decipher it himself. (It was to ask him if he would like another CGS in view of criticism).[1]

Tuesday 5 October 1915

A stack of telegrams from all quarters. The chief facts:—that 10th Division was to leave as soon as the Salonica anchorage reasonably secure, that Mahon was

1 Orlo marked this 'omit'.

to command that and yeomanry regiment coming from Egypt, that his force was to be separate from French and as soon as he left Mudros would cease to belong to our force, though we should continue to be responsible for supply till new base formed. Orders for Mahon that he is to communicate with WO on getting established at Salonica and not to advance or undertake any military operations without orders from home.

The 4 yeomanry brigades at sea are to remain in this force.

News telegram says Russia delivered ultimatum to Bulgaria requiring her to dismiss German officers or Russian Minister would leave Sofia, and another wire from WO said that on October 1, Black Sea Fleet bombarded Zonguldak etc. for 5 hours.

Work considerably delayed this morning by CGS taking cipher to answer Kitchener's very secret wire of last night. Pollen and he soon got hung up and had to send for me, so it really came to my sending it. Much time lost. A personal matter. Bearing out remarks made in this diary. Aeroplane sighted, and went once to dugouts. One bomb dropped towards K beach. Some shots fired but no hits.

8 p.m.: *Albion* arrived Salonica with 2 battalions and HQ advanced base. Troops landing at 2 p.m.

10 p.m.: Very urgent wire received from Athens that Venizelos in a private note to Elliot said he was afraid he would have to hand his resignation to the King. What next?

Major Watson joined O as GSO3.

Walked with Deedes after tea.

Wednesday 6 October 1915

Very hectic morning with telegrams. The wire from Athens said the King came to Athens yesterday and sent for Venizelos, and told him that in his speech of the 4th—in which he opposed those who wanted only armed neutrality and denounced venerability of Greek Press—he had gone too far. Venizelos replied he had always told the King that if attacked in Chamber he would speak out clearly and defend his policy. King said he could not support his policy to the end. Venizelos thereupon tended resignation. Venizelos told Elliot and French Minister that there was no chance of compromise. He did not know what would happen, but thought a coalition of all opposition leaders. He would not support them unless they undertook to support Serbia if attacked by Bulgaria, but might tolerate them rather than bring about revolution or general election which would mean demobilisation.

Elliot also wired that in Venizelos' view with which he agreed troops ought to be landed at Salonica as soon as possible to show that Venizelos's resignation had no effect on our policy. Did not know what successors would do but thought a partial demobilisation likely. In that case question of getting enough troops to Salonica would be difficult.

Later in the morning O'Beirne, Minister at Bucharest, wired he was asking for his passports owing to rupture of relations.

After lunch urgent wire from Proemial saying that owing to Venizelos' resignation question of landing troops at Salonica was again very doubtful. Had asked Admiralty to stop all troops starting who had not already left, and sent orders for Mahon if started to return Mudros, if not, to remain Mudros. Whole situation therefore very muddy. Mackensen is down in Bukovina with a force threatening Rumania. Press news from WO indicate heavy fighting in France, and better news from Russia, who has apparently taken offensive in centre and south, while in north seems competent to deal with Hindenburg's heavy guns.

Aspinall gave me to read very interesting letter from Dawnay written from WO on September 23–25.

He had been in full activity seeing authorities. Saw the King on the 17th who asked a great many pertinent questions including why elderly generals were sent out. Could not understand optimism of Chantilly and Saint Omer.

On 21st talk in WO with DMO, Carson and Winston. "With Winston in the room it is easy for anyone else not to talk too much". Winston pressed the project of an expedition to Asiatic side, and if French wouldn't, tell them we would. He wanted to dash 10 divisions ashore to push on Chanak and had no notion it would take any time to land divisions complete with necessary transport on open beach. Carson said little but had no objection to any undertaking on sufficient scale but "would be party to no more bickering".

Bulgarian situation was by then getting threatening which led to consideration of sending troops to Greece. Two courses: either to push here in as large force possible or reduce our commitments here and send to Greece.

On 22nd saw Winston for 2 hours in House. Found it hard to make him understand importance of making decision as to Asiatic plan at once, so that necessary problems can be solved, even though decision conditional on result of offensive in west.

... Winston gave his version of inception of Dardanelles campaign. He wanted to reduce Constantinople with fleet alone and still thinks could have done it with loss of 12 ships. If then unsuccessful prepared to bring fleet away. Last thing he wanted was to commit any army to that theatre. But after he had lost 3 ships, it was decided against him to make a combined naval and military expedition.

In evening saw Sir Edward Grey. Found him evenly balanced between 2 alternatives, but leaning towards sending a force from Gallipoli in answer to Venizelos' appeal.

Saw Lloyd George and Winston at Munitions Ministry. Impressed on Lloyd George need for ammunition. Lloyd George said factory would be at work almost at once turning out 25,000 a week, and working up to 300,000 a month. Promised to reach 500,000 a month. Dawnay tremendously impressed with new Stokes trench mortar, great simplicity and throws out 15 lb HE at great rate. Also new fire squirt.

As to question of drafts, he says "drafts don't exist. There is no real provision made for the maintenance of the armies. Almost all recruits are bundled into new units, made up into new formations, and the "draft-finders" are as bare as Mother Hubbard's cupboard. Eventually Kitchener will be forced to break up some of the new formations for drafts—or it looks so; and even then, if the war doesn't stop almost at once, the wastage cannot by any possibility be replaced except by compulsion. So at last it seems to me and AG2a concur. My own private guess is that if the offensive in France is not fully successful, Kitchener will go for compulsion at once—but that he wants to see if a result cannot be reached in the west first".[2]

Sir Ian over at Helles today, but we have sent on instructions about Mahon etc. to IGC and VA. CGS says he has won a bet of £10 from Sir Ian over the behaviour of Bulgaria.

The French are to make a combined bombardment of Chanak quays and Greek works at 4 p.m. today by aircraft.

Aspinall obviously thinks, and with some reason, that Dawnay is at the bottom of this denuding of our force to send to Salonica, which has brought us such rebuffs and

2 Orlo marked this 'omit'.

seems to have ended in a diplomatic victory for Germany. A passage in Dawnay's letter says that when the Bulgarian news began to get serious, he got nervous, and went and had a long talk with the DMO which resulted in a scheme for sending troops to Salonica. A letter from Glyn this week fills this in by saying "Guy Dawnay has drawn up such an excellent scheme and the DMO is backing him up (!) for sending troops to Salonica; they will be much better employed there than at Suvla".[3]

Thursday 7 October 1915

Very much quieter day as regards wires. A long one from Elliot describing his rather inconclusive interview with the King: as the result of which he said he was less depressed about situation, but that, until he had seen M. Gounaris on the question whether Greece would help Serbia if attacked, the only certain thing was that the King was determined to keep neutrality as long as possible. When Elliot pressed him on what Bulgaria would do if Germans were victorious and asked him if he didn't think the first thing they would take would be Kavalla, the King evaded the question. He also protested that none of his new Ministry could properly be called Germanophile. Said that disembarkation of allied troops could proceed but refused to let any discussion as to military plans take place between the allies and Greek General Staff. In evening wire came from Proemial saying move of 10th Division to Salonica was to proceed.

Friday 8 October 1915

Short wire came from Elliot reporting inconclusive interview with Zaimis, who said question of helping Serbia if attacked by Bulgaria would be considered in Cabinet today. Allied embassies have left Sofia.

3 Orlo marked this 'omit'.

Spent the day walking with Powell to Panaghia. Day rather grey and cloudy with bursts of sun and stuffy. But enjoyed ourselves very much. Three perfectly howling cads, officers in the Yeomanry were to be seen at Christo's.

Saturday 9 October 1915

Very quiet day and very little news. Germans say they have penetrated Serbia at 3 points. Two French divisions have cut Beauséjour-Challerange railway at St. Marie. After tea took a last walk with Powell who leaves tomorrow to be DAA & QMG of 42nd Division. This loss of him and Vitale leaves me rather solitary.

Sunday 10 October 1915

Lovely day. Powell left by 8.30 trawler. News that Serbians had evacuated Belgrade and enemy were established south of Sare between Shabatz and Belgrade. Not much other news. Elliot reports that 3 of new Greek Ministers positively stated to him that Greece would maintain neutrality unless attacked.

Before dinner very urgent wire to Admiral from Admiralty asking largest number of British troops in addition to present force at war establishment he could support with his present resources. What does this mean? It looks as if home authorities were considering abandonment of Salonica scheme and thinking of another push here as a counterattack to German attack on Serbia.

Two new arrivals in O mess. General Smith as BGRA and Captain Peyton of 60th, successor to Powell.

Monday 11 October 1915

Grey damp day. Germans claim to have penetrated Serbia on front of 250 (?) miles. The generals under Mackensen are Gallwitz and Kövess, each with 8 divisions. GS telegrams indicate that before long, Rumania will be compromised.

General Sir Ian Hamilton at the door of his hut, October 1915. Hardly what one has in mind when they think of how a General lived during the First World War. Soon after this photo was taken, Hamilton was recalled to London and replaced by General Sir Charles Monro (Family collection).

Very pleasant ride with Barttelot after lunch; lovely afternoon after thunderstorm. Very little work in evening. Dawnay returned with King's Messenger looking very well.

Tuesday 12 October 1915

Not much in morning wires except one from Bucharest which said:—Germans not yet firm enough on right flank of Danube to build bridges, but this is only a matter of time in view of their numerical superiority. Moreover Serbians, as he heard from various sources, are disgusted with their treatment by the allies, and not disposed to make sacrifices in north while Bulgaria attacks their one remaining line of communication in south. Germans must continue their advance both on account of need for communication with Turkey and prestige in Balkans. They are therefore committed to a campaign which may place them in an awkward military situation with communications open to attack by Rumania at short notice. He was still of opinion that Rumania might side with allies if they gave assurances of vigorous offensive, though the best course open to us was he thought attack on Dedeagach, Varna and Burgas. The possibility of Rumania's coming in would almost become a certainty if Dardanelles forced in 2 or 3 months. Otherwise impossible for her to replenish supplies. Nothing known here of intentions of allies, and at present even our most warm supporters are depressed. Well may they be.

I had hardly finished deciphering above telegram than I was called in to encipher an answer to a very secret wire from Kitchener which arrived from Kitchener yesterday with instructions that only Sir Ian was to decipher it. Assumed the answer was supposed to be seen only by him. But CGS had written it out and, being unaccustomed to ciphering called me in. The contents are too secret to be committed to writing but they were surprising and dramatic and not likely to fade from my memory.[4]

Up to now have only seen Dawnay a short time and only heard scraps of information. The gist of what I gather of his impressions so far is as follows:—The ensemble is rather depressing, and people in England are rather depressed. There is no "man" to be found. Kitchener really controls the situation by keeping everyone else in the dark. The FO quite taken by surprise by Venizelos' fall. Government trying to pull together but quite in the dark as to what to do. Lloyd George threatened to resign if conscription wasn't brought in, but was quelled somehow. The WO very stupid and dilatory, and the only office really bustling is the Ministry of Munitions. Rather astounding to hear that

4 Kitchener had asked for Hamilton's views on estimated losses if Gallipoli was evacuated; Hamilton, consulting the general staff, replied that it would be a disaster, potentially half of his force. (Ian Hamilton, *Gallipoli Diary*, Vol. 2, pp. 249–253).

Asquith's speech saying there had never been a shortage of munitions was put on Kitchener's table before delivery, and he wrote on it "I quite agree with everything you say"! He is the one man who stands between the country and conscription. As regards the offensive in France it failed, though Omer and Chantilly were absolutely confident they would break right through, and nobody at home ever saw the last glance of hope. They were right in as much as they argued "we know the Germans can't break through our lines, why should we be able to break through theirs". Casualties about 50,000 British and 150,000 French. British used gas.

Dawnay also much disquieted by financial situation. Says bank has been badly handled, and the loss on American exchange shows the state of affairs (½ pence in the £). Also nobody in England economizing. Says if we don't look out we shall be busted.

Shall ask him further questions later, meanwhile there is a lot of food for reflection in what I have written today. The struggle, as it has seemed to me from the beginning, is one between 2 great forces, one of which *must* prevail. If the Zeitgeist is with Germany she will prevail, as England has in former days, morals, gentlemanliness and everything else notwithstanding.

A very quiet day as regards work. Walked after tea. My rubber boots arrived from Lawn and Alda.

Wednesday 13 October

No wires of interest in morning, only a very biting wind.

After lunch walked for an hour with Dawnay hearing his views on the immediate future. His view, like mine, is that things are bad, and that we are at this moment not far off being beaten. The financial situation is bad and the Balkan situation distinctly threatening. He didn't think Kitchener had brains enough to cope with things, and confessed that he could not understand exactly what Kitchener's game *was*. He seems to have thought very highly of Lloyd George and Winston who really are both dead keen on beating the Boche and don't care how they do it, what they spend nor whom they offend, which is not the case with some of the other Ministers. McKenna, he thought, was doing well.[5]

He is of the opinion that the idea of sending a force to quell the Bulgarians was right since, if there *is* to be a push here, it will be some weeks before it could be properly assembled, meanwhile if by our presence at Salonica the Greeks could have been induced to stop Bulgarian aggression, Rumania might have come in too, and the Balkan question settled. As it is, he mightily blames the FO for allowing Venizelos' fall, which he thinks could have been avoided, and which makes the Balkan situation very much worse for us. However, his idea for the future is another effort, or if necessary, a series of efforts, properly supported, to carry Sari Bair and win the Maidos-Kaba Tepe line, on the ground that the Turks in this small theatre must give way before repeated pressure. No advance to be made beyond that line, but to be held with a small force as a kind of Torres Vedras, and the rest of the force to be taken away, though this might not be possible until the end of next March. Anyhow that is the plan he hopes will be adopted. It is interesting to compare this with the telegram sent to Kitchener yesterday.

Thursday 14 October 1915

Blithering cold wind all day. Felt rather miserable till I got to bed. Preparations for move to the other camp are beginning. Not much news. Bulgaria and Germany attacking Serbia simultaneously.

5 Orlo marked this 'omit'.

Friday 15 October 1915

Part of O Section and office going over to new camp today. Wind blowing still but not quite so cold. News telegram says Delcassé has resigned, and French people are not satisfied with handling of Balkan question. Bucharest wires that Turks said to be concentrating 200,000 troops at Adrianople to reinforce Bulgaria. Am reading *Guy and Pauline* a second time.

Walk with Peyton in afternoon. Military Attaché Salonica sends information Sarrail has a French division and a reserve brigade there but no instructions. Serbians pressing him to send up a strong a force as possible but he is afraid to do much yet.

6.45 p.m.: Wire from Kitchener saying that the following cipher is personal and very secret, and only to be seen by Sir Ian. What this may portend, heaven only knows.

Saturday 16 October 1915

The following wire in question turned up at midnight and was deciphered by general before breakfast. It was nothing less than a bombshell saying: "At a council of war held last night it was decided that although the Government fully appreciate the gallant manner in which etc. etc., it was advisable to make a change in the command. General Monro is being sent to relieve you and is bringing chief of staff so Braithwaite should also return. Birdwood should replace you till Monro's arrival".

So there it was. Sir Ian and the CGS *dégommés*, unstuck without a shadow of warning, the Operations section in the throes of moving, and all the handing over to be done at short notice. Wire was sent to Birdie to come over at once, though he was seedy, and Chief saw Admiral who will send him direct to Marseilles tomorrow. It was a rather exhausting and depressing day for many of us. I had orders not to move to the new camp, so stopped all my kit. No telegrams arrived at all, and after lunch the CGS told me to go. So I routed out my servant, who got the things across and actually into my tent at the new camp by 6.30. He really is an excellent man. My condition was made no better by my tummy being distinctly out of order. Before tea Gascoigne, Barttelot and I walked over here across the sand and had tea in Q with Gascoigne, all feeling rather faint after that sandy walk on a stuffy afternoon. The office was too full for me to find any room and there was nothing to do but wander about rather disconsolately till dinner. Went to bed early.

It is strange to reflect on the *dégommage* of Sir Ian and the CGS, which I think a good thing, sorry as I am for them personally. Sir Ian wired home to his wife: "Coming right home, Monro succeeds me. Don't be downhearted for I know I have done utmost with means given. I am quite cheerful. Love …". I sent that in cipher. The truth is that Sir Ian never did anything of himself at all; as Dawnay said yesterday "if ever we had *had* to ask his advice on anything, imagination faints at the probable result". Let us hope Monro who has done very well in France will do better. The CGS also was no real use: he had not the necessary brain for this job. So another bunch of those who came out in the *Phaeton* will have left. The general, Pollen and his 2 ADCs go, also CGS and Val. Possible Churchill is left behind rather disconsolate. The bomb fell at a particularly difficult moment, because it necessitated a great deal of copying out of telegrams etc., so that Sir Ian and Birdie should have some material. So Moberly was full of work getting it all done. How the general situation will be affected there is as yet no means of judging. We don't know if any more troops are being sent, and we know nothing of the size or aim of the Salonica force.

The new camp is still extremely rough, and all kinds of things want doing. We want to move our sleeping tents which are on the other side of the stream to the offices. The mess is still rather upside down, and half the stores have not turned up. The kitchen is still without shelter, and there is a general air of house moving and depression about. From the office side of the camp a little way up the slope there is a really beautiful view right over to Asia, and the ensemble is rather like camping in low dolomites with the sea in the distance.

Sunday 17 October 1915

Slept pretty well, though tummy still dicky and decided to starve for a day. Grey and showery day. A few telegrams after breakfast. At 12.30, Sir Ian, CGS and ADCs, and Pollen came over to say goodbye to us—a rather painful business. We all turned out in belts to shake hands with them. The general shook me warmly by the hand and said "goodbye cipher, we have done a lot of work together". To us all he said "goodbye to you all. Do as good work for my successor as you have for me". Poor Val was very much affected. Dawnay said to me he was glad it was not the CGS who went without the Chief; there had been talk of that at home and the opportunity was offered to Sir Ian (in that first very secret telegram) of getting rid of CGS. This Sir Ian refused to do. CGS then wished to offer to resign, if it would give more confidence at home, but Dawnay strongly urged him not to.

Nothing of comment rest of the day. Grey and cloudy and rainy. It becomes obvious how bitterly cold winter will be. Great discussion whether we shall move mess from its present site. Decided against, but general move to shift living tents to the other side of the stream.

Monday 18 October 1915

Wet morning after a wet night. Better inside. Chose place for my living tent after breakfast. Very little work, morning or afternoon. After lunch worked with Ashley on site for our living tents. Barttelot and Hony working there too. The site is certainly protected from northerly winds though exposed to south. The view is magnificent. Felt very much better for the exercise. At 3.30 Churchill put a gang of Greeks on for us, who did a lot more levelling. After a good deal of upping and downing "O" mess is now moving to vicinity of an abandoned house part of which will be used as kitchen, and part as smoking room. Our stores are still missing, but Watson and Barttelot are taking up very energetically the business of helping Hony make a good bundobust about servants, get a mess sergeant etc. Barttelot is an awfully good fellow. I like him more and more every day. I discovered quite recently he is an ardent musician and apparently quite a proficient violinist. Another good addition to the mess is General Smith, the BGRA, a burly man of 6 ft 4, who has an amusing manner of talking and is generally cheery. Peyton the newest arrival of all strikes me as rather an ass, and I don't believe he will stay long here. As Barttelot is going to O(a), Peyton not being considered efficient enough, I am going to have to try to get made GSO3 in O(b). I suggested it to Aspinall after tea today, and he seemed to regard the situation favourably, though he said no new appointments could be made till new CGS arrived.[6]

The present state of affairs is that Birdie is on the *Cornwallis* rather seedy, and the DQMG[7] is acting as CGS. No news yet of Monro. Serbians report detachments of

6 Orlo marked this 'omit'.

7 Major-General Ellison.

Bulgarians have cut Orient line at Kranyo, and threatened it at Kochanka. Kranyo due south of Nish. Also concentration in Strumnitza Valley. Sarrail is pushing a whole division into Vardar Valley west of Droina.

After dinner NA[8] turned up and with him Glyn, both from Salonica. NA seems to have enjoyed his fortnight there. Glyn reports authorities at home are still flapping in the wind about that show. King's Messenger bag brought a very interesting letter from Gregg, telling me incidentally both Schooling and Bull were working in the WO cipher room. The letter written on October 9 said that they had had a hell of a time in C2 during last fortnight. For several days the daily total was between 80 and 90, and one day touched 97. The Salonica affair didn't give us a spare moment. The authorities much exercised over the Balkan situation. How many men can Germans send against Serbia? What is Greece going to do? How long will it take the Germans plus Bulgars to drive the Serbians west of railway? How long to repair railway? How long to get munitions to Turks? These questions, intimately connected with safety of our force, exercise the powers that be a good deal.

Speaking of offensive in France he confirms generally what we know, but says we still haven't enough ammunition—not enough to blaze away regardless of the "number of rounds on the lines of communication at 12 noon". Our gas and smoke seems to have been fairly useful. There is a new CIGS now, Sir Archibald Murray, and the whole GS of the WO is to be reorganized and more men of experience in present day fighting to be brought in.

Nothing doing in East Africa. Mesopotamia expedition depends largely on Germany's invasion of Serbia.

8 Captain Mitchell, RN.

Tuesday 19 October 1915

Still coldish but quite pleasant sun in the middle of the day. Stomach got very tiresome.

All shaking down well in the new camp. The new sites for sleeping tents are very popular now. Several others have marked claims, and the Greek labourers were clearing all day. My tent was put up on my terrace after lunch, and I moved in in the afternoon.

Took a short walk up one of the hills. Just before dinner a wire came from Proemial addressed GHQ, saying "wire your views on situation in Gallipoli and on future operations". Odd not addressed to Birdwood. Aspinall went to see General Ellison who is acting CGS, and told me he kept him there till quarter to 12, talking all the time.

Wednesday 20 October 1915

Very good night in new tent, which certainly is well protected from northerly wind. Going to starve all day. News wire from WO said allies and Serbians had inflicted severe check on Serbians[9], and telegram ... said Bulgarians were evacuating Strumnitza. So far so good. News telegram also said Carson had resigned, which I don't like, if he was so strongly against "tinkering". Nothing much to record for rest of day. Had to keep very quiet owing to tummy and to starve.

Thursday 21 October 1915

Wire from Athens says Greek General Staff hold that for Greece to help Serbia would be simply to court destruction, and that however many troops allies send they will not arrive in time and could be better employed in France or Asia Minor. Greek Government will therefore adopt neutrality benevolent to allies. News telegram shows that Serbians

9 Sic: Mackensen's forces.

are being very hard pressed by the Germans and Bulgarians. Latter seem to be advancing on both sides of Nish, while Serbians are falling back to south in front of Germans.

After sent of[f] Birdwood's answer to request for appreciation of situation, which was entirely Birdwood's own work. Following is a summary:—Position seems to me much the same as that in France, we faced by lines of trenches which can only be taken by assault. Troops in good heart despite sickness, but wastage still 20% per month. Of the three zones, no advance possible at Helles, all further attempts there having been given up for some time. At Chunuk Bair Turks hold higher positions all round Australians and continual showers of bombs would be too much for assailants. Only hope of carrying that position is by mining, a lengthy operation, but matter now being taken up and extensive galleries prepared. Best chance of advance along Kiretch Tepe together with attack on Ismail Oglu Tepe. By this means might hope to reach Ejelmer Bay and eventually win all Anafarta ridge. Troops at present on peninsula if brought up to War Establishment, would be sufficient, but there is not nearly enough ammunition. Suggest for commencement 250,000 shell all calibres, half HE, 200,000 Stokes mortar shell, and 50,000 50-pounder trench howitzer shell. It must be remembered that our troops are much affected by sickness and not really capable of extreme physical exertion. Should therefore have two more complete divisions. In any case the operation would be costly and success could not be guaranteed. No use landing troops elsewhere. Best chance a really large force at Yukyeri Bay to push up through Eren Keui to Narrows. Not so opposed to Enos as formerly but understand naval objections very strong. In any case, if this new force is to be sent, it must be sent *at once* for in bad weather only 30% of days fit for landing troops.

Present numbers: 125,000 Turks with 85,000 at close call against our 85,000 rifles.

Also came this evening significant wire from Kitchener, saying that operations in Serbia may lead to increased supply of ammunition to enemy, we must therefore dig deep defences like those of Germans. "My advice is dig".

Friday 22 October 1915

Bleak cold day. Wires from Athens (1) Serbian Prime Minister wires that, although defence has hitherto been satisfactorily maintained, catastrophe may soon occur unless allied troops can shortly render effective assistance. (2) Only 30,000 Bulgars facing Greek front, the force at Strumnitza having gone north to take part in an attack on Istib. Greek and Bulgarian officers had recently met and agreed to do everything to avoid Greco-Bulgarian complications on frontier. This significant of Greek attitude. (3) Report (Samson) that Turks were preparing to send 150,000, which might be increased to 200,000, troops to help Bulgarians. Two divisions had been withdrawn from Peninsula. *Goeben* now fully equipped and coaled.

Tummy much better today. Barttelot has gone to O(a) and handed over O(b) work to Peyton. Wonder if I shall get any chance at O(b).

Now rereading Galsworthy's *Man of Property*. Am a little disappointed. Galsworthy's rather cold prepossessions spoil all his work for me.

Wet and beastly day from afternoon onwards. Nothing particular to do. After dinner played chess till 12 with Colonel Tyrrell. Rained all night and was very cold. The dampness of the air in a wet tent is beastly. But one must always think how very much worse it is in the trenches.

Saturday 23 October 1915

Rain ceased this morning. Short clamber on hills after breakfast to get up circulation. In afternoon took vigorous and very jolly walk alone, exploring to new valleys in the west of the island. After tea a wire came from Proemial in answer to the appreciation sent by Birdie saying he wanted also our opinion on the matter of resistance of stronger attack. After dinner I composed a draft reply to that in verse "M.F-999".[10] Some success.

Sunday 24 October 1915

Very wet and cold on waking. Rain steady till after lunch. Few ciphers. Assisted Watson getting gun emplacements on to his maps. I like him—a cheery, nice fellow. ¾ hour walk on hills with him and Peyton before tea. Met Birdwood out of doors after tea. He greeted me kindly and said he had liked my last verses, which Aspinall had shown him. Last night a new cipher officer arrived in Bass' place. He is also called Williams. Stoutish man about 40, who smokes cigars. Seems capable and has been in Government of India, don't know in what capacity.

News that *Marquette*, carrying 29th Divisional Ammunition Column, and another transport, sunk off coast of Thessaly. The Italians seem making a general push, while Russians in centre continue to do well. Meanwhile Germans pressing Serbians hard. It is given out in press telegrams that we have offered Greece Cyprus as price of participation. Confirmed that Carson resigned on Near Eastern question, not conscription. As to the latter, news that King has issued an appeal to the nation to come forward.

10 Annex 4.

Monday 25 October 1915

Bright sunny day but feeling rather piano with an upset stomach. Nothing occurred.

Tuesday 26 October 1915

Warmer day but grey and overcast. King's Messenger letters arrived bringing me a fur waistcoat and a cardigan from Mother and Father, and jolly letters. Father's gives details of the Zeppelin raid. Three bombs dropped in Lincoln's Inn. All Father's and Sir F's windows broken, and Hunter and Haynes' wrecked. Newspapers of 17th seem gloomy, and *Sunday Times* has article by Ashmead Bartlett saying what he thought pretty straight. Garvin all for sending 300,000 men to Balkans at once. Barttelot's letter says country is depressed.

Sent off our wire on the situation here looked at from point of view of defence. What it came to was that trenches could be made impregnable, but there are 4 difficulties. Lack of material—some asked for on August 21 only just arriving, bad physical condition of troops, congestion at Mudros, and no facilities on beaches. Reserve areas harder to protect owing to difficulty of scattering troops and fact that enemy commands them from observing stations. As for beaches, little can be done except deal with enemy's artillery, for which we want lots more 60 pounders and heavy howitzers. Of 8 60 pounders, 6 are out of action owing to non-arrival of important parts asked for many weeks ago. But even if more were available, no space except at Helles to conceal them. Not a particularly cheering wire, but seems to me to be true. If enemy were able to bombard our beaches night and day we could do nothing.

Hony down with the trots, but I better, having applied to the medico, who produced an apparently successful draught to be taken before meals.

After tea Aspinall showed me though I had to read it very quickly, a draft appreciation of the whole situation here as it now is, the whole general outlook having changed since the force first came out, when the gaining of the Narrows would, in conjunction with pressure elsewhere, have brought the Turks to their knees very soon. As it is, our hopes have been dashed. The pressure in the Caucasus, in Bagdad has come to an end for lack of troops and the whole Balkan situation has changed. The question is whether even the gaining of the Narrows would bring us appreciably nearer our aim of beating the Germans, or even the Turks. It is suggested that since the war has now a certain popularity in Turkey and Germany has a means of getting through munitions, it would only be a first and easiest stage. To gain any definite result probably it would be necessary to beat the whole Turkish army and take Constantinople.

In any case what has to be considered is the future of this force. There are 3 courses open. (1) To make another attack on the Narrows. (2) For this force to maintain itself in a defensive position as well as possible. (3) To cut our losses and withdraw.

If (1) is decided on, it cannot in any case be done before next spring. The only means of success would be to make simultaneous attacks on Sari Bair and Achi Baba (the former to be pressed home) and to land a force of 2 divisions fully equipped with transport south of Yukyeri Bay to make for Chanak. To do this it is estimated that a force of 250,000 troops would be required with corresponding ammunition, besides men enough to bring our present force up to war establishment and 20% reinforcements ready in Egypt. This would mean sending out from home during next 5 months 400,000 men. This includes 10 new divisions, men to maintain present force during winter, to bring it up to strength, and to provide reinforcements.

This would of course mean tremendous strain on mercantile marine. Also the time taken to disembark troops is so long, that the problem of maintaining the force here during the winter would anyhow have to be considered. To feed and maintain a largely increased force here during the winter months would be impossible. So that, though, if another attack *is* to be made on the Narrows in the spring, preparations to concentrate troops in Egypt must begin *at once*, it is also necessary to consider (2) on its own merits.

Here the main question, as already stated in last telegram to WO is the protection of our beaches. If enemy can get enough ammunition to bombard them day and night position would be hopeless. We have nothing like enough guns for counter-battery, and if we had we have nowhere to put them, for all the concealed positions are badly needed for reserve areas, stores etc. Anzac alone is so situated that enemy's guns cannot make it entirely untenable. To make certain, therefore, of being able to maintain the defensive through the winter, Suvla must be rendered free from shell fire, if not Helles as well. To do this we should attack along Kiretch Tepe, with a view to seizing Anafarta Ridge from Ejelmer Bay. To do this should want 2 new divisions and enough ammunition not only for 3 distinct operations (250,000 rounds) but enough to leave us the normal field allowance when that was expended.

(3) The abandonment of our campaign would be costly and difficult, but could be done, if to be done, better in our own time *than* under pressure. It would probably cost 50% of force and 60% of guns on the peninsula, but could begin unmolested and in secrecy. If to be done at all, the sooner the better (The paper went into further details on this which I had not time to read).

That is the summary of considerations which I think just. What the government have got to weigh is the possibility of another attack on Narrows, if worthwhile, and the uselessness of this force if kept here without that end in view, against moral and political effect of withdrawing with heavy loss.

Wednesday 27 October 1915

South-westerly wind strong, but ever so much warmer, sun but hazy. No woolly waistcoat required. Wire this morning from WO to say that base at Alexandria was to be much increased, and that all forces in Levant would draw ammunition, stores and supplies from there, also an increased force in Egypt. Monro bringing General Walter Campbell as QMG, and General Ellison, present QMG, if can be spared to proceed at once to Alexandria, to reconstruct increased base as GOC Base. The 1st Division now en route and embarking at Marseilles, to be followed as soon as ships available by 22nd Division. Great relief of Aspinall and Dawnay, who were fearing Ellison (whom Aspinall calls Pooh Bah) would be made CGS—in which capacity he has been acting since Braithwaite left.

The medico's draught have much improved my health. After lunch had a jolly clamber in the hills with Barttelot. At tea it was settled that B should take over main duties of mess president which will be a very good thing. The Commander in Chief arrived in the Bay and saw Corps Commanders. To come ashore tomorrow.

Thursday 28 October 1915

Still warm with a southerly wind and cloudy.

A perfectly imbecile wire of 7 pages of cipher from Kitchener in answer to Birdie's wire giving points about the defensive situation. It consisted of a number of futile remarks, e.g., that all demands for material and gun parts had been met but perhaps they had not arrived, that officers who were not working wholeheartedly should be removed, could we not build bomb proof communication trenches on beaches, congestion at Mudros was a matter between us and Navy. The prize remark apropos of the condition of troops was "I cannot help thinking digging would be beneficial for troops in the condition you mention". He is sending 1 more battery of 60 pounders, the best lieutenant colonel Royal Engineers he can get, and, vaguely, extra ammunition, and will do his best about drafts. Kitchener is a *very* stupid man and I have no faith in him.

Shortly after 9, the new Commander in Chief, Monro, came to camp, with the new CGS, Lynden-Bell. There was a general handshaking and considerable bustle and excitement. Peyton, who was talking to one of the ADCs, says they are all sick as mud at being sent out here from their comfortable châteaux in France. Poor things, this is a warm day, and they don't yet know what they are in for. Monro is a big, heavily built man, with a grizzled moustache. One funny thing was that when maps were demanded as they were at once, the new map section under that idiot of a brigadier general proved to be quite inefficient. There was no set of trench maps available and all O were running about hastily trying to put a set together.

The excitement quieted down and a normal day was passed. Birdy sent a short answer to Kitchener's futility of this morning, and Monro wired that 20 company commanders each ought to be sent at once to Byng and Davies: this was absolutely essential.

Aspinall had a walk with Lynden-Bell in the afternoon, who looks a very capable man and who, Dawnay says, has a lightning brain. I gather from him and others that Monro was expected by Kitchener to leave for here at about 6 hours' notice, but flatly refused to leave until he had learnt something about the situation, so he had 3 days in London.

He didn't want to come as he was very comfortable in command of the 3rd Army. They have had to leave their châteaux and come to a cheerless winter in desolation, and they haven't brought beds or camp kit. I walked with Dawnay after tea to see R. Buxton who is very seedy in the hospital at K beach—a wretched place. On the way talked over things with him.

Apparently Monro has come out here as Commander in Chief of the Aegean with a free hand. He is to go both to Salonica and to Egypt and report on the situation there too, and then make up his mind on the course of operations. What Dawnay dreads, and of course may happen, is the decision to cut our losses here and withdraw as best we can. They will have to look sharp about it, because the preliminary investigation and decision will take a month, and then we shall be in December, when sea operations may be none too easy. On the other hand, this force is doing no good here unless it is going to make a real big push forward next spring. So at any rate there will be a good deal of interest in watching events during the next month, and I daresay I may have to accompany the generals when they go to Salonica and Egypt. The Germans have already joined hands with the Bulgarians, and Lord Lansdowne has stated openly he feared the Serbian army had little chance of withstanding the combined attack of Germany and Bulgaria. Dawnay and I agreed on the right estimate of the people at the helm at home. Muddle and discord. Kitchener a stupid bully. No help to his generals, stupid at appointments, allows discord to go on between General French and others. What I say is it will serve us right as a nation if we are thoroughly beaten, because we haven't come up to the scratch in national unity, in producing great men, in organization. Our dead weight against Germany is still enormous, but there seems nothing animating it.

Friday 29 October 1915

Still fine and warm. CGS lame through tumbling over tent peg last night in the dark. Quiet morning. Walked in the hills by myself all the afternoon. Quite summer warmth. It seems as if things would be different now to the old friendly days when the GS came out with Sir Ian, the effect of which days lasted all the time he and Braithwaite were with us. Now these people come among us as strangers; lords from another country, and rather by way of getting us out of a mess. The CGS, DAG, QMG are all going to mess with the Commander in Chief, so we shan't see much of them.

After tea, a wire came from Kitchener in the following words: "I hope you will send me as soon as possible your report on the main issue in the Dardanelles, viz. staying or leaving. Of course the setting free of the Turks now held in Gallipoli will be considered as well as the likelihood of the Germans getting through transit to Constantinople which seems to be almost inevitable".

Kitchener is always in such a hurry. How can a reasonable man expect Monro to have formed an opinion yet? But it is significant he no longer sends such a query "ultra-secret, decipher yourself".

Saturday 30 October 1915

Beautiful summer-like day. The Chief started early and made a tour, going to 8th Corps, Anzac and Suvla. Apparently very successful. Aspinall says he is a charming man to go about with, with a very good memory for faces seen long ago. Dawnay meanwhile hard at work on some appreciation for the CGS who is still confined to his tent. Dawnay told me Chief was rather worried at being hustled into giving his very important decision: Dawnay thinks people at home still don't know what to do and are playing with the idea of inducing the Greeks to come in. On that connection one wire this morning was significant: it was from WO asking for immediate report on what horses and mules here and in Egypt were available for pack transport. The French Government has fallen, and Briand is forming a ministry with Galliéni as Minister for War. *The Nation* says Asquith is to make a speech on Tuesday which will throw a new light on the Balkan situation. Dawnay thinks that the die will be cast for evacuation here for the purpose of getting more troops to help Serbia, a decision that would seem foolish, because it will be impossible to get up sufficient troops quick enough to be any use. If that is the case, and evacuation here were decided on the ground that anyhow this force would more useful elsewhere, there is no *desperate* hurry, and we had better have time to make complete arrangements first.

More and more does this whole expedition seem to take on more colour of a national tragedy which is approaching more nearly to its climax. If we do have [to] go, the story will then be complete. So many lives, so much gallantry, so much energy and wealth uselessly expended. If on the other hand we stay, I cannot see what we are ever going to achieve. The Bulgarians have taken Pirot and the line from Orșova to Vidin seems to be clear, and intelligence shows that an increased number of German officers have been sent to Gallipoli.

Finished today Joseph Conrad's "Victory"—a very absorbing story, and the psychology both of Axel Hept and the girl Lena, very fine studies. But the villains Schomberg, Jones and Ricardo rather melodramatically repulsive, and they are not the kind of people one would usually be much interested in, and therefore much of the art expended on them is rather wasted. All the technical achievement, which is as fine as ever, does not quite compensate for this.

The Russian novelists continue to show the bizarre and hideous as somehow belonging to ordinary life; in this story Conrad doesn't, and the effect is nearer to that of Poe's tales.

Sunday 31 October 1915

Beautiful day, no events. After lunch tramped in the hills and had a charming ramble over new paths. Our wine turned up from London, so several of us indulged ourselves with fizz for dinner, thinking it a good thing not to put off too long enjoying what we had. After dinner, strains of "Hoffmann" suddenly struck our ears: the gramophone had at last arrived. Quite a pleasant surprise and we sat trying it till after 9.

After tea sent off our MF 800 to Lord Kitchener doing it by myself in Aspinall's tent. Nobody else but Aspinall in O saw it. A tersely expressed and very lucid telegram, putting Monro's view clearly. Summary as follows:—(1) Troops on peninsula, except Anzac, too weak and ill-trained for further efforts. (2) Turkish positions, with advantage of position and observation, very strong, daily improving, can only be carried by frontal attack. (3) We have no room to distribute new divisions nor to deploy sufficient force of artillery, which even if available would have bad observation. Weather. (4) Therefore no further hope of success from attack. (5) On purely military grounds I recommend evacuation of the peninsula. Estimate of losses cannot be stated at present either by me or by Admiral. (6) Against loss of prestige would be set advantage to this force of a few months' training in Egypt.

9

'THINGS AT HOME ARE IN A DREADFUL STATE OF CHAOS'

DECISION-TIME, NOVEMBER 1915

If the general conditions at Gallipoli were not intolerable enough, gales and thunderstorms during early November damaged piers and grounded lighters. The weather did improve for a few weeks but then returned with fury; heavy rainstorms and a sudden drop in temperature brought floods, a blizzard and even snow. This was such a contrast to the customary blistering heat of the summer. Flood water filled trenches and gullies. The deres and nullahs, which usually contained barely more than a thin trickle of water, were turned without warning into fast, gushing torrents. When the temperature suddenly dropped there were reports of at least 250 British soldiers dying of exposure or drowning. Over 5,000 more had to be evacuated, suffering from frost-bite and hypothermia. With an approximate casualty rate of 860 per week, holding on through winter was estimated to cost some 15,000 casualties, some of whom would not be able to fight again. The hope that dysentery related sickness may drop during winter was offset by the reality that frost-bite was on the increase. The winter weather was fickle and the casualty rate worrying, both of which became important factors in the decision-making regarding evacuation.

All three of Gallipoli's Corps Commanders reviewed General Monro's earlier report to Kitchener. Birdwood was against evacuation, though he agreed with Monro as to the grave disadvantages of the Allies' position on the Peninsula. He was concerned about the risks, especially the impact that withdrawal might have on the greater Indo-Muslim world. Byng, by contrast, was in favour of evacuation, indicating that the withdrawal from Suvla should be made sooner rather than later; and before the Ottomans made it compulsory. Davies fully supported Monro's views. Kitchener, however, remained undecided, and continued to explore various schemes for keeping a presence at Gallipoli. Orlo, who was privy to these machinations, discusses the many complexities in his diary.

Kitchener arrived on 9 November. His discussions with Monro, Birdwood and others were informative, but the three-day inspection of Helles, Anzac and Suvla, was particularly significant. He was shocked by what he saw. Now fully informed, Kitchener concluded that Monro was correct. Gallipoli either needed reinforcement, or the campaign had to end. Kitchener, however, was also anxious about the deteriorating situation in the Balkans and made a follow-on visit to Salonika. This cemented his decision that Salonika trumped Gallipoli in strategic importance. On 22 November he cabled London, informing the Government that he had reluctantly reached the same conclusion as Monro. The final decision about what to do with Gallipoli, however, resided with the Cabinet.

Realising the negative impact the Allied withdrawal from Gallipoli could have on British prestige and interests, Kitchener was desperate to strike back at the Ottomans quickly. Various schemes were considered: most were quickly discounted, including a plan to march on the Bulgarian capital, and another to use the navy once again to force the Dardanelles. One scheme developed by GHQ staff was to conduct a landing at Alexandretta, in Syria, with view to severing the Ottoman communications south of Turkey's Taurus Mountains. The Ayas Bay Scheme, as it became known, would have needed French support due to Syria being a French country of interest. Dividing Turkey from its Arab empire was hoped to encourage an Arab uprising against its former master, thereby keeping the Ottomans engaged and Egypt safe. Kitchener concluded that if progress on the Gallipoli peninsula was impossible and the Dardanelles couldn't be forced by naval action, what other alternative was there to counter the German-Ottoman threat? Some believed that Egypt would be better defended in Egypt—not in a new expedition—and therefore urged that expanding the Suez Canal defences should be a priority. In Kitchener's mind, the answers to these questions were serious: to get it wrong might mean losing the war.

Whilst British politicians prevaricated over the decision to stay or go, the consequences of Bulgaria joining the Central Powers and Serbia being occupied were becoming increasingly apparent. The opening of an uninterrupted land route between Berlin and Constantinople had already manifested in the supply of heavier artillery and more reliable ammunition to the Ottomans. The relative lack of modern Ottoman artillery and a shortage of munitions meant that the MEF previously could continue to exist even though their rear areas were under the intermittent menace of shell fire. Now with a direct land line to their German allies, with the impact that this had on all manner of ordnance supplies, Ottoman shells were dropping on areas that had been previously considered relatively safe. It was evident that the Ottomans were being supplied with new and heavier guns and to counter this the British had no answer. This made the idea of holding onto Helles with a smaller force challenging, unless the Ottoman force could be pushed back from the range of the beaches.

All the schemes, including striking at Ayas Bay, were eventually rejected by the government, a decision they made with overwhelming support from senior military leaders. It is not to say that the British Government was not apprehensive of a German-Ottoman onslaught upon Egypt; they were, but they had another way to address that. Since July 1915 Britain had been progressing talks to persuade the Arabs to join the Allies in the fight against the Ottomans. The Hussein-McMahon correspondence between the British High Commissioner in Egypt, Sir Henry McMahon, and Sharif Hussein of Mecca was the vehicle for that negotiation. In exchange for opposing the Ottomans, Sharif Hussein would be granted an Arab independent area that stretched from the Mediterranean to modern day Iraq and from the Indian Ocean to Syria. With the failure of the Gallipoli campaign all but certain, British negotiations for an Arab deal accelerated. This negated the need for the Ayas Bay Scheme, as an Arab Revolt, supported by the British, would satisfy Britain's aim of protecting its interests in Egypt.

There was despondency amongst the old-hands inside GHQ, including Orlo, who felt that GHQ itself was dying along with the campaign. They were further disheartened when on 23 November, Monro, who had been a popular commander, was transferred to command all forces in the Eastern Mediterranean. The force on the Gallipoli Peninsula was renamed the Dardanelles Army, and Birdwood was given command. Birdwood's headquarters, which contained a mixture of old and new staff officers, was known as Army Headquarters (AHQ). Monro's headquarters, which continued to be called GHQ MEF, formally oversaw the campaigns at Gallipoli and Salonika, but in a practical sense, most of the work concerning Gallipoli was undertaken by

Birdwood's staff. In many respects, therefore, November effectively marked the end of GHQ's existence. Even though the Cabinet had not yet made up its mind, evacuation—and the end of the Gallipoli campaign—was looking more likely.

* * *

Monday 1 November 1915

Jolly day. Orders for me to accompany General and CGS tomorrow on their trip to Egypt and Salonica to report on situation.

However, a wire arrived from Kitchener soon after 5 in reply to our MF 800[1] which asked if all the Corps Commanders agreed with Monro's view. Also giving extract from a letter of Maxwell's dated October 20:—"If we can and do evacuate peninsula effect will be disastrous, unless of course we knock the Turks elsewhere. It is a great strain on the Turks to maintain their Gallipoli army and if we can hold I think we ought to". Kitchener asked if Monro had considered these points and where Turks were to be engaged elsewhere. Also said Government must have estimate of loss before them in considering Monro's proposal, so he must send it as soon as possible.

This wire has led to the postponing of our departure for 24 hours. Generals Byng and Birdwood have been specially sent for, arriving at 10 p.m., and Aspinall has gone over to see General Davies who is seedy. The object is to get their views.

Dawnay, who is coming to Egypt too, has been engaged all day drawing up an appreciation of the strategical position as regards Salonica. The curious thing is that, from our intelligence, our government seem to be entering on

1 Telegram sent to Kitchener on 31 October. See previous chapter.

definite commitments in Greece, but tell us nothing about them and are supposed to be waiting for Monro's report before they do anything. Yet Monro is going to Egypt first, where he will meet Maxwell alarmed about the Mahommedans, not to Salonica. So far as we can make out, things at home are in a dreadful state of chaos and indecision and discord. Our letters for the week October 16–22 came tonight and all tell the same story. Harold[2] is very gloomy and so is Dawnay's wife who sees and hears a good deal. The newspapers are all up in arms and the Cabinet obviously divided. Lloyd George intriguing against Asquith and nobody really fit to lead. If we only had a strong policy we could easily strike out a winning line, no doubt at some cost, but as it is—.

Dawnay's wife reports J. Pease as saying, financially, the war couldn't last after Christmas.

Letter sent to Admiral today about forming joint naval and military committee to prepare a complete scheme for reembarkation "so as to be prepared for all eventualities".

Tuesday 2 November 1915

Considerable movement of generals during night. Byng finally turned up about 1.30 and was then told to go back to *Cornwallis* till the morning.

This morning a wire, addressed Egypt and repeated here, announced that 22nd Division had been diverted to Salonica and that 28th Division was to be despatched there as soon as they could possibly get out of Egypt. This confirms our suspicions that the government had entered on definite commitments with Greeks, and here is our Commander in Chief without the least idea what is their policy. I await developments with interest.

Another lovely morning.

2 Harold Beresford Butler.

A long and very secret wire arrived from Cairo for Tyrrell saying that as the result of negotiations initiated by the Sharif of Mecca, the High Commissioner had sent to him a definite proposal on behalf of England, in which England undertook to support independence of Arabs, excluding certain not purely Arab districts, Damascus, Hama, ... etc., and to offer them advice and assistance and secure sacred places against aggression, if Arabs would form alliance with us, recognize that our interests in Bagdad and Basra required special administrative provisions, and of course turn out the Turks. This information was sent with reference to certain secret negotiations now in progress in which "No. 1" and our bureau in Switzerland are playing a great part, by which Syrian troops are to desert to us and Syria to rise. The Sharif's answer cannot come before November 9 but an Arab officer and others of his party have agreed to proposal and are ready to act on it. Great secrecy necessary, since, even now, the Sharif's life is in some danger.[3]

Query, how this might be affected by our withdrawal here, and what use it would be unless we could send a large force to Arabia.

After tea sent wire MF 805 in answer to Kitchener's query of last night. It began by giving the views of the 3 Corps Commanders as stated in writing. Birdwood was against evacuation, though he agreed with Monro as to the grave disadvantages of our position. His Indian experience led him to fear result on Mahometan world. He thought effect on morale of our troops would be bad, and it would be necessary at once to launch the force against Turks elsewhere though he failed to see where this was feasible. Also he thought the dangers of the actual operation were

3 Orlo marked this 'omit'.

made too hazardous by the approach of bad weather conditions. Byng plumped for evacuations, saying he thought Suvla could now be evacuated voluntarily and cheaply, whereas with German help to the Turks it might be made compulsory and costly. Davies said "I agree with General Monro's views".

Monro continued:—"I have given anxious consideration to Maxwell's views and my decision, which is unaltered, is determined by the judgement how we can best employ our force. As said before, the force here except ANZAC is unfit for further offensive operations till rested and further trained. The longer it remains on the peninsula the less efficient it will become. My decision is a certain degree determined by the above consideration but I also strongly hold that we must be in full strength at the vital points. I think we should remain on the defensive in Egypt, collect all available forces there (without impairing operations in France which I regard as the main theatre) and strike wherever attacked. I hold that our course of military action should be governed by our military resources: opposed therefore to any further landings and frittering away of our troops. I think it is not appreciated how immensely difficulties of landing on beach are increased by the introduction of quick firing artillery, heavy ordnance and multiplication of stores necessary for maintenance. As regards estimate of losses have consulted Admiral and Corps Commanders. Much depends on number of lighters, tugs etc. available besides other factors already mentioned. They all agree in estimate of between 30–40% loss in personnel and material. I am inclined to agree.

Wednesday 3 November 1915

Jolly morning. Up at 6.30 and dressed to allow Ashley to pack. Had a cup of coffee and porridge in Chief's mess and started to pier at 8 a.m. having borrowed a brassard from Aspinall. At 8 a.m. horrified to find the motors had disappeared and started to run, but relieved very soon to come on the whole party walking. All aboard the *Chatham*: Chief, CGS, Dawnay, Butler (30th Lancers) and myself. Had some more breakfast in wardroom and spent a pleasant idle day and received my first anti-cholera inoculation. The only drawback to this ship is that she burns coal and with a headwind the quarterdeck is almost unbearable for the cloud of clinker dust from funnels. Walked and talked a bit with Dawnay after lunch. He thinks Monro will be given command of Salonica push and Birdy left with smaller staff to hold the peninsula; doesn't think government will face evacuation. Personally I think it would mean their fall. The CGS talking to me in the morning said: "One thing we want is a good Secretary of State for War. This fellow is really a civilian and doesn't understand the soldier's view". We got a wire, futile as usual, late at night saying "I hope you and I will discuss matters as soon as possible with Maxwell. I am sending him information for you".

Dawnay would like to see a really big force sent to Salonica provided it could be done in time. His view is that we must go for the *Germans* wherever we can, and not fritter away strength away on the Turks.

Monro, I gather from Butler, thinks he that he will be recalled after expressing his opinion.

Thursday 4 November 1915

Slept well on a camp bed in the alleyway. Comically aroused at 6.15 by Butler who said there had been an explosion of gas in his cabin. What had happened was that a bottle of Scrubbs' ammonia had fallen on the floor and bust. Spent 2 hours on bridge. Glorious calm weather. Enciphered 3 telegrams to be sent. Most important to

Aspinall as representative of Chief on the Reembarkation Committee. Instructions: Scheme to make on assumption (1) that guns could only be reembarked during period for preliminary arrangements. (2) Sufficient guns must be left ashore to enable us to hold out against determined attack for say a week of bad weather. (3) Main embarkation of troops must be superior to all other considerations and as rapid as possible, not exceed 48 hours.

Another to DQMG to begin withdrawing all unnecessary animals from Helles and prepare to accommodate resting troops at Mudros and Imbros (up to 25,000).

Arrived at Alexandria soon after 4. Three generals came off to meet us. Generals Egerton, Inglefield and Wallace, much to the annoyance of Commander Hardy who had wished them to wait at his house till the General came ashore. On shore General Briggs, commanding 28th Division, was also there. However we got off in our special in good time and reached Cairo about 8.15 p.m. Here Sir John Maxwell and his ADC, Walford, met us, and took us to Shepheard's [Hotel] where we have a suite of rooms and a sitting room. We all dined sumptuously in the General's sitting room, including Maxwell, his ADC, and the lieutenant Royal Navy who has come up with us as an extra ADC from the *Chatham*. A wonderful jump from GHQ to the luxury of Shepheard's and iced champagne and the best rooms. After dinner Monro went off to talk with Maxwell, and Walford was commissioned to take Butler, the Navy and myself round the town. We certainly couldn't have had a better man than Walford, who seems to take himself round the town pretty often and to enjoy it. He is a semi-Belgian with a knowledge of all the languages of Europe, and speaks English with the accent of a Cook's interpreter, which sounds odd from a cavalry lieutenant. We went first to the Kursaal[4] where we saw a very blameless show, juggling, a *very* stout troupe doing part of Acts 2 and 4 of Carmen and finally, 2 knockabout acrobats. Thence to the Café Petrograd. Things have changed a bit since I was here last, as drinks can't be served after 10.30 and no dancing is allowed. At the Petrograd, not a bad little upper room, we had iced coffee and talked French to a couple of nothing very particular, and a violin and piano played and at times a creature chanted songs in unrecognisable Italian. Thence to get a drink we [went] to the Pension Adele. Madame Adile (Tellier), a wonderful old dragoon with a bass voice opened the door of our flat and in we walked. We had brandy sodas and 3 of the pensionnaires entertained us meanwhile quite agreeably. A dark girl of Italian extraction, she spoke all languages badly, seemed to think me promising. After a blameless sojourn I assured her that *la prochaine fois.*[5] Butler was also enjoying himself hugely, chiefly in imitating G.P. Huntley, which he does rather well, and Walford would have stayed out all night if we had given him half a chance. But we didn't and were in bed by 2 a.m.

Friday 5 November 1915

Did very little all the morning except a little shopping. But Dawnay went and spent the morning at the WO. I saw him just before lunch and lunched with him. He hadn't got any information out of the WO but had some momentous news. That is (1) the Chief is ... to command an army at Salonica while Birdy gets command of the Dardanelles, (2) as a *great* secret, Kitchener is coming to Alexandria himself, though he will remain on board the ship, to see us on Monday, and that is why we are staying here over the weekend.

4 Amusement park.

5 Translation: 'next time'.

Dawnay is very disheartened. As he says, what is the good of sending out a man here as Commander in Chief and the moment he gives his opinion, taking him off? Dawnay had come to have the very highest opinion of Monro, who, he thinks, has a fine grasp of things and gets at once to essential points. He is most disappointed at this latest display of Government ineptitude, especially as even now they seem to have no fixed plan. Birdy, a slippery little customer, has got what he has been playing for all this time, and now it remains to be seen what he will do. It will be very uncomfortable at GHQ, and Dawnay and Aspinall will hate it.

Quiet afternoon and walked after tea with Tennant in Esbekieh Garden. Received invitation by telephone to dine with Bigham at the Residency which accepted. Went there at 8.15. Handshake with MacMahon[6] who was dining out. The other guest was General Cox, now a KCMG. Bigham in great form and kept up a ceaseless stream of questions all the evening. Left about 10.30 unfortunately with tummy ache. Tummy not behaving as well as I hoped.

Saturday 6 November 1915

After breakfast drove with the Chief and Dawnay to the Gippy[7] WO where we interviewed intelligence department to glean information about Salonica and Alexandretta—there is some idea of landing at the latter and defending Egypt by holding the railway. I took down the information as it came. Then back and wrote it out. General says 4 divisions are being moved from France: 22nd, 26th, 27th and 28th. The Serbian position looked at on the map is not at all encouraging, for the Bulgars have already penetrated a long way and the country we should

6 Sir Arthur Henry McMahon. (Orlo usually, thought not always, wrote 'MacMahon'; we have edited it for consistency).

7 Slang for Egyptian.

have to defend is all inhabited by Bulgars and practically no good roads.

Slept in afternoon and sat about, inside not being very grand. Just before 5 a wire came from WO which upset the powers pretty considerably. It was to say that Generals Lynden-Bell and Campbell had been appointed to MedForce and should take up their duties at once. A complete staff had been despatched to Salonica including Howell and Clarke. *(He does not like Howell).* His force to consist of 5 divisions and be one corps. So the WO after sending out a good man, because his opinion is unpalatable, promptly relieve him of that command, give him a smaller one, separate him from his CGS and generally make themselves unpleasant. Both he and Lynden-Bell are much cut up. So is Dawnay. Dawnay has written a strong letter to Hankey intending it to be shown to Carson pointing out the rottenness of the whole thing, and making clear that *all* the commanders in Gallipoli were agreed on the military situation and need for withdrawal, while one, on political grounds, with which he has nothing to do, deprecated it. Moreover the government, instead of saying that *they* could not agree on political grounds and ordering Monro to carry on, give him a fall and turn him on to an expedition, the policy of which has never been made clear. News from Mahon yesterday showed that 30th Brigade was in camp north-east of Lake Doiran on the right of French. Had 20 casualties from shell fire, but not engaged. 31st Brigade going up on 8th and 10th. 29th Brigade still at Salonica. 22nd Division now disembarking.

In the evening dined alone on terrace overlooking garden with band. Afterwards there was a dance at which looked on. Some quite pretty girls and nice dresses. Met one of the Lamberts who is in artillery of Mounted Division.

Sunday 7 November 1915

Really meant to see something of Cairo today but the gods willed otherwise. Went round with the Chief to HQ about 10.30. Obviously some conversation about trains and times going on. Then about 11.15 heard our plans had suddenly been altered. Kitchener is going to Mudros instead of Alexandria and we are to be there to meet him on Tuesday. Also, McMahon and Maxwell are to come too, all on the little *Chatham*!

Orders were that the ADCs, servants and I were to return to Alexandria by 4.15 train, while all the rest came in a special at 10.30 p.m., sleep on train and come off at 6 a.m. My servant and Lynden-Bell's of course gone off to see pyramids and couldn't be found. Hope they will turn up. In spite of all, I walked up to the Citadel and saw the Mosque of Mehemet Ali before lunch.

Lunched with Dawnay, who agreed with me it was a good thing Kitchener was coming to Mudros, for then Monro and Maxwell could put their case well against Birdwood's. He thought it showed that the whole things was in the melting pot again, and that, as I suggested, Maxwell has probably been wiring in a good sense to the effect that an evacuation of Gallipoli together with an offensive in Syria would be the best plan. Dawnay told me that this morning Monro decided to resign rather than take the Salonica job on Kitchener's terms. This may now not be necessary.

Off punctually and had uneventful journey. The embarkation officer met us with motors and brought us to the quay where embarked for *Chatham*. Have just had supper in the wardroom. Ships' officers quite exercised as to accommodation of all these notables. Hear that submarines have been very busy off this coast during last 48 hours.

Monday 8 November 1915

Generals Monro, Maxwell, Lynden-Bell, with Sir H. McMahon, with Anglesey and Bigham as ADCs came on board at 7.30 a.m. and we started at once. After breakfast had a stroll and talk with Anglesey on deck, a very pleasant fellow. Does Maxwell's cipher work and very long hours. Read Flaubert's *Tentation de Saint Antoine*. In the morning a submarine scare; as I came on deck saw the ship turn a complete semi-circle, but it turned out that the object she was making for was a porpoise, not a periscope. Another alarm just as we sat down to lunch owing to Bandy Butler, up on the bridge, leaning against the alarm buzzer handle and so sounding "action" for the whole ship. After lunch talked in the charthouse with McMahon, who is a Savilian. Told me he had always been strongly opposed to the Dardanelles expedition and done all he could to stop it. Said he had never seen 2 more depressed men than Sir Ian and Birdwood when they started off on it. He is a great friend of them both and spoke to me very warmly of Birdwood. He hoped Kitchener was going to bring some definite data with him for them all to go on, but agreed with me that it was difficult to get anything out of Kitchener. Dawnay tells me that the 2 generals and McMahon while on board have been arriving at a general entente as to the view to be laid before Kitchener, and they all agree that the Dardanelles force is no use where it is. The idea would be to go for the railway near Alexandretta, and when the first half of force was in a firm position there proceed with your evacuation of Gallipoli. The advantages of such a plan would be (1) A smaller force would be required than that on the peninsula, (2) It could be landed in instalments as required, for any Turkish concentration against it would be slow, (3) Its wastage would be smaller and supply easier than on the peninsula, (4) It would stir the Arabs to break away from Turks, (5) It would absolutely safeguard Egypt.

Bigham, Dawnay and I talked in the afternoon; Bigham babbling on unceasingly on all kinds of subjects. Bigham showed me a copy of Raymond Asquith's lines on the young girl of today, which are extremely clever, and end by describing her as "Voluptuary, virgin, prude and plump".

Dawnay tells me Kitchener has 5 people with him but not known who they are.

Tuesday 9 November 1915

Rest of voyage uneventful. Dropped hook at Mudros soon after 2. Kitchener not yet arrived. Arrangements had been made to house all our party on various ships but this proposition was resisted, our notables wishing to keep together and go on talking. The Vice Admiral, Wemyss, and Altham came aboard. Also Aspinall bringing King's Messenger letters. Birdwood arrived in evening and came to confer with our party.

The news of what had been going on here is fairly astounding. As soon as we had gone Kitchener sent a series of telegrams to Birdwood which would be laughable if the matter were not so serious. The day we left he wired:—"You know Monro's plan. Nothing would induce me to agree to evacuation. You are to command the force and Monro will go to Salonica. The Navy will force the Dardanelles. You will reduce your front as much as possible and collect every man you can, and Maxwell will collect every man he can, and we will land a force to seize the Bulair Isthmus and feed the Navy, if the Turks have not already surrendered". Birdy, who has behaved very decently indeed, replied by saying he thought it much better for Monro to remain in command, and refused to make it known in any way that there had been a change in command. About 12 hours later another wire came from Kitchener to Birdwood:—"The Admiralty have refused to let the Navy attack the Narrows. I am afraid after all there is nothing for it but evacuation". Not long afterwards a third telegram:—"I cannot bring myself to agree to evacuation, you must just hang on as best you can". And that man is our Secretary of State—a nation's hero! Then Kitchener started, and a wire came from Asquith saying "Nothing will be definitely decided till Lord Kitchener arrives. Meanwhile make all your plans for evacuation". So that's that, and very exciting for Aspinall.

At the same time, as Dawnay told me, there is a big proposal from the French on the tapis which would be alternative to the general scheme agreed on by Monro, etc. It had obviously been refused once at home, but might still be carried if strongly supported. This is to make a really big affair in Serbia, letting the Germans get through to Constantinople if they liked but then proceeding to make things very hot for them. The plan would be to land up to 250,000 troops eventually at Salonica, including an Italian contingent, and march on Sofia, practically forcing the Greeks to come in, while at the same time the Russians landed 150,000 on the other side and brought in Rumania. Dawnay thought there was a great deal in this plan, but it would mean concentrating every effort on such an expedition. All the Gallipoli troops would have to be withdrawn but since it would be about 2 months before they were wanted, they could then be taken back to Egypt, reorganised and trained. He was afraid, however, that Maxwell and McMahon might not like that scheme, because it would mean giving up their set-off in Syria for the withdrawal from Gallipoli. He would therefore have given a good deal to be at the pow-wow after dinner last night. Knowing that by tactful handling he could probably get them all to pull together, but rightly distrusting the diplomatic abilities of Lynden-Bell.

Wednesday 10 November 1915

Do not yet know what was arrived at last night. Since breakfast, and before the various bigwigs went off to see Kitchener on the *Lord Nelson*, there has been a great deal of subdued agitation, Monro, McMahon, Maxwell, Lynden-Bell, Dawnay and Bigham, all walking up and down in various pairs talking vigorously in low voices: rather like the lobby in the House of Commons. Finally, Monro, Maxwell and McMahon got off by 9.45, the latter having had 15 minutes' start. The news that Sir Archibald Murray, the CIGS, is with Kitchener has apparently depressed them all very much. Meanwhile the ship is coaling and there is nothing for me to do.

It appears that the conference last night was completely successful, and if its plans are carried out the country may yet win the war. Birdwood came in and McMahon promptly took the reins by cross-examining him as to what he thought he could do in Gallipoli. Birdwood has a hazy mind and it soon became apparent that he couldn't really say how far he hoped to get and with what loss. "Anyhow", said McMahon, "what good is it going to do when you do get there?" Birdie hummed and hawed a bit and was again hazy, and at the end of it all McMahon rapped out "What it comes to is this, it's no damned good at all". Thus, the meeting arrived at a general agreement that the Gallipoli peninsula was no good. The big Serbian scheme was not considered apparently, because it had definitely been rejected at home, but they went on to consider the Alexandretta business. Here Maxwell got a little tiresome saying we ought to go to Alexandretta itself and seize the pass above it. But here again McMahon was very much on the spot and convinced him that it would be impossible in winter.

The Ayas Bay scheme was therefore agreed on.

There was a little irritation this morning, because McMahon got ¼ hour's start of Maxwell in going to see Kitchener. All off the ship by 9.45. Dawnay and CGS went with General Campbell to *Aragon* for a committee.

For me the day wore on very uneventfully till 4.30. Ship was coaling and all the officers came to lunch exactly like sweeps.

At 4.30 I was summoned to the *Lord Nelson*, where in the captain's cabin I found a lot of ciphering going on. Monro, Birdie and McMahon were hanging about. Fitzgerald and Storr, Kitchener's secretaries, were being very important and busy, and Bigham (who has the true Buckingham Palace back bend and nose poke) was helping with the ciphers. I assisted him in sending Kitchener's wire to the Prime Minister giving the results which was my first news of how things had gone. It was a longish wire of which the gist was as follows:—

"Met everyone here today. As you know the chief difficulty is, in case of evacuation here, to find some set off to keep the Arabs and Mahometans at rest. Both Maxwell and McMahon strongly of opinion something must be done. The most effective method is to land at Ayas Bay and hold the railway by Alexandretta (here followed a few details). All are agreed here and Admiral is working out naval plan which he considers feasible. Let the staff work out any objections to this plan on which all here are agreed. It would be essential to move 2 more first class divisions from France in addition to the 6 already ordered and the Indians for Mesopotamia. Then the 28th and 27th would remain in Egypt and an equivalent number to them (RND, 53rd and 54th) would be moved to Salonica from Gallipoli. If this is agreed to utmost secrecy must be observed, 27th diverted to Alex. and 28th stopped in Egypt".

Girodon was at the meeting. Talking over with Dawnay

and Aspinall later, and after the grand dinner party given to the generals by the Admiral, the state of affairs appears to be something like this. The actual round table meeting didn't last long, but Kitchener was closeted with Maxwell and Birdie (both his own men) for a long time. The principle of Alexandretta has clearly been adopted, and though Kitchener probably couldn't be made to consent to complete evacuation of Gallipoli, the fact that troops would be sent from there and also the military pressure will probably make that unavoidable. E.g., a wire was sent last night to Byng asking how many men could be spared if he held his low ground with detached posts. He replied that the reduction could only be small. Detached posts would take time to make, the beaches would have to be defended by an inner line. Then 3000 could be spared, but if enemy artillery were increased any line would be untenable. Also, as regards Salonica, it appears we are pledged to the French to send so many men, but we are going to send useless ones from here, and it appears certain that such a small force will be unable to do anything and will finally have to come away.

Intelligence shows that the Serbian army is demoralised and Germans have joined forces with Bulgars. Austro-German force is about 750,000. Germans bent on beginning to attack Egypt soon, and some troops withdrawn from Western Front have arrived in Vienna. Meanwhile Germans failed before Riga and Dvinsk and Russians have assumed offensive all along line.

Finally, what is particularly pleasing is that, though nothing definite has been said about a Commander in Chief for the whole Levant, Birdie seems to have persuaded Kitchener to leave things as they were, and our old Monro is said to have made a very great impression—Fitzgerald going about saying "He's a really great man" and Kitchener seizing him by the arm and saying "Now, come on forward with me, you're the very man I want etc., etc." which is quaint after recent events. But that is the very best thing that could have happened, and may lead to his being Commander in Chief of the whole Levant.

The impression here is "*Tout va bien*"[8], and that Kitchener having accepted the principle of right doing will be driven to do it properly and not shilly shally.

Had to go on to *Aragon* after dinner to send a wire. Had a drink with Aspinall and NA.[9]

Thursday 11 November 1915

Kitchener gone ashore to see hospitals, etc. Goes to Anzac tomorrow, to the great horror of his secretaries who fear he will be hit. Maxwell and McMahon want to leave for Egypt as soon as possible. Dawnay and CGS have gone to do staff work on *Aragon* and I left here. So also Bigham who much chagrined McMahon should have gone ashore without him.

Very uneventful day for me. Remained in *Chatham* all day, but in evening dined with Sir J. Maxwell and Anglesey as Wemyss' guests on *Europa*. Pleasant dinner but very sleepy afterwards.

From 3 a.m. to 5 a.m., was up deciphering 2 wires from Mahon repeating wires from Elliot which had already been received. But these particular wires were important as making a new factor in the situation which was, I believe, the chief subject of the conference yesterday afternoon. The Greeks are misbehaving and Elliot says the situation is grave. What happened was that when the French Minister called on the new Prime Minister, the latter spontaneously said that if Serbians were driven into Greek territory they would have

8 Translation: 'All is well'.

9 Captain Mitchell, RN.

to be disarmed. The French Minister after vainly arguing that this would be shabby treatment of allies asked what would happen if British or French troops were in similar case. The Prime Minister replied they too would have to be disarmed whereupon the French Minister got angry and said that any such attempt would be regarded as a hostile act and that the Greeks had better demobilise. Elliot went to see the Prime Minister who said there had been a misunderstanding. He had only said that French and British troops if pursued by enemy into Greek territory "ought to be" not "must be" disarmed. There was no unfriendly intention, but the Greek Government only desired to maintain neutrality and wanted allies to relieve them of the embarrassing position, in certain eventualities, of not maintaining it and wished that allied staffs would put forward some scheme by which this could be done. Sir F. Elliot had replied that since the allies were paying for the Greek Army they were not going to be threatened by it; that he would have to refer to FO but thought formation of any scheme unlikely. What the Prime Minister apparently has in mind is the neutralization of the railway with a few miles for either side. Elliot thinks such a scheme futile and impracticable, especially as Germans would have to be a party to it. He regarded situation as grave, especially as an evening paper had said that Prime Minister's declaration was given at German orders. He recommended immediate and firm action, that an allied squadron should be sent to Piraeus and that former assurances of benevolent neutrality allowing free ingress and egress should be required to be renewed in writing for publication, failing compliance supplies should be stopped. This might lead to revolution against the King. At same time, subject to military requirements, urged that troops, who are too late to save Serbians, should all be withdrawn to Salonica ready to move in any direction.

Before going to bed found Dawnay who had been over to see Aspinall on *Aragon*, rather fed up. Aspinall is apparently becoming very jealous, and saying he was kept out in the cold, etc. while Dawnay was the man people applied to and also very cross with Dawnay for letting the powers go on with the Ayas Bay scheme, since in his opinion the only possibility now is to evacuate peninsula at once. Dawnay says rightly that that may be so, but it would have been quite useless to say so at first, as the authorities, afraid of Indian and Egyptian mutiny, would never have considered evacuation without some set off. The question may be settled as regards Salonica by Greek action, and the great thing is to get the evacuation principle decided on somehow. As regards jealously, of course there is something in what Aspinall says. Dawnay's opinion on the strategical situation *is* more considered than his and rightly; at the same time Dawnay has done nothing to push himself forward, and it was purely his doing that Aspinall became a GSO1, major and lieutenant colonel.

Friday 12 November 1915

Kitchener, Maxwell, McMahon and party gone off to see Anzac in a destroyer. No plans seem definitely to have been agreed on yet. Dawnay was up till 2 a.m. writing an appreciation of the Gallipoli situation, showing why we couldn't get on there.

Kitchener and co. couldn't land at Anzac so went to Helles, and hope to go Anzac tomorrow. So we are stuck here another day.

Aspinall came on board and I heard him talking over situation with Bigham. Aspinall's position is that the landing at Ayas Bay, which Buckley told him must be 4 divisions in 5 days, was a pure military impossibility, since there was nothing like enough small craft to land them so quickly with their transport. At the Gallipoli rate of landing and with the Gallipoli allowance of boats the landing of one division takes 14 days. The idea was to land there before withdrawing from here, then where are the small craft coming from? Aspinall's view is that the Ayas scheme is as bad as this and shuts up as many men without killing any Germans. He says that we want to beat Germans and there are only 2 possible courses here: either to withdraw entirely from peninsula and undertake big scheme against Salonica, or to do the Asiatic shore push as Girodon wants. If there is an Indian and Egyptian mutiny, well that won't end the war, but the war will end if we defeat the Germans. Bigham, from the diplomatic point of view pointed out how wedded McMahon and Maxwell were to a quid pro quo, that the telegram about Ayas had been sent to the Prime Minister, and that by adopting the most stiff-necked attitude we shall lose Monro and be saddled with Birdie. He inclined to think that it would be worthwhile to keep Monro and even fail at Ayas. What strikes me is that people like Kitchener, Maxwell and McMahon *will* run things their own way on political rather than military considerations and that their politics are not good enough to beat those of Germans.

Dawnay's answer to Aspinall's view is that so far as the GS is concerned the only thing necessary is for them to keep their mind on the fact that, politics apart, the Ayas Bay operation is militarily possible, *given certain conditions.* If these are not fulfilled, then they can't help it, but he considers it foolish to do anything to hinder opinion from hardening in favour of evacuation by taking up a stiff non possumus attitude about Ayas Bay.

A very interesting telegram from Elliot, sent yesterday, arrived today—repetition of one to FO in which he presses very strongly for immediate firm measures to show Greeks that the British danger is nearer than the German: stoppage of all money and supplies, fleet to Piraeus, 300,000 men to Salonica.

After dinner played poker and lost 14/7d though enjoyed it very much.

Saturday 13 November 1915

After breakfast to *Aragon* to inquire about some cipher wires, then to *Lord Nelson*, where I came in for some ciphering, assisting Berry, who seems more or less installed there as cipher officer. Incidentally saw the great Kitchener just before the party went off to Anzac. Gathered some very interesting information.

(1) Wire from Creedy giving position as regards Greece up to date. All money and supplies to be stopped till situation clears. The dissolution decree ready but not actually signed. Cabinet disposed to agree that fleet should be sent to Piraeus. French Government asked what they think of Elliot's suggestion to call for written assurances. Greeks given to understand that to lay hands on a single allied soldier compelled to retire on Greece by military exigencies would be fraught with gravest consequences. "Things appear to be fast going towards an ultimatum to Greece".

(2) I, with Berry, enciphered an important wire from Kitchener to Asquith. I gathered from it that the Cabinet had answered Kitchener's last by pointing out all the objections to the Ayas scheme which Aspinall sees (his views apparently shared by CGS and Monro), and suggesting that Egypt would be better defended in Egypt. Kitchener replied by saying that all these objections had been foreseen. The political effects of the Germans and Turks to

carry out their intentions would probably jeopardize French and English possessions and be so enormously far-reaching that political considerations outweigh military disadvantages of Ayas scheme. "Maxwell, McMahon and myself must be admitted to know the difficulties of the defence of Egypt. By defending Egypt in Egypt we should be throwing Arabs into hands of Germans, having serious internal trouble which would spread to Algiers, Tunis and Morocco, endanger French and English possessions, interruption of internal communications, and close Canal for long period. All this unless we are committed to massing of so many men and resources in Egypt as to give Germany an opportunity of gaining her aims in the West. As regards military objections answers of "Monro and General Staff" were (1) Turkish concentration could only be slow according to intelligence. (2) Line held would be 50 miles, but 2/3 of this marsh and mountain, so usual numbers of men per yard not necessary. (3) Reembarkation easier than at Gallipoli. Kitchener went on to say "I would ask the GS, if it is recognized that the defence of Egypt in Egypt is doomed to failure, if progress in the peninsula is impossible and Dardanelles cannot be forced by naval action, what other alternative to that proposed is suggested to meet the Germano-Turkish menace. I would point out that very valuable time is being wasted and that a decision as to our future action is urgent".

As regards Monro, CGS, Dawnay, Aspinall and Tyrrell, they have been doing very hard work all day, and disapprove of Kitchener and his reference to the opinions of "Monro and his staff" which they were not. However the difficulty is that they have been instructed to draw up a reasoned answer to the WO's objections, they themselves, especially CGS, Tyrrell and Aspinall heartily agreeing with the WO objections and wanting Monro to make a firm stand, while Monro is rather disposed to say that he must abide by instructions.

Asked Dawnay tonight how things stood. He replied: We have said that in our opinion to remain on the peninsula is a matter of serious danger. The Egyptian party who have Kitchener with them will not hear of evacuation without the set-off at Ayas, owing to their views about the defence of Egypt (which Dawnay thinks all bosh). So Monro and they are required to work out a scheme of which they don't approve, and they take the line that they will carry out the scheme provided so many men, guns and stores can be put ashore within a certain time. The possibility of this depends on the Navy. Aspinall and Dawnay are convinced the Navy can't do it. What the Navy will say they don't know. That is how it stands till tonight. As regards Salonica they have made up their minds to bring the troops away. A wire from Mahon last night reported considerable success on the French left. Enemy coming on in dense masses lost heavily from machine gun fire and forced to retire. Serbians recaptured Tetovo.

Today news received that Winston had resigned. The Committee for War in Kitchener's absence are Asquith, Lloyd George, Bonar Law and Balfour. It has been announced that if unmarried men don't come in by November 30th, compulsory measures will be adopted to take them before married men.

Played poker again tonight, no luck at all. Lost 26/–.

Sunday 14 November 1915

Eight months yesterday since I left England. Returning

when? This odd life on board ship at Mudros continues. Kitchener and party off to see Suvla, fresh southerly wind blowing which will toss them a bit. Church parade on board; did not attend, nor did Harke, the assistant surgeon, whose views agree with mine, and who very much objects to the compulsory religion of service: he a parson's son. Later went to *Lord Nelson* to get right a corrupt cipher which Storr and Berry had failed at. Very simple job. To return at 6 to encipher long wire from Kitchener. WO not yet replied to Kitchener's wire of yesterday, but apparently Cabinet and GS are sticking to their views. Moreover the French are intimating that any action in Syria nearly concerns them, and that no action must be taken there except in full consultation with them, and preferably majority of troops to be French. Rather amazing we should have made all those plans without consulting them. Opinion seems coming towards coercing Greece. Elliot wired Mahon that he wanted Kitchener to come to Greece as King would much like to see him. Dawnay thinks only way to get out of all these muddles is to agree on *some* policy, get Kitchener and co. out of the way, and carry on till brought up against sheer impossibility.

Saw a wire from Clayton to Maxwell giving summary of Sherif's answer. Pretty favourable, claimed that Damascus and ?[10] were purely Arab, would leave Mesopotamia out of question for present, also demanded a subsidy. The rest of telegram contained summary of long and strong objections made by India to the whole scheme, especially as regards undertakings with regard to Basrah and Bagdad, and also saying directly that they had no trust in the Arabs at all nor had the people of India. Another pretty little divergence of opinion.

10 The question-mark is Orlo's.

Expecting that Kitchener was going to send a long wire home when he returned, Storr asked me to come to *Lord Nelson* at 6 and stay to dinner, which I did. The Admiral was entertaining everybody and Wemyss and Girodon. Quite a good dinner and fizz. I sat at small table with 2 Flags, Paul and Fitzgerald. Kitchener however didn't send his wire, so I dined under false pretences and returned to *Chatham* at 10.

Monday 15 November

All day on board *Lord Nelson* from 9–6. A good deal of work. Lunched in wardroom and had tea in *Triad*. All the morning there was a Council of War in after cabin: Kitchener, Admiral and all the generals (why Birdwood?) and McMahon which lasted till lunch. As no door between this and the dining room, I often caught glimpses of them and heard bits of their talk. Old Monro was sitting opposite Kitchener with that very solid look on his face which I wish I could draw.

As I read through all the telegraphic correspondence that had passed since Kitchener started I saw that what Kitchener said to Birdy was "I will do all I can to enable you to hold out as I think the evacuation of the Dardanelles would be a frightful disaster". He went on to say Birdwood was to command and went into details of troops. Birdy replied he hoped Kitchener would leave Monro in command till he saw him (Birdy), for unless things went much better, the Corps Commanders would all be wanted on the peninsula, and he must be with his men. Kitchener idiotically wired to the CIGS: "Birdwood telegram seems to me very depressing. He must be ill. Find this out".

I found that since yesterday something of note has occurred, namely, that our government had received a formal communication from French government to the effect that they could not agree to the proposed operations at Alexandretta, thinking them quite impracticable. The Prime Minister also wired yesterday that Kitchener's telegram would be considered at meetings (a) of French and British general staffs, (b) French and British governments. Meanwhile wanted to know what view Kitchener took of evacuation and of proposed naval action in Greece.

The Greek Minister had been informed that to attempt to disarm and intern Anglo-French troops would be an act of hostility and treachery.

Three telegrams of importance were sent during the day as a result of conferences, etc.:

A. As regards naval action. It would undoubtedly be a serious thing for Greece to lose her fleet, and this could be assured by action in Bays of Salamis and Phalerum. Salonica could be secured if a force there could prepare defence before fleet action. Owing to presence of 2 Greek Army Corps, the 4 divisions up the line would be left *en l'air*[11] if Greeks cut line, but they could not put up more than an equal force if French could disengage from the Bulgarians in time and assure their retreat to Salonica.

B. The position on the peninsula. The Turkish positions exceedingly strong and could be held against a very serious attack. Communications of our force, owing to distance of base, want of harbours etc., very bad, and this cause chiefly due for failure to gain strategic point across peninsula, without which it would be useless for the Navy to attempt Narrows. Everyone has done wonders both on land and sea considering the great difficulties. These trenches well dug and cover good, and I think the line could be held against Turks even with increased ammunition but if

11 Translation: 'in the air'.

Germans sent German force, could not be defended owing to want of depth. Evacuation now being carefully and secretly prepared, and could in my opinion be done with even less loss than estimated though an operation of great difficulty and danger.

C. The real result of the conference. If Ayas Bay is rejected because of French objections and disembarkation of force. Admiral and I met to consider what scheme we could best propose to you. Generals Monro, etc. present and all agreed on the following:

1. No other point at which to prevent Germans carrying out their announced project, unless by putting utmost pressure on Bulgaria and Greece and massing 400,000 men at Salonica, but this extremely unlikely to attain our object.

2. As to evacuation decision could not be wisely taken until results of naval action against Greece were known. Admiral would like to keep Helles.

3. Defence of Egypt on the Canal must be risked. The defences of Egypt would have to be very greatly strengthened and considerable force employed. Whether this force could not be more usefully employed at Ayas Bay is a matter for grave reconsideration.

Tuesday 16 November 1915

Again to *Lord Nelson* by 9. Find Kitchener has had to get more off his chest about the Ayas scheme. He is convinced that to let it go is to see the East in a blaze and a force in Egypt so large as to impair an allied position in the West.

He therefore sent a wire to the Prime Minister which

began something like this:—"The decision about to be come to appears to me to have such a momentous effect on the future of the war that I should like to place my opinion on record, as it may, I think have a great effect on the loss of the war by the allies". He then proceeded shortly to say that with Germans having fulfilled their announced intention, East in a blaze and vigorous offensive of allies intended for next spring impaired, if war has to last through winter of 1916/17 without any decision or improvement of our position, he greatly feared that some of allies if not ourselves would not stand the strain.

Also wired he had seen Elliot who wants him to go to Salonica and Athens. He doubted if his going to Athens would do any good as Germans had complete control, but thought he ought to go Salonica at once to see Sarrail and our officers, and was leaving tonight unless he heard to contrary for Salonica.

Just after lunch he wired to Edward Grey that if Ayas Bay scheme was to be given up owing to French "sentimental objections", would it not be well, on precedent of allotting Constantinople to Russians, to allot Syria to France after the war. Perhaps we should then be allowed to operate in future French territory for our own defence against dangers from which they cannot guard us.

I hear we are also off to Salonica in *Chatham*, and that Kitchener is unlikely to come back.

Talking after playing poker with Dawnay last night he expatiated on the comicality of the Greek situation. Almost unbelievable we are *paying* their army.

Dawnay holds that events have proved the wisdom of his persuading Chief and CGS to play with the Ayas Bay scheme, as without it there would never have been the pow-wow, and the hardening of opinion in favour of evacuation which seems practically settled. Dawnay says they, the staff, are putting forward an alternative scheme to attack the Turks in Syria *from* Egypt across desert, as a reply to the Egyptian party.

Stayed on board *Lord Nelson* to dine. Great special dinner in wardroom at which Kitchener himself was present. Merry time, but had to be cut short at 9.30 to go on board *Chatham*. Berry was also with us. Have begun rather to take to Berry, who is a fellow of King's, and was Keynes' tutor.

Just before dinner 2 wires came from London. One saying "take special precautions for personal safety". The other from Prime Minister saying "I and some of my colleagues are going Paris tonight to confer with French government. Will wire you decisions without delay. In the meantime postpone any visit to King of Greece".

Dawnay told me that the Chief's post has been properly settled. He is Commander in Chief of forces in Levant not Egypt, and a new staff is being made out for him. Aspinall to stay with Dardanelles force, Dawnay to go with Monro, and Neill Malcolm to be sub-chief. I think I shall be Monro's cipher. Wonder if we shall have GHQ in Egypt. Monro is sending a good wire to CIGS, which is result of an appreciation he has shown to Kitchener and with which Kitchener agrees. He says he considers advantages of retention of force on peninsula no longer commensurate with drain on resources. Turks under German guidance could either hold us there with a small force and proceed to Egypt or Bagdad with whatever army they could collect, or else make a serious effort to drive us out of our positions and then proceed to east with enhanced prestige. McMahon's view, however, being that to evacuate without attacking Turks elsewhere would have disastrous effect on Moslem world, he had consented to favour the Ayas scheme with its dissemination of force.

General Howell from Salonica reported to Kitchener

today. He drew a very gloomy picture of things, saying Greeks were obstructive, water scarce, food and accommodation at famine prices, and our camps split up among Greeks and officers not allowed to view ground for defence purposes. Situation very critical and cannot continue under present condition.

At 10.30 p.m. set sail for Salonica with General Campbell on board. Kitchener and co. in *Dartmouth*.

Wednesday 17 November 1915

Arrived off Salonica at about 8 a.m. Cloudy morning and freshening wind. Salonica a picturesque town coming down from hill right to foot of sea. An old castle with wall at summit, and many minarets. Hills all round, which command the town. Very bad for reembarkation in face of an enemy.

Went ashore for 2 hours with Bigham and saw an old mosque which was crowded with refugees. Town rather smelly and fearfully crowded chiefly with soldiers. Sea rather rough and breaking right over sea front. British HQ at dirty little hotels. Came off and went on board *Dartmouth* at 2.30 where stayed to tea. Sent in cipher Sarrail's view of situation not at all hopeful. Says he must have more troops from France and cannot retire far because roads very bad, and railway service also bad and run by Greeks. The general sprained his ankle badly and the captain hurt his foot getting into boats in rough sea.

Thursday 18 November 1915

Much colder, north wind, but calm and sunny. Lovely day and could see Olympus well. On board *Dartmouth* after breakfast doing telegrams, but the long expected one from Prime Minister did not turn up. Stayed to lunch and returned to *Chatham*. Decided we are to return to Mudros tonight. If Monro really *is* Commander in Chief we shall have HQ at Mudros, Byng will command at Salonica and Wilson at Suvla.

Birdwood wired Fitzgerald today hoping we should hang on at Anzac. CGS much annoyed at this backstairs play.

Sailed at 10 p.m. Played baccarat after dinner. Won 11/–.

Neill Malcolm on board, who is to be BGGS.

Friday 19 November 1915

Arrived at Mudros about 7 a.m. After breakfast Monro went off to be x-rayed—result very satisfactory. Meanwhile IGC arrived with wires for Fitzgerald, so I went off with him on board *Lord Nelson* to decipher them. I stayed in *Lord Nelson* all day till after 10 p.m.—having all meals on board in wardroom.

In the morning 2 important wires arrived.

(1) From Prime Minister saying Cabinet thought Kitchener ought to go to Athens to persuade King of Greece [that] Greece will do herself no good by persisting in present attitude. (According to wire from Elliot yesterday the King said he would never come in but would not intern allies). Kitchener rather annoyed at having to go to Athens, but decided to go tonight. He thinks he will do us no good, Tino[12] having made up his mind.

(2) Prime Minister says at Paris conference it appeared French were suspicious we were not landing troops as quick as we might to support them. It was pointed out that this was not the case, but we agreed in pursuance of our engagements to send 26th and 28th divisions at once. Object of this—in spite of inevitable congestion—to safeguard the town and

12 King Constantine of Greece.

secure retreat of troops before naval measures were taken.

(3) Kitchener wired saying he intended to appoint Monro to command overseas forces outside Egypt; Birdwood for Gallipoli and if troops to remain in Serbia; Byng at Salonica, if to come away, Mahon to get them off.

(4) Maxwell has news Senoussi are giving trouble in Egypt, which worries him and the Kitchener party.

Birdwood was sent for and arrived at 2, staying to dinner, but the result of this did not appear. Kitchener rather fidgety all day, waiting for some definite Cabinet decision. He at first thought he would go straight on from Athens, but McMahon persuaded him to decide to return here for a day. McMahon simply won't leave Kitchener, and has gone to Athens too—dragging Maxwell, who is bored to death, with him. McMahon is a conspirator who doesn't want to let Kitchener go till a definite policy is settled out here.

Just in time about 8.30 p.m. 2 important wires arrived from the Prime Minister.

(1) As a result of Paris conference, Government have decided against Ayas Bay. So leave that out of any further considerations. Can you now give us your considered opinion on evacuation in whole or part?

(2) Line to be taken with King. We are not coercing him to join us. Internment will be an act of war. Try and impress on him Germany will lose war, that we and Russia are only at beginning of their efforts, that our determination is unchanged, and our resources unexhausted.

At 10.25, I left for *Aragon* where we are for the present. Smells badly.

Saturday 20 November 1915

Very uncomfortable day on board *Aragon*. Coaling made the ship worse than usual. Atmosphere horribly smelly and food pretty bad. Very little to do and couldn't get off for a walk. Met Montagu[13] who was on his way to Alexandria. Also Drake, an Eton contemporary, whom I hadn't met since 1902. He is MLO here. After dinner played picquet with Malcolm. No particular news. General getting better.

Sunday 21 November 1915

Cold and very rough. Doing telegrams till 11 p.m. *Dartmouth* expected at daybreak but had not turned up by 12. Conditions of work here with no office pretty impossible.

On board *Aragon* is Colonel Williams who has come out again having recovered from his wound. Is much delighted because CGS has promised him first vacant brigade.

Dartmouth with Kitchener turned up in afternoon but no developments. Very rough day, hear they had bad voyage.

Monday 22 November 1915

Quiet morning, went to help on *Dartmouth* after lunch, where I learnt what had gone on since I lost sight of Kitchener.

(1) Result of interview with King of Greece. King said he was really anti-German but would on no account involve his country in war with the central powers. Would fight Bulgaria later. No intention of hostile act against allies at Salonica, but position would be very difficult if Bulgars pursued allied troops over frontier, as Germany had intimated that to attack Bulgaria would be an act of war and Greeks could not very well remain passive. Complained bitterly of

13 Lord Herbert Montagu-Douglas-Scott.

Venizélos and treatment of Greece by England. The Greek staff officer, Metaxas, showed that Greece had a very lively fear of German attack on Egypt where Greeks have large interests, and were very anxious for allies to concentrate on defence of Egypt.

(2) Important wire sent this afternoon to Prime Minister giving considered opinion on present situation including Dardanelles. Began by saying that German intentions might have been thwarted by pushing at Suvla and landing at Alexandretta. As it was Egypt would have to be defended in Egypt with grave risk from Moslems, etc. Position was such at Salonica that troops would probably have to be withdrawn. As regards Dardanelles, evacuation of Suvla and Anzac necessary; troops to be concentrated and to some extent refitted on Imbros, Tenedos and Mitylene. Helles to [be] maintained for present. Thus Turkish forces will be kept in neighbourhood; effect of withdrawal not so bad as if all were taken at once to Egypt; Helles could not be used as submarine base nor could heavy guns mounted in mouth of Dardanelles. Horne going down to Egypt to consult on defence of Canal with Maxwell and McMahon. Kitchener himself to return as soon as he received agreement to this wire, to report to WO and give effect to policy. (n.b. Kitchener has chosen Malcolm to be BGGS in Egypt, thus taking from Monro his carefully chosen man who knows all about Salonica and nothing about Egypt.)

(3) Wire to WO giving requirements for defence of Egypt. Line of defence to be 12,000 yards in advance of Canal, defence not to be purely passive. Water

arrangements to be made at once and light railways. Artillery to complete all troops including MedForce to be sent to ¾ scale per mile in Flanders. Heavy gun positions to be made and connected by railway. 15 companies Royal Engineers to be despatched. 2 divisions cavalry to be sent at once from France with British infantry to follow. Aeroplane establishment proportionate to force.

Thus, if government agree, the great and perhaps final step in our policy is decided—contrary to Lord Kitchener's opinion.

Tuesday 23 November 1915

Nothing very much. Went on board *Dartmouth* in afternoon to stand by to decipher the telegram from government but though I stayed to dinner nothing arrived. Understand that a wire did arrive later saying government agreed to evacuation of peninsula including Helles. Kitchener and co. left about 3.30 a.m. next day for Naples on his way home. Maxwell and McMahon with General Horne left in *Chatham* for Egypt to begin the arrangement of defences.

From Prime Minister to Lord Kitchener (extract)
10234 cipher
23/11/15

Your 91. Final decision will be communicated to you after Cabinet meeting tomorrow. War Council after full consideration approve evacuation including HELLES but stages and method of evacuation must of course be left to judgment of Commander on the spot.

Wednesday 24 November 1915

Certain amount of work here. More members of the staff turned up i.e., Robertson who is GSO2 in O(b), a very pleasant fellow. Also Tyrrell and Herbert Scott.[14] It seems as if I am to be the GSO3 in O(b) if my not having a unit doesn't stand in the way.

Dined with Birch on board *Ortolan*, to play accompaniments. A very comic evening. The tenor was an Australian from Sydney who with a filthy production could scream up to B, but sang very out of tune. We did "Goodbye Summer", "Come into the Garden Maud", and a lot of other rot. The other was a baritone who sang unpretentiously sentimental ballads of ballad concert type, but pleasant. They sang the duet "Excelsior" in all seriousness, till at the end somebody in the saloon below blew the foghorn, whereat the tenor threw down his music. Another comic thing was that after I had played Chopin's "Polonaise" in C minor, a rather screwed engineer officer said "Thatsh war I call shacred music".

Thursday 25 November 1915

Beginnings of a cold. King's Messenger arrived with a fortnight's mail. Great congestion of letters but very welcome. Good news of all at home. Work, conferences etc. Nothing much settled, but instructions to be issued to Birdie to prepare scheme for evacuation of whole peninsula in case of receipt of definite instructions. NA[15] arrived. Glad to see he had got DSO. Heard I was mentioned in despatches. If that is an honour it was very poorly earned in my case. Gillman, the new BGGS arrived (seems a pleasant fellow too).

14 Lord Herbert Montagu-Douglas-Scott.

15 Captain Mitchell, RN.

Friday 26 November 1915

Strong south-westerly wind which towards evening developed into gale with heavy rain and lightning. Walked with Dawnay on Mudros in afternoon fearfully dusty but invigorating on hills. Gather I *am* to be GSO3 in O(b) and to go Imbros tomorrow to see Moberley, collect files, etc.

Saturday 27 November 1915

Sailed with NA and Captain Lambert in *Redpole* destroyer for Imbros at 11 a.m. Wind from north-east quiet passage till near Imbros. Then squalls began and as we rode in Imbros harbour there was heavy sea, heavy rain and bitter wind. K Beach looked very uninviting. Arrived in camp at 4 and so to tea. Found O mess had started a fireplace, very comforting. Very pleasant to be among old friends again, but bitter cold. Found my tent had been down on Friday night and was wet through. Bed put into Barttelot's tent. Merry dinner and played bridge with Barttelot, BGRA and Watson. Lost 11/–. Found AHQ[16] with several grievances against GHQ, and Barttelot very fed up with having little work and little news. Bitterly cold night with snow and wind. Slept in 2 waistcoats and socks, mittens and cap. Feet still cold.

Sunday 28 November 1915

Very cold all day, with much wet in morning. Spent a good deal of time with Moberley looking over files and taking over, etc. Short walk with Barttelot and Hough.

Part of sunken ship pier at Kephalos destroyed and wire from Suvla to say many officers and men sick from

16 Army Headquarters, Dardanelles Army (i.e. the senior Headquarters supporting Birdwood's new command, and responsible for planning the Gallipoli evacuation). GHQ continued to support Monro, who now presided over Gallipoli and Salonika.

exposure yesterday. Very little prospect of sailing tomorrow, for wind beastly. Walked down in afternoon to see effects of storm. Kephalos Bay a really pitiful sight. Every small boat or ship is ashore, also one large water tank steamer. 1 T.B.[17] ashore, and all pinnaces and cutters piled up and covered with seaweed. Some smashed. The concrete road to pier very badly damaged. Serious situation, because if another ship not sunk at once, there will be no place of refuge for small craft from Anzac, and troops from Anzac or Suvla could not be concentrated at Imbros. Played game of chess with Hough. After dinner poker at which lost 7/–. News from Anzac that Lone Pine had been heavily shelled with 12″ shell and 100 casualties chiefly from men being buried in tunnels.

Monday 29 November 1915

[No entry]

Tuesday 30 November 1915

5 degrees of frost in night but wind quite dropped and sea calm. Cloudless sunny day. Some doubt as to how it would be possible to get away. At first the only chance seemed to be Wemyss coming over to conference in destroyer. But at 10.30 hearing trawler would be ready at 11 decided to take the certainty. A great hustle to get servant and baggage ready but successfully pushed all into car, walked down myself and eventually all got on board. We are escorting submarine *H3* whose speed is delaying us. Most perfect day and sun when up was warming: lovely view of Samothrace and Asiatic mountains capped with snow. Only scratch food. Fear we shall not be in before 9 or 10 and it will be freezing cold. Arrived at 9. Not so cold as expected owing to stillness.

17 Tug Boat.

10

'A REALLY GREAT FEAT OF ORGANIZATION'

EVACUATING GALLIPOLI

It was not surprising to anyone, least of all Orlo, when on 7 December the War Committee finally decided to evacuate the Gallipoli Peninsula. Rather than leave all at once, however, withdrawal would be a partial affair. Anzac and Suvla, for instance, were to be abandoned, but Helles was to be retained for two reasons: the Royal Navy believed that its occupation would help restrict enemy submarine activity in the Dardanelles; and politicians felt that evacuating the whole peninsula would amount to a full admission of defeat. Retaining Helles, reasoning went, meant that it could still be used as a base for a future operation, and would keep the best part of 200,000 Ottomans tied down to the area, thus preventing them being deployed elsewhere. In any case, purely from a practical standpoint, the Royal Navy didn't have enough ships to evacuate all the three sectors simultaneously.

The challenge of how to evacuate Anzac and Suvla of its 83,000 troops, 186 guns and 4,895 animals, and as much of their equipment and stores as possible, wasn't taken lightly. It would be an enormous task. The evacuation plans envisaged either a fighting withdrawal to the beaches, secured by fresh defensive trenches close to piers, or a withdrawal based on deception and cunning. With opposing trenches separated by the smallest of distances, the danger lay in the Turkish reaction to an evacuation. If they knew, the Ottomans would almost certainly increase their shelling of the beach embarkation points as well as conduct disruptive attacks across the whole of the front. Because of this risk, Birdwood and his staff favoured the deception plan: they would try and conceal the evacuation until the very last moments and then get off quickly.

The evacuation plan, written by Birdwood's staff, was undoubtedly a brilliant piece of work that combined rigorously and detailed planning with a considerable imaginative effort to 'fool' the Ottomans. The evacuation was to be carried out in three stages: a preliminary stage to remove all surplus personnel, animals and vehicles not necessary for the winter campaign; an intermediate stage that would remove all personnel, guns, and animals that were not absolutely necessary for the defence of the positions; and a final stage (which required two nights), to evacuate the reserve and rear-guard elements. Throughout, every effort would be made to maintain the appearance of normality in everything the soldiers did. Clever means were employed to simulate the presence of men, guns and stores where there were none. Indian muleteers continuously drove their carts, throwing up huge clouds of dust, so that it appeared as if a consignment of stores had just arrived. Rifle and artillery fire was to cease unless there was an attack, to get the enemy used to extended periods of relative silence, just as it would in the last hours of the evacuation. Trenches were held by as few men as possible, their presence supplemented by uniformed, scarecrow-like dummies made from straw-filled old jackets and hats. On the beach the illusion of stacks of wooden ration crates was created by means of constructing an outer framework only, making it appear that the massive piles were solid. Stores that could not be evacuated were buried, rum jars smashed, and water tins holed. Even games of football and cricket were played in the overlooked reserve areas to give the impression that everything was normal.

In a masterpiece of military planning and execution, Anzac and Suvla were successfully evacuated during the night of 19/20 December. On 20 December Lieutenant-General Davies, commanding VIII Corps at Helles, received news of the successful evacuation. It didn't take long before the shelling at Helles increased as more Ottoman batteries began to arrive from Anzac and Suvla, their gunners determined to make their presence felt. In support of the Ottomans the timely arrival of an Austro-Hungarian four-gun 15cm howitzer battery and a 24cm howitzer battery, the latter with 1,200 rounds, added to the daily hate. The Austro-Hungarian's opened fire for the first time at Helles on 24 December. Their presence known, this put paid to any idea of hanging on to Helles; with the Ottomans now able to focus their efforts, Helles would soon become untenable. But could the ruse that was played out so well at Anzac and Suvla be repeated?

The British at Helles followed the same template as that adopted at Anzac and Suvla. Once again, the number of men in the line was thinned and guns removed, leaving roughly half of the original force, 17,000 men, to be evacuated on the night of 8 January. It had been decided that the French would be withdrawn entirely; this made the final evacuation easier by leaving only one nation's army, and not two, to be taken off the beaches, avoiding the complications and potential for misunderstandings in carrying out so complex an operation. Still, though, planners wondered whether they could get away with the ruse a second time. The Ottomans were suspicious that the British were withdrawing, but they didn't know when it would happen. Opposite them were only four divisions: the 13th, 29th, 52nd and the Royal Naval Division.

Everything they did was meant to give the impression that life was normal. Guns and troops were still landed during the day, but under the cover of darkness the garrison was being withdrawn.

Finally, on 28 December, Monro received news that the War Committee wanted Helles evacuated as soon as possible. With this news Orlo wrote 'so this ends the final chapter of the Dardanelles tragedy, and may it not prove, as I fear it will, a bloody one!' What the British feared was a turn in the weather or an all-out attack. They would receive both. The first of their worst nightmares came true on 7 January 1916, just thirty-six hours before Z-Day, the final day of the evacuation. Following a remorseless bombardment on the British trenches, and then the detonation of two mines, an Ottoman infantry attack targeted the Gully Ravine section of the line. Luckily, it was repulsed by a withering fire from those still manning the front-line trenches, supported by the guns of the Royal Navy. The British were enormously relieved that the attack had not been pushed home as on that day their total numbers at Helles stood at only 17,000, with 63 guns in support. Any sustained effort by the Ottomans would have certainly broken through. That night, further challenged by a storm that washed aways some piers and grounded lighters, the last 2,300 men and nine guns were evacuated. All surplus stores and all horses and mules not required for moving the last guns were destroyed and the surplus ammunition was buried or packed into the natural caves at the back of the beach and fused, ready for detonation after the last men had left. All the wagons and vehicles that could not be embarked were parked on the cliff edge for destruction by naval guns. Positions were selected for a stand on Hunter-Weston Hill, but the enemy did not take alarm and so these positions were among the last to be evacuated.

When the Ottomans realized that the evacuation was in its final throws, they began to bombard the trenches and beaches; too late, they were empty. The British warships responded with a last goodbye and gesture of defiance by shelling Achi Baba one last time. The Ottoman bombardment lasted until about 6.30 a.m., followed up by an infantry advance; but by the time they had got through the trenches the transports were already long gone. The evacuation of allied troops from Helles on 9 January 1916 marked the end of the Gallipoli campaign. Orlo ended his diary the next day. The peninsula was once again fully in Turkish hands. On 12 January the Dardanelles Army was broken up at Imbros, the majority was ordered to Egypt, along with Monro's GHQ, ready to strike again.

In Orlo's words 'so ends more brightly the doleful chapter of the Dardanelles expedition.'

* * *

Wednesday 1 December 1915

Busy day. O(b) still in great state of chaos owing to want of clerks etc. Find that since I was away Kitchener has wired saying that evacuation still under decision by Cabinet and that such of his instructions as referred to that were cancelled. We replied that nothing had yet been done, but pointing extreme urgency of acting at once if we are going to evacuate owing to weather. As regards Salonica, Sarrail is preparing to retire on Salonica moving about December 10 but Mahon is very apprehensive that his plan will leave the British force north of Lake Doiran in the lurch by its having to wait so long, in view of Bulgarian concentration at Strumnitza in which Sarrail refuses to believe.

Gillman away at Suvla inquiring into results of blizzard. Bernard arrived as GSO2 in O(a). Find he was my contemporary at Eton. Scott ill with asthma. Myself trying to get files in order all day.

Thursday 2 December 1915

Very busy all morning. One wire home to say Wemyss had asked if Navy forcing Narrows would help Army. Our answer: no it would not. Another report on casualties at Suvla owing to storm. 6000 altogether. Causes flooding of rivers then frost. Mahon wires again very apprehensively of Sarrail's plans. Reply strengthening his hand. Various O(b) work most of the day, feeling after effects of cold rather heavy.

In evening "clear the line" wire from Proemial.[1] "Cabinet been considering Dardanelles position all day. Strong feeling against evacuation owing to political consequences. If the troops now at Salonica up to 4 divisions were put at your disposal for offensive at Suvla to gain depth and higher ground, would this operation be possible? Navy would cooperate with offensive. WO and Admiralty now engaged on working out transport direct from Salonica to Suvla, which will be sent to you. Only new consideration affecting position is defeat of our troops south of Bagdad. Turks following them up which renders it imperative they should not be allowed to gain another success".

Action taken on this was to send wire to Birdwood repeating portion of this and asking for his view.

Friday 3 December 1915

Birdwood's answer was that it could be done, but a great deal of additional RE stores, hutting, roofing, etc. would be required and additional supply. Wire in from Salonica indicated Mahon and Sarrail were concerting plans for retirement on Salonica. The wire sent to Proemial was

1 Telegraphic address for Lord Kitchener.

most excellently couched. The Chief gave it as his opinion that the operation as suggested could have no reasonable chance of success. There was not enough of the right artillery, i.e., howitzers, no material or supply, the element of surprise would be absent, the 4 divisions could not be disembarked simultaneously and the enemy's fire would be trouble. A purely local success might be gained but would not really ameliorate the position. Naval cooperation would be useless, and in any case preparations would take some time which at this season is an impossible condition.

Walked over Mudros West in afternoon with Bird and Hart Davies: stiff walk of 6 miles. The multitude of camps a fine and interesting sight. Mudros certainly one of the sights of the world.

Lieutenant Gammell joined as GSO3 O(a).

Read file of *Times* up to November 19. Winston Churchill's apologia very good. It is rather frightening how much is being publicly talked about the Balkan situation, evacuation, etc.

Saturday 4 December 1915

Very characteristic wire from Kitchener in answer to ours saying "please send me views of Byng and Birdwood on the proposal, as former told me with certain numbers of fresh troops he could improve his position". Why will he never trust the good man on the spot? Anyhow, as we already had Birdwood's views, Gillman was sent in a destroyer to see Byng and get his. Meanwhile we wired Birdie's views and asserted that we adhered to our view, the essential point being that no possible advance at Suvla done at short notice could be of any real value in ameliorating our military position, and that the expedition would in any case take 6 weeks to prepare which would land us in middle of bad weather.

Total blizzard casualties about 10,500, 4,211 of which frostbite, some very bad cases.

Mahon wires more hopefully of joint measures regarding Salonica position. Bulgars have entered Monastir, and Germans expected very shortly at Uskub.

Saw private letter from Mahon to Commander in Chief about Salonica situation. He doesn't like it at all. Says 10th Division are very bad, and after exposure to very severe cold had never seen such a dejected lot. Chief reason bad regimental officers who have no idea of looking after men. Commander good, staff moderate.

Miscellaneous work all day till tea kept me busy. O(b) work a teasing job because one is always switching from one thing to another and perpetually interrupted. Also had to take a turn of assisting with ciphers, which were rather congested.

However, in spite of the rather difficult situation, the discomfort of working on this ship and all, the staff is very cheery. The CGS, a regular bluff, loud-voiced hearty soldier, sets a fearfully hearty tone. At lunch he never stops bucking in a loud, rasping and cheerful voice. Gillman, the sub-chief, is a very nice man too, quiet but amusing, and Robertson is a capital fellow too, and Bernard, who is still seedy with jaundice, is likely to turn out very well.

Dawnay looks a bit weary. This indecision of the Cabinet and Kitchener rather wears him. Precious, precious time is being wasted, and no telegram they send shows that the government realize that sudden sallies implying disembarkation *cannot* be made with any chance of success.

Sunday 5 December 1915

Muggy day. Walked in afternoon at Mudros West with Orr and Armstrong, dull. Gillman got back at about 2 a.m., and result of his visit was a wire expressing Byng's opinion the gist of which was that under present conditions the doubling of troops at Suvla would seriously complicate matters and supply an excellent target for the enemy. What he had formerly said was that with fresh troops and more howitzers he could undoubtedly advance on the left.

Wire from WO to say that French and British governments would meet provisionally at Calais to decide on Salonica question. Meanwhile disembarkation there has been stopped. French retirement of 2 forward divisions in Serbia has begun. Artillery activity on British front.

Letters from Mahon show he is considerably anxious about position of 10th Division, and afraid it will be left *en l'air*[2] by the French, especially as it is in a bad state owing to casualties from exposure.

No further communication from WO.

Monday 6 December 1915

No wires from London of import. Wires from Salonica: (1) fearing the retreat of 10th Division will be exposed. (2) Greek GOC has orders to resist all attempts contrary to Greek summary. Wire from Athens that Colonel Napier, formerly Military Attaché at Bucharest and Wilson, KM, had been captured on December 5 in Greek steamer by Austrian submarine. Part of despatches saved![3]

System started by which all officers in GS are to go for a walk daily either morning or afternoon. Walked in afternoon with Berry.

2 Translation: 'in the air'.

3 They were on the Greek steamer, *Spetzia*. Both became prisoners of war. The Foreign Office correspondence that Wilson was carrying was also captured.

Tuesday 7 December 1915

Received long wire from Proemial, that at meeting on Saturday with French Government, British Government declared they could not consent to keeping a force at Salonica and was of opinion preparations should be made without delay to evacuate the port. Greek Government should be informed military necessities compel allies to occupy and prepare for defence necessary strategical points but should receive assurance that these measures agree with intention not to violate Greece's sovereign rights. This declaration accepted. Massing of Bulgars confirmed. Our opinion asked about Sarrail's demands, whether they affect sovereign rights of Greece. What demands should be made? Mahon to discuss plans for carrying out this decision. Monro to report on movements and orders of French. Unnecessary impedimenta to be sent Alex. "I think you should proceed Salonica to assist Mahon in carrying out this negotiation and give weight to his arguments and to insist with Sarrail on release of transports now held up".

Wire from Mahon, that yesterday evening Bulgaria after a heavy bombardment attacked 10th Division. Trench lost but recaptured. Mahon with 10th Division reports he may want another brigade. State of health 10th Division serious. 23 officers and 1633 men come to base since December 1. French withdrawal going slowly but well.

Chief decided to go to Salonica this evening, and sent wire to Proemial giving briefly his views on Salonica problem:—our successful withdrawal depends on Greek attitude. They could make our position very difficult. We should offer them all possible consideration. Difficult to see how we can make any demands for protection not infringing sovereign rights. Two courses open: (1) To announce to Greeks our intention of occupying territory and doing what she will consider infringement. (2) Give assurances of our intention to withdraw as quickly as possible and tell them that if they protect their frontier we shall take no steps to occupy a covering position. Commander in Chief thinks latter offers more promise.

I went ashore for walk in morning, and on return found I was to accompany Salonica party in *Chatham*. Finishing up work all afternoon and left *Aragon* at 6.30.

Party: Commander in Chief, Lynden-Bell, QMG, DAS, Dawnay, Butler, Orr, Bridges and self. Cheery meeting with *Chatham* friends. Out of the harbour by 8.45 p.m.

Wednesday 8 December 1915

Late arrival owing to thick fog. Did not drop anchor till 9.45 a.m. in harbour. Thick fog all day which cleared away about 6 p.m. This delayed the conference arranged with Mahon and Sarrail. About 10.30 a.m., Granard came on board with messages: (a) bringing news of 10th Division which had been attacked again yesterday, line broken and 31st Brigade went back in disorder, 1 battery lost, possibly 2. Moral bad. Reforming on Crête Simonet. But night quiet and French retirement going slowly but well. Mahon wired home saying he thought situation critical and French blindly optimistic, and that we should clinch bargain with Greeks before they know of our bad position.

Mahon came on board at 2.30 and Sarrail at 4.

Mahon brought wire from WO which reached us also in AW cipher at 4.30. 10770 cipher: "The Cabinet has decided to evacuate the positions of Suvla and Anzac but to retain Cape Helles for present. You should act on this without delay. I need not say that this decision has only been reached after the most earnest consideration and with greatest reluctance, but the government feels that the exigencies of the situation render this course inevitable".

We wired Birdie at 1800 to carry on with operation and

subordinate everything to avoidance of delay. Another wire later that only islands of Imbros, Lemnos and Tenedos to be used.

Situation complicated by French wishing to relieve the Colonial brigade at Helles, Wemyss wishing another Admiral to take his job on, and Cipher T being apparently compromised.

Result of talks with Mahon and Sarrail was a long wire home urging a rapid decision be taken as regards defence of Salonica. Situation much complicated by fact that French government are trying to get decision to evacuate reversed and do not wish Greeks informed of arrangements to evacuate. Mahon and Monro think Sarrail blindly optimistic: also he has no orders, and though he has free hand in disposition of troops will have no hand in negotiations with Greeks as regards our position at Salonica. This is being done by French Minister at Athens apparently in a very high-handed way which is likely to put up Greeks' backs, and make our position more difficult. Colonel Pallis is coming here tomorrow, but he is supposed to be hostile and have no full powers, so nothing much is really hoped from negotiations. Message received late at night that 31st Brigade had been compelled to abandon its positions at dusk, and 30th Brigade had conformed. These brigades and 2 battalions of 29th Brigade moving back on line Pazarli-Dedeli. General Herbert and 2 battalions arrived 24 hours too late to save situation.[4] This exposes French right badly. GHQ wire the evacuation committee are meeting Birdie's representatives at 12 tomorrow.

Thus the Old Man's predictions of 5 weeks ago are absolutely realized. We are forced to evacuate Dardanelles and Serbia, and worst of all both at once. Nothing *could* have

4 The Battle of Kosturino.

been worse arranged, and one can hardly help wondering if anybody at home has any sense at all. The Dardanelles should have been evacuated 4 weeks ago, if not a great deal earlier but the government couldn't face it. Dawnay thinks this will be the death blow of the government and that there will be an unholy row in England.

Meanwhile these are hectic days.

Nevertheless played poker tonight and lost 15/-.

Thursday 9 December 1915

Pretty busy morning. At 10.30 Wilson and Fairholme arrived to see Chief. At 12.15 Mahon and Adye. Wires about ciphers sent off, also another wire to London about Sarrail's attitude, and saying that unless an agreement was come to with French government as to joint withdrawal and communicated to Mahon in same terms as to us, we could not release transports as desired. Sarrail and Pallis did not come here this afternoon, but a conference of Pallis, Sarrail and Mahon was held in the afternoon. Mahon came back to report result at 7.30. Sarrail formulated his demands, i.e. evacuation of Vardar and Kara Burnu forts. Defence of frontier by Greeks, and assistance to allies; and other measures for effective defence of town. Pallis said he would forward these claims to Athens but stated clearly that unless allies gave assurance to quit Salonica Greeks would not oppose Germans and Bulgars, though they would not be definitely hostile to us. Mahon elicited fact if Bulgars came near their present camps Greeks would move away. Greeks on other hand gave definite assurance of assistance if we would give assurance of leaving as soon as possible. Pallis said reconnoitring for defensive positions would be considered breach of neutrality, but Mahon received orders from Monro to do so. In his wire home Monro reported that Sarrail seemed to be playing his own hand, holding that his military career was associated with continuance of this campaign.

Friday 10 December 1915

Still fog. Have not caught one glimpse of Salonica since we came. We determined to sail today at 4 p.m. to reach Imbros 7 a.m. tomorrow and return to Mudros at 1. However 3 wires came from Kitchener in Paris at 11.30 which delayed us. From them it appears 2 governments are informing Greek government today that a free hand should be given to our 2 generals here to reconnoitre, select and prepare defensive positions to hold Salonica, and instructions given to Monro to act at once. Allied troops were to retire on Salonica as quickly as possible and take up defensive positions round the town, and all steps were to be taken at once to defend it. Pallis was to be informed today of allied demands, and the disembarkation of troops was to be hastened to release transports.

Thus they have done their very best to make the job as difficult as possible by making these 2 very difficult operations coincide. No small craft is available from here for Dardanelles, and we are going the way to risk open hostility from Greeks. Dawnay said he had great fight to get general to say in a wire home[5] that Secretary of State must realize that course he was taking might lead to open hostilities by the Greeks, and that troops now here would take at least 10 days to be ready for field owing to method of

5 Orlo provided a footnote for this entry. Wire said (went 1630) "Steps being taken to carry out your instructions and Pallis will be informed accordingly this afternoon. But you must realize that the action you order may precipitate open hostilities with Greeks in areas far from favourable to us. Our troops owing to way in which transports loaded cannot be got ashore complete in a state to take the field in less than at least 10 days. Mahon being told that forces up north must act as retarding force in order to gain time".

loading transports. At the same time Chief refused to send a wire (drafted by Dawnay) saying plainly that Wemyss' resignation was due to Roger Keyes, and that we feared that owing to Keyes' influence we might not get whole-hearted cooperation from Navy. Mitylene not to be used for evacuated troops.

6.30 p.m.: As things stand at present we sail tomorrow. CGS has gone ashore with the written instructions to Mahon on lines of Kitchener's telegram. Chief is rather worried, and Dawnay both over-worked and worried over the way things are being done, dying to get over to help at Dardanelles, and despairing rather of the state of things here.

News of position at front satisfactory. General Gordon arrived and taken command.

The Chief dined in the wardroom this evening and it was made a special and very cheery function, fizz and so on: the old man enjoyed it and it did him good in taking his mind for a while off present worries. The evening was an odd mixture of jollity and seriousness, for the Rear Admiral came at 9 o'clock and Howell with him to talk about things, and a long cipher wire was prepared before dinner which Orr and I did in 2 spells just before and after dinner.

This wire gave the position up to date: i.e., that the demands according to Kitchener's instructions had been made to Pallis, who noted them to forward to Athens but had absolutely no powers. The GOC Greek forces had been informed that our 2 mobile brigades ashore would move to defensive positions north of town and that we counted on him to prevent our action leading to collision with his troops. Pallis had promised to do his best in this respect.

Also said to the Secretary of State that our action must necessitate proclamation of martial law and control of whole district and administration jointly with French for which we presumed authority would be sent.

What happened after dinner, as Dawnay told me was this:—he himself had been much worried all day at the precipitancy of the measures being taken and afraid that if they led to open rupture Kitchener would round on the Chief. So before dinner he represented this urgently to CGS, and persuaded him and Chief that Greeks should be told of our intentions to act in accord with Sarrail, but that for 24 hours we were ready to consider any alternative proposals to secure the same end; this especially refers to the securing that Kara Burnu and Vardar forts should be made innocuous to Navy. However when Admiral and Howell came on board, they were both for informing Greeks they were taking immediate action, sending bluejackets and marines ashore at 6 a.m. and so on, and were obstinate against objections, bringing CGS and Chief with them. Dawnay however, got Cunliffe-Owen into a quiet corner and found that he agreed with his (Dawnay's) view that they were going too fast, and finally Dawnay drafted a short note to the GOC Salonica Army saying that as regards the Vardar and Kara Burnu forts we associated ourselves with General Sarrail's demands but at same time we were ready to consider alternative proposals for 24 hours. He slipped this to Chief and suggested he should sign it, and to his surprise Chief did so at once. Howell went ashore with these instructions and 1½ hours' talk might have been saved. Dawnay's view was that we ought to delay a little to give Kitchener a chance of getting us a wire today in answer to our recent ones. If none came, then we should be in a much better position if things turn out badly.

CGS said Sarrail at his conference with Pallis behaved very fiercely, shook his fist at Pallis, and at the end said "Franchement je ne suis pas amiable".[6]

6 Translation: 'Frankly I am not in agreement'.

As for Dardanelles, two things occurred today:

(1) A wire from Gillman saying Vice Admiral had received wire from Admiralty which made him think Birdwood and Byng had not properly realized results of attack on Narrows and wished to see Birdwood from whom he seemed to have the impression something was being kept back. Gillman had not wished to accentuate this impression by making a strong protest. We wired back at once: "Cabinet's instructions were quite definite. Birdwood is not to discuss military situation with Vice Admiral who must be told that Chief's orders alone govern action of troops".

(2) Wire from GHQ asking decision on: (a) since Navy objected to using Tenedos as much as Mitylene, could troops for whom no accommodation could be found on Imbros or Lemnos be sent direct to Egypt? (b) Could Birdwood send 2 brigades of 29th Division to Helles and if necessary 54th or Mounted Division?

Dawnay on his own answered "yes" to both.

The evening ended up very cheerily with whisky and soda and ping pong. Bandy[7] was in great form. I finally got into bed at 1 a.m.

Saturday 11 December 1915

No developments in the night. Decision taken to sail at 4 p.m. to Imbros and thence to Mudros tomorrow. Wires sent accordingly.

9.45: Fog again today. No sign of the town from the ship.

7 Captain Richard Butler.

Colonel Fairholme and General Wilson came to see General in morning. About 11.20 General Mahon came to report. Reported position at the front satisfactory, and was given written instructions to push on the defence of Salonica.

A batch of wires went off at 4 p.m. the chief of which was embodying Mahon's report and the instructions given him.

We tried to sail at 4, but the fog was so thick that we had to drop anchor at 6, just inside the gate.

Played auction bridge with Orr, Harke, and Paymaster. Won 500 by good cards and bad play.

Sunday 12 December 1915

Sailed at 7.30 a.m. Quiet and peaceful voyage. Reached Imbros 5.30 p.m.

Birdwood, Aspinall and Mitchell came on board at 6 p.m.

Our wires to Proemial: (a) on Salonica situation, (b) Senegalese went 7.30 p.m. and 10.30 p.m. respectively.

Monday 13 December 1915

Sailed from Imbros 2.30 a.m. dropped anchor at Mudros about 7.30 a.m. Came off to *Aragon* 9.30 and 10 a.m. Found enormous mail for myself including 2 sacks of parcels, the Fortnum & Mason things from Lady Pollock[8], my lining to Burberry, and my darling's lovely Xmas present of a chamois leather waistcoat, which put on at once.

Working at War Diary etc. all day.

No particular news. The weather is still calm and the intermediate period is going on, though tonight's weather report announces expectation of high winds. Dawnay beginning to get rather worried about the evacuation. The Navy isn't playing the game. Wemyss egged on by Roger Keyes is doing all he can to get government to order a joint naval and military attack. Tonight he forwarded to

8 Orlo's mother-in-law.

us a copy of a wire he had sent to the Admiralty giving views on the military situation at Helles after evacuation of Suvla and Anzac which he had no right whatever to express. What he wants is a joint attack to capture Achi Baba. Dawnay and the others exceedingly annoyed.

Tuesday 14 December 1915

Busy day. Evacuation during interim period going on steadily. Weather today magnificent, calm and sunny. Chief got up on deck and walked about. Busy at War Diary. Sent brief opinion to WO on Admiral's wire that we had no opinion of it. Later in the day the WO wired it all back to us asking our opinion, the brigadier general shortly replied we had already answered and did we want any more.

Struggling all day to get level with War Diary.

Wednesday 15 December 1915

Robertson seedy in bed, so had to run O(b) with Gammell to help me, rather a harassing day which only quieted down after dinner.

The Chief very cross about brigadier general's answer of yesterday and spent 2 hours of his own and Dawnay's time concocting still stronger objections to Admiral's scheme beginning: "I think it would be better if Admiral confined himself to expressing his opinion on naval matters". Copy sent to Admiral.

Urgent wire from WO saying *certain* information received that Austro-Germans meant to attack us at Salonica in collusion with Greek General Staff and Greek Army would leave slowly so as to hinder our defensive preparations. Orders to send this by safe means to Salonica. In afternoon, Tyrrell went off on destroyer taking copy of this wire and instructions to Mahon, to take with Sarrail all necessary measures.

Nothing else of any very great import, but a great deal of telegraphing on various matters, sending of troops to Egypt, etc.

Thursday 16 December 1915

Quieter day in the office, though a wire of some import went off, summarising an appreciation to be sent off by King's Mesenger tomorrow. Gist of it was that a definite policy was now necessary with regard to forces in the east. The army in Dardanelles worn out and very deficient in transport and artillery; in fact in an inextricable muddle. The Salonica army in no position to undertake a big offensive and cannot be reinforced from Dardanelles. A large number of troops in Egypt without staffs or formations. Whatever is going to be done with this force, no time to be lost in preparing it for its special task, whether in Egypt or Balkans. To re-equip, rest, and train it will take some months. Urgently desirable to take Salonica troops back to Egypt as they are doing no good.

Walked in the afternoon with Bernard, and at tea had preliminary mess meeting with Owen, Deedes, Bernard, Williams and self. Decided to get some stores and furniture. Collecting £5 a head.

Up till 1 a.m. doing War Diary.

Friday 17 December 1915

King's Messenger bag in. Busy morning opening letters. Interesting private letter from CGS to DMO.[9] In answer to a still more interesting one. Following are 4 extracts:

After saying he couldn't see what good Kitchener's visit had done—"Nor do I understand how the government propose to excuse themselves when the truth comes to be

9 Major-General Charles Edward Callwell, Director of Military Operations, War Office.

known for not taking your chief's advice when he recommended retirement from the Dardanelles".

Of Salonica:—"The French rushed us into this tomfoolery". "I despair of getting the government to make up their minds about Dardanelles. They are doing their best to make a difficult position absolutely impossible. We have 4 enemies to contend with—the Boches, the Turks, the Bulgars and HM government—and the last is the most deadly".

A very calm day again, excellent for operations. Stayed on the ship all day, but read *The Times* in afternoon. Commander in Chief's appreciation went off to WO with an appendix showing how hopelessly mixed all the supply and artillery units of the force are at this moment. G. Lloyd turned up again after long absence. Up rather late again trying to get square with War Diary. Tiring day.

Saturday 18 December 1915

Very calm day again. Nothing gone wrong so far. Had a rather less worrying day, though Robertson is still in bed. Walked in the afternoon with Dawnay: he is obviously pretty anxious about this operation, and not sleeping well of nights. He is very much afraid that if this comes off the Helles garrison will never get off at all. Another wire of the Admiral's forwarded to us re: Achi Baba, to which excellent reply was sent. Admiral said that if his view was not accepted he thought Helles ought to be evacuated at once. In this Monro said he absolutely agreed, but had always understood retention of Helles was determined solely because of the Navy.

Also sent a long wire to WO on subject of command of our troops and reinforcements for this force that go to Egypt. Our intention was to appoint Inglefield to command them all. Maxwell wants to organise them all into temporary formations for use "in emergency". WO wired that troops in Egypt were to be under Maxwell's command. Our strong protest pointed out that it would be impossible to carry on, and that we should never get any reinforcements and never know where we were. Suggestion is that Altham should both be GOC Levant Base and IGC. The real necessity is to get rid of Maxwell in which the staff at WO agree: but it can't be done so long as Kitchener is there. Now that French has given way to Haig in France (and became a Viscount and Commander in Chief of Forces in England) the hope seems to be that Robertson will go to the WO and really take Kitchener's head under his arm.

Sunday 19 December 1915

Woke up with great relief to find it had been a calm night. Everything apparently gone splendidly so far. This night's quota, 20,000 in all, reembarked at Suvla and Anzac, and 12 guns at Suvla. Turks seem to have twigged to nothing at all. Today and tonight are the anxious times. If all goes well again, we shall really breathe freely tomorrow.

Total evacuations intermediate stage were:

Suvla: 13,765 and 32 guns
Anzac: 11,768 and 59 guns
Total: 25,533 and 91 guns

Important wire from WO on policy at Salonica, answering our wire based on summary of situation. (1) No prospect of big offensive in Macedonia and realized that impossible to reinforce from Dardanelles. If more troops and heavy guns needed Salonica they must come from France. Policy to hold on to Salonica for the present, but may withdraw later if French can be persuaded. (2) It is hoped to make defence of Egypt very active. Troops being sent there from France and England.

The final night of evacuation of course began at dark, but it was almost impossible to get up much excitement because we were so far away and all reports were so uniformly satisfactory. There were a good many short reports during the night, but the gist of all was that on 20 December… [continued on next day]

Monday 20 December 1915

…all of our troops both at Anzac and Suvla had got off without the Turks discovering it. All guns but 12, of which only 5 of any import, all wounded. Some stores and 50 mule carts left at Anzac. Some big mines exploding under Turks' positions after we had left caused them casualties and they opened heavy rifle fire which lasted until 7.30. They also shelled our positions (which were empty) heavily. At 12.15 they shelled the front line at Anzac, and it was not till the end of the day that they realised the situation and occupied our positions. This ends a really great feat of organization, helped by wonderful weather. I would like to have heard the language of the Germans when they found out what a chance they had missed. The *Aragon* was full of generals etc. all day who had come off. It is, of course, a sad reflection how many lives were spent and gallant deeds performed fruitlessly at Suvla and Anzac, but one cannot help being tremendously glad they are abandoned. The force can now be rested and refitted and be made ready to strike somewhere really useful. We propose to send Anzac to Egypt as well, but the whole question of the command in Egypt is troublesome.

Another wire sent home today advocating abandonment of Helles as soon as possible, to save expense and transport, and use the force better elsewhere.

The 29th Division have now gone to Helles to take over French line, which they are leaving. They will be relieved as soon as they can, but 42nd Division will be first to be relieved. Proposal to reorganise 8th Corps into 11th, 13th, and Composite division of RND, 42nd and 52nd.

Tuesday 21 December 1915

Nothing much to enter. Gammell sick and Robertson still away, so forced to remain in office all day. Congratulatory telegram from the King, printed with others in a special order of the day. Pretty busy, and no time to read or write letters.

Wednesday 22 December 1915

Calm fine day. Same conditions for myself, Gammell and Robertson still being away. *But* a great surprise in store for us all in two telegrams that came this morning, which changes all our plans and makes it certain we shall not go to Castro. Two telegrams attached to this page [see below]. Commander in Chief I believe was very annoyed, and Lynden Bell personally furious. A very urgent message was at once sent in Monro's name asking as a personal favour that Lynden Bell and Campbell be allowed to return to France with him. The move of course of this command to Egypt is an excellent one, though Archibald Murray may not be much of a general. He was CGS to French, then sent home, and has lately been CIGS. The obvious thing seems to be that Sir William Robertson has gone to the WO and is generally taking charge. The changed tone of WO telegrams lately made me suspect as much. The Kitchener note was quite absent from them. So now we are off to Alexandria, and will live a town life again. It will be very odd to be spacious again and civilised: rather like the WO in a foreign country. There will be a tremendous lot for O(b) to do: switching off on to a wholly new set of subjects. Rather a pity I have so much warm clothing and stores.

Nothing else much up to 7 p.m. Nor for the rest of the day. News that V Beach had been rather heavily shelled with 6″.

From WO Deciphered 1600/21
For Gen Monro Recd 0730/22
11254 cipher

The evacuation of Suvla and Anzac and the withdrawal on Salonika having been successfully accomplished, a reorganization of the command in the Mediterranean appears to be advisable.

As long as Cape Helles is held Birdwood will remain in command of the Dardanelles force, and now that Salonika is clearly defined as a defensive operation the command will remain with Mahon or such successor as may be appointed.

In these circumstances the task for which you were specially selected having been successfully carried out, the Government fully recognizing the value of the services you have rendered wish you to resume your work as an army commander in France. Haig has taken over command from Sir J. French and you have been nominated to command the 1st Army.

The defence of Egypt requires the reorganization of the commands there. Maxwell is fully occupied with the internal military affairs of the country, and it is necessary to appoint a general in complete control of the defences of the Canal and in command of troops detailed for that line.

General Sir Archibald Murray has been appointed to take over this duty and he will also supervise Helles and Salonika with HQ in Egypt.

From Proemial	Deciphered 1725/21
For General Monro	Recd 0730/22
11260 cipher	

Our 11254 cipher of today.

You will proceed to France with your personal staff and on your departure will direct the HQ staff of the Mediterranean Command to proceed to Alexandria to await Murray's arrival. Murray probably leaves England about Dec 28.

The excellent thing about today's news is, of course, the fact that it takes away troops from a useless sphere and gives them a chance of resting, reorganizing, filling up and being trained into a really first-class fighting machine which will eventually kill Boches. Egypt, the training ground, will be simply stiff with soldiers and in that way rather tiresome. The idea of most savants is that by next April we shall all be in France, any invasion of Egypt being either over or impossible by that time. It is interesting to note the predictions expressed earlier in this diary that this move would be forced on the authorities.

As to Salonica, Dawnay thinks that there will be no fighting there, and that once this is realised at home the troops there will come away too. But it doesn't seem certain that the Bulgars won't come on; and Sarrail for personal reasons wishes to stay. But the Germans have lost their chance now. Our defensive line is already very strong and could only be carried with huge loss. In another fortnight it will be impregnable. There are 5 British divisions there: 12th Corps, 22nd, 26th, 28th Divisions. 27th and 10th, 16th Corps under General Mahon. Three French divisions under General Sarrail. They urgently need transport, which is held up in France by want of shipping, as 2 Indian divisions and Cavalry Corps are being shifted to Mesopotamia, and other troops to Egypt. It is interesting to hear that, whereas at first the British were very unpopular with the Greeks and the French could do no wrong, now the Greeks are fed up with Sarrail, who has a very uncertain temper and is a damned liar, and are beginning to feed out of our hands.

Thursday 23 December 1915

The CGS delighted. Kitchener wires that as a special case, Monro may take him and Walter Campbell back with him. So now we have no masters. Gather we shall all go down on Tuesday, and wire sent to ask Murray where he wants his HQ. No other wires of much import. Salonica wires that private and personal message from King of Greece says Bulgars will advance.

Gammell and Robertson still away.

Another consideration regarding yesterday's decision is that Maxwell is at last put in his right place. He remains responsible for the internal defence only. The Levant Base will be commanded solely by General Altham, on whom the forces will demand direct, he being only under WO control. So all the fuss about the command of MedForce reinforcements, etc. is settled.

Nothing very exciting rest of day. Spent time in writing letters, reorganising files, etc.

Further excitement, however, in the evening as a wire came from Kitchener saying "Suspend action on my 11308". i.e., the wire saying CGS and QMG could go to France.

Birdwood was finally wired for to come here tomorrow to take over, as Chief and co. were sailing in *Euryalis* on Saturday to Marseilles. Birdwood and 2 of his personal staff were to come down to Egypt with GHQ and hand over to Murray.

Friday 24 December 1915

All arrangements again cancelled. WO wires that Monro is to remain in command till Murray arrives and hand over to him personally, disposing of GHQ as he thinks best. This of course is the proper course, but why couldn't the WO think of it before? So now Birdwood is put off, and we sail all together (probably) next week, unless Murray is to come up here. Another wire answering the query about location of GHQ, said Murray must go first to see Maxwell in Cairo, and hoped to have HQ in neighbourhood of Ismailia, but could not say before he got there.

News message today reports Kiggell is CGS to Douglas Haig in France.

Nothing of any very great import during rest of morning and afternoon. In the evening at dinner time another wire, rather bomb-shell-like in nature turned up signed Chief WO, a signature which is very significant.

Clear the line

From Chief W.O. Deciphered 1620/24
To Chief Medforce Recd 2003/24
11399 cipher

Your CM80 of Dec. 15th

You are authorised to make all preparations necessary for the rapid evacuation of position at Cape Helles subject to condition that no steps are taken which will prejudice our power to remain there is so decided.

To discuss what this portends is not necessary, and it throws some light on the rapid change of orders regarding our departure. Birdwood was at once apprised and told to take measures. This naturally caused a bit of excitement for the 3rd night in succession.

At 11.30 p.m. made punch for a select company with brandy and rum sent by Alice. A most excellent and much appreciated brew. Present: General Marshall, General Gillman, Dawnay, Bernard, Herbert Scott, Smith, Hough and self.

General Sir Charles Monro and Lieutenant-General Birdwood discussing evacuation of Helles on board HMS *Cornwallis*, 25 December 1915 (O.C. Williams, IWM).

Saturday 25 December 1915

Christmas Day and perfect weather. Hope shall never spend another in such circumstances. Code telegram from WO says all letters and telegrams dealing with military operations to be addressed CIGS and not Secretary WO. Significant of new regime at home. Also telegram from Chief WO that all evacuated troops were to go to Egypt as soon as possible, where their organisation to be taken in hand as matter of extreme urgency for protection of eastern frontier. Photo taken of Chief and GS. Hostile aeroplane dropped a few small bombs in sea around the ship.

Major-General Lynden-Bell (left) walks with his chief
General Monro (O.C. Williams, IWM).

Lovely afternoon. Walked on shore with General Campbell. Dawnay rather worried all day over several things:

(1) Appreciation of situation in Egypt. WO evidently getting very anxious and want things hastened. Byng to go down at once to reorganise, also Godley and the BGRA.

(2) Stavros move of the Salonica army.

(3) Sudden decision for GHQ to embark on *Ascanius* tomorrow to sail early Monday morning. Commander in Chief, CGS, etc., Dawnay and I go down in *Cornwallis* on Tuesday. All arriving 30th.

Christmas dinner more or less cheerful. Wire came late last night saying WO were sending 46th Division to Egypt and not Indian Cavalry Corps.

Also amusing wire from Maxwell answering our intimation of arrival to await Murray. "This is 1st intimation of Murray's coming. Have arranged HQ Canal Defences at Zagazig." Poor man if he thinks we are only HQ Canal defences he is much mistaken.

Last of all came wire from Secretary of State saying that after further careful consideration couldn't allow Lyndell Bell and Campbell to leave MedForce.

Sunday 26 December 1915

CGS on hearing above sweated with rage. But it is a jolly good thing for us even if he only stays a short time. Maxwell was stiffly wired to, giving extracts from WO instructions to us. A good deal of flurry and scurry owing to need for finishing things off. Also Birdwood is fighting so hard to keep 29th Division that he has not obeyed our orders to inform GOC 29th Division that he is going to Egypt. We wired to him to do so, and if 42nd Division was too weak to strengthen by one brigade, 11th or 13th.

Nothing else particular. The advance party of GHQ embarked on the *Ascanius* during the afternoon, leaving Dawnay and me behind, and we had a lot of work to do one way and another, for these sudden moves and interregna usually mean doing a lot of hearty and important work with a much reduced staff. Finally got to bed very tired and slept rather restlessly.

Monday 27 December 1915

Perfectly heavenly day. One seaplane came over at 2.30 p.m. and dropped a bomb somewhere. A few ships opened fire.

General Birdwood came at 12 and had a long talk with Commander in Chief which it is to be hoped put things as straight regarding his command as we could put them pending more definite decision from WO. At present his position is a bit ridiculous, for he really only commands 8th Corps which has its corps commander. He is also fighting like the devil to keep the 29th Division for a bit and relieve 42nd Division at once, which is reported in a very bad state and its GOC, Douglas, badly in need of rest. The only decision arrived at was that if we stay at Helles the 29th Division comes away; if, on the other hand, orders come to withdraw the 87th Brigade should come away last.

Rather quieter day on the whole, our wires of yesterday having choked off cipher telegrams almost entirely; but Dawnay cumbered with much saving.

In the evening the Commander,[10] PMO and Gregory of the *Chatham* came to dine: we presented them with the joint silver salver with all our signatures on it. Quite a handsome piece of plate.

Today to my great surprise Vitale turned up again, looking much better, though still not particularly well. He has since become a major. Hope he will eventually come down to Egypt. Says things in Italy are going splendidly.

Tuesday 28 December 1915

A good many wires came in the morning including one from Chief to say that we were not to leave till important telegram arrived. Also wire saying that Maxwell had been instructed that he would command all troops in Egypt till arrival of Murray, and in consultation with Monro would see about reorganisation. Sent home another message strongly pressing evacuation of Helles to be decided on. King's Messenger arrived but no letter from Alice.

All morning and afternoon clearing off the work: very busy time which left me fagged out. Finally the Chief and co. went on board *Cornwallis* at 4.30, Dawnay, General

10 Commander Raymond Fitzmaurice, RN. Commanding Officer, HMS *Chatham*.

Campbell and I staying behind. At 5.20 the expected wire came, as follows:—

"From Chief, WO to Chief, MedForce. The government has decided that the position at Cape Helles may now be evacuated. The withdrawal should be carried out as soon as practicable but at your complete discretion". This was addressed to us and repeated to Birdwood.

So this heads the final chapter of the Dardanelles tragedy, and may it not prove, as I fear it will, a bloody one.

Dawnay and I couldn't get off to the *Cornwallis* before 7. When we did it was decided at once not to leave for another 24 hours and to send for Birdwood and inform Vice Admiral at once.

Curiously, as I was writing to Marquis this afternoon I got a letter from Major Taylor, his CO telling me that Marquis had been wounded on the 24th and put on a hospital ship on 26th; deep flesh wound left arm, slight wound in back, and fragments in both legs. No complications. I wired in code to Reynolds to inform his people. So he is well out of it, though as it turns out a day or two more and he might have got off unwounded. But then he wouldn't have got home, as I expect he will.

Usual watch dinner in wardroom and to bed early, very tired. Dawnay, Bridges, 2 ADCs and I are sleeping in forward cabin in iron cots as put up for wounded. Quite all right.

Wednesday 29 December 1915

At 11 a.m. Birdwood and Aspinall arrived to confer with Commander in Chief as to final arrangements. QMG and DIGC also there. First day of preliminary stage to be tomorrow. It was decided to remain at Mudros to see Vice Admiral on 31st and then make for Alexandria. In evening played for Dell, assistant Pay, to sing. Quite nice.

Thursday 30 December 1915

A good many wires, etc. in the morning about nothing particularly exciting, but it kept us busy. War Diary in afternoon. Lovely sunny afternoon, splendid sunset. Walked a good deal up and down with Bridges.

Friday 31 December 1915

Vice Admiral turned up with suite, followed by Aspinall and Birdie and NA.[11] Final conference about 12.15 p.m. Then sent wires announcing our departure at daylight tomorrow. In afternoon, which was sunny and really warm walked with Gammell among camps at Mudros West. Heaven send it be the last time I set foot on Lemnos Island! After tea auction bridge with Padre, Courage and another. Won 2 rubbers. After dinner poker, suggested by the Padre, who wears ordinary lounge suit and naval cap with cross instead of anchor. He played a lion's game at penny ante and 1/– rise. Sat up to drink a glass of rum punch and hear 16 bells rung to see new year in. Evening a little spoiled because captain stopped the piano when general went to bed. As 16 bells were rung there was a tremendous booming of steam whistles all over the harbour, and Very's lights going up on shore. So to bed.

Saturday 1 January 1916

Sailed about 8 a.m. coldish north-easterly breeze blowing. Wire before we left from Gillman at Alexandria to say that Maxwell had no definite orders from WO question of command not settled, and could not make decision as to HQ till we arrived at Alexandria. Calm voyage. Auction bridge before dinner again won rubber.

11 Captain Mitchell, RN.

Sunday 2 January 1916

Uneventful day. Some rain. Wire from Birdwood to say all going well and Davies full of confidence. Drank new commanders' health in fizz in wardroom.

Monday 3 January 1916

Arrived Alexandria 8 a.m. Gillman came on board. No news but that King's Messenger had gone down in Persia but Bigham was saved. He would be.

General, CGS, Campbell, ADCs, Scott and Bridges going up to Cairo straight, intending to sleep one night. General wouldn't go till he had copies of certain telegrams for his despatch, also Birdwood's despatch. Finally he had to go without them and when all the copying was done I dashed after him, found his train had left, borrowed a motor and went to Sidi Gaber station where met their surprised view when they arrived. Then back to *Majestic* where got a room with Gammell. Found nobody had any work to do but all well including Robertson. Lunched excellently and went out later with Gammell, who enjoyed himself immensely. We bought several things, had hair cut and shampooed, then had tea at Baudrot's—cakes and strawberries and cream, finally dined very well at Mohammed Ali Club with Gammell with first-class lot of Chateau Larose '78 (only 7/–). Played pills later. Saw Montagu there, and 2 MPs, Hicks and Mason. On getting back to hotel after 11 heard we were all to go Cairo tomorrow with office. Such are the sudden changes of this campaign: nothing ever happening as expected.

Tuesday 4 January 1916

Some rush and scurry and worry and off on a wet morning in 12 train to Cairo. Arrived at 3.30 more worry and scurry. All officers at Shepheard's, Servants Kasr-el-

Nil barracks. Servants and kit got all separated, and some servants didn't find their home in the barracks till 9.30 p.m. Meanwhile heard we were to have offices in the old Army HQ of Egypt, Maxwell and co. having moved to the Savoy. No work to do. Walked with Robertson and Bernard, and bought gorgeous red hat. Excellent dinner, some talk and so to bed. Cairo swarming with seemingly idle officers, and too many females. As unlike war as anything you could imagine.

NB: My appointment appeared in General Register Office for December 27 no. 66 appointments. "Capt. OCW cipher officer at GHQ to be GSO3 GHQ to complete establishment".

Wednesday 5 January 1916

The Chief and co. were to have left for Alexandria by night train to meet Murray on arrival, but not knowing when Murray was coming they put this off. Also a sharp wire sent home showing Chief's indignation at being refused a battleship to take him Marseilles.

Spent all morning at Headquarters—bare building, no furniture, telephones, etc. Few telegrams came. Dawnay and others convinced that GHQ MedForce is now a washout. Maxwell has a complete staff who know their ground and it is obvious they don't want us. Nobody wants us and we have no work to do, yet a new commander is about to arrive. The whole position is impossible and ridiculous. Salonica runs itself and Maxwell runs Egypt, and GHQ MedForce seems dying in rather undignified convulsions. It was CGS' doing we were all bumped down here to give ourselves some *locus standi*[12] when Murray arrives, as CGS went out to Zagazig and flatly refused to set up GHQ there.

12 Translation: 'place of standing'.

At office till 3.30 with Hough doing odds and ends then with him to the bazaars and tea at Groppi's.

Once more to office before dinner.

Dawnay rather pessimistic about present situation, and we all agree that the present state of Cairo and Egypt is a scandal. The place simply swarms with staffs, who are quite unnecessary, and the assembly of females at Shepheard's is appalling. Hosts of young (and old) idlers turn up and lounge there at tea and dinner time and when one considers that war is on the whole thing is disgusting. As Dawnay said, he wears his brassard to show he has no connection with the army in Egypt.

Murray arrives at Port Said on the 8th, and we hope he has some instructions. Most of us are convinced that either Maxwell's staff or ours must go. Apparently WO so annoyed with Maxwell for not beginning defences of Egypt earlier that they have flatly decided he is not command the defence force; on the other hand Kitchener won't consent to his being pushed out altogether *as he ought to be*. So some *modus vivendi*[13] has got to be arrived at.

The Admiralty refuse to send old Monro to Marseilles in a man-of-war, though he rather indignantly demanded it.

Thursday 6 January 1916

A few wires of no very great import. Dardanelles wire evacuation going on satisfactorily but high wind on evening of 4th made work impossible. 14,500 evacuated, all French infantry and all but 25 guns. Night of 9/10 provisionally fixed as final night.

Spent most of day till 6.30 p.m. at office with usual intervals; we are not so very uncomfortable in our very bare quarters, as chairs and tables are plentiful enough.

13 Translation: 'mode of living' (i.e. they needed an arrangement that worked for both parties).

Suffering from a rather tiresome relaxed throat. Bridges painted it with nitrate of silver after dinner.

No particular developments, except that a wire came from London to Altham saying that he would be IGC under Murray when he arrived. This is thought to be symptomatic of defeat for Maxwell, for if Altham *is* our IGC he comes right out of Maxwell's command and the institution called Levbase dies.

Sub-chief and DAS gone off to pay a hurried visit to Canal Defences before Murray arrives. This delay in Murray's arrival has certainly given us a little time in which to get together and start some kind of work. O(a) are hard at it over the artillery question and maps; and today 'I' arrived in Alexandria. CGS and Dawnay dined at our table tonight: CGS stood champagne. Wire from Alice saying "all well" which very comforting seeing I have had no news of her for over 3 weeks.

Friday 7 January 1916

Throat still pretty sore. Office as usual. Telephone was up, and started arrangements by which Robertson and I make our own tea. No particular news. Dardanelles Army reports calm weather and all going well. Enemy shell busily and hostile aeroplanes active. They bombed AHQ at Imbros yesterday and in neighbouring mule camp 26 men and 130 mules killed or wounded.

Heard from Montagu. Hospital Malta telegraph about Marquis: "Multiple wounds. Condition quite satisfactory".

Robertson says that in Monro's recommendations I am down for Military Cross. This I find hard to believe and shall think no more about it.

Weather very chilly again today and chamois leather waistcoat very comforting.

A wire was sent today to Chief WO saying that we are inclined to believe in Salonica's view that no hostile attack was contemplated and again urging the advisability of withdrawing our troops before they became a serious drain on our resources.

Saturday 8 January 1916

Wire from London Wemyss appointed to Naval Command as regards Canal. Wire from Dardanelles Army HQ, owing improvement of weather decided to advance final period by 24 hours. Turks shelled line heavily yesterday: bombardment heaviest yet experienced on peninsula and considerable damage to parapets and communication trenches. Remaining guns retaliated and Navy gave valuable support on left flank. RND heavily shelled from Asia. Turks attacked Fusilier Bluff but easily repulsed by 39th Brigade. Normal programme proceeding.

Salonica wire about aircraft raid by 5 aeroplanes. Casualties so far reported 5 killed and 13 wounded. Further wire said that Turks attacking 13th Division suffered heavily and that aeroplane reports that naval fire on left flank very accurate and did much damage. *Edgar* fired 1000 rounds and *Wolverine* all she had.

Saturday night dance at the hotel. Horrid sight especially this being last night of evacuation of Cape Helles. Spent an hour in my room struggling with primer of Arabic.

CGS showed me today that he had recommended me for Military Cross and had written opposite my name:—"An officer of rare attainments. Though not a soldier before the war, he took over the duties of GSO at a time of great stress with conspicuous success". It is this recommendation that really gratifies me whatever be its result.

Sunday 9 January 1916

Hurrah! Great news from Helles. "Evacuation completed 4 a.m. No French casualties. One British wounded. All howitzers evacuated and guns with exception of 1 6″ gun and 10 obsolescent 15 pounder guns and 6 heavy and practically worn out French guns. All guns left were blown up before withdrawal".

So ends more brightly the doleful chapter of the Dardanelles expedition. The whole force is now free to strike elsewhere, and the Germans should be correspondingly depressed. It is also pleasing that all is done before Murray arrives, which he does at 1.30 today, so that old Monro goes home with complete success in his pocket.

Now the chief point of interest is the reorganisation of the force in Egypt. All of yesterday Dawnay and co. were elaborating a new scheme of command, the gist of which was as follows:—

There will be under Commander in Chief, a GOC internal defences and military governor, a GOC Western Force, a GOC Eastern Force of Egypt, IGC. The military government to be the channel of communication with government of Egypt. The IGC to approach government of Egypt through him. IGC to be at Alexandria, and command of Eastern force and communications Cairo–Ismailia, Ismailia–Port Said–Suez to be directly under GHQ. Small reinforcement camp at Cairo, but Altham to be kept out of Cairo. Byng to be military governor and GOC internal defences with small staff. Eastern force 3 corps, and Byng to do duties of Commander, lines of communication defences. This of course disposes of Maxwell altogether who, it is rumoured has resigned. But it *may* all be beating the air if he hasn't and if he is left with equal powers to Murray.

Further wires regarding the final evacuation of Helles are attached:

PRIORITY SECRET
FROM: GENERAL BIRDWOOD
TO: GHQ
D.O. 819 9/1/16

Naval difficulties of embarkation last night greatly increased by weather though at sunset the sky was cloudless and meteorologist confident of little increase in southerly winds. The weather suddenly grew worse after 2000 and at 2300 wind had increased to 35 MPH. From midnight onwards only just possible to use piers and lighters and impossible to carry out programme of embarking troops in destroyers along the side of sunken ships at 'W' Beach owing to connecting pier being washed away. Embarkation at Gully Beach became impossible. One lighter went ashore there and remainder of troops had to be marched to 'W' Beach for embarkation. In spite of these difficulties programme at 'W' and 'V' was completed by 0230, and by 0400 above mentioned troops from Gully Beach and all beach parties had been safely embarked. Total numbers evacuated between 8pm and 4am were 17,000 men and 33 guns. A hostile submarine was reported off Cape Helles about 2100 and about midnight HMS Prince George after embarking 2000 men reported she had been hit by a torpedo, which did not explode. Total numbers evacuated since December 28th are—exclusive of French—38,100 men, 121 guns, 3,100 animals. French 4,000 men and 72 guns. French embarkation carried out by their own navy. French also greatly assisted by us embarking some of our animals. General Brulard left peninsula on January 2nd with his infantry leaving remainder of French artillery under order of GOC 8th Corps, thus simplifying difficulties of command. I am especially indebted to him for all his loyal cooperation throughout the withdrawal which has greatly facilitated my task. If permitted I should like to recommend to His Excellency, as a special case, he might be granted a KCB.

Murray arrived today but did not take over formal command today. We gather that though he has temporary rank of general, he has a delimited territorial sphere of command.

Dined very pleasantly at the Turf Club with Robertson. Excellent port.

Monday 10 January 1916

Sir A. Murray, whom I have not yet seen, took over command. His instructions are that he commands all formed units in Egypt and supervises Salonica force, but that his command is roughly limited by a line drawn from north to south 5 miles west of Canal. Maxwell responsible for internal defence of Nile Delta and western frontier and commands depots: IGC and lines of communication to eastern front under Murray. So there will be a lot of adjustment to do between the 2 staffs. The Eastern Force consists of 3 corps:

15th Corps—31st, 11th, 13th Divisions under General Horne

ANZAC—under Birdwood

9th Corps—46th, 29th, 10th Indian Divisions under Byng

That leaves 4 Territorial Divisions, and 2nd Mounted Division and South African Infantry Brigade not allotted to Corps.

Note from CIGS says that our force constitutes strategic reserve of Empire, and will supply troops if needed for Mesopotamia, India or France. France decided to be the main theatre of war for England. Our ultimate destination therefore must be France. Sarrail is given supreme command at Salonica. Maxwell's staff and Dardanelles Army staff will be somewhat broken up. Some of Dardanelles Army staff go to 15th Corps, Aspinall is GSO1 of 46th Division. GHQ goes Ismailia.

Distracting day. In evening dined with Throckmorton whom I saw last night. He looking very fit and brown, with 1st Mounted Brigade. Had been at Suvla but escaped with nothing worse than a bomb wound in neck from accident at a bombing class.

Here I shall close this volume of my diary which ends on a note of great hope for the future. Asquith has spoken warmly of our achievement in the House, saying that generals, etc. would be recommended for special recognition. Very warm wires from the King and Kitchener.

* * *

Postscript, from Orlo's diary

Conversation with Dawnay and Pollen in Shepheard's Hotel, 16 January 1916, elicited following facts regarding Sir Ian Hamilton's recall and other matters of interest.

There is no doubt that Ian Hamilton, rightly as he was recalled, has a legitimate grievance at the way he was treated. Had the authorities told him straight out that they wanted a change in the interests of the nation, and given him some recognition for the landing, he would have been justly treated. As it was the Cabinet behaved badly to him.

In the first place, as Lansdowne told Pollen, and as Kitchener told Ian H. there was division in the Cabinet,

After Gallipoli, Orlo transferred to the Operations Section of GHQ, Egyptian Expeditionary Force. Here he is at Ismailia, 1916 (Family collection).

and to some extent the recall was decided on to bring about unity. L. George, McKenna and Bonar Law and Carson had made up their minds that I.H. must go. Also the 3 latter were arch anti-Dardanelles, and Kitchener was very anxious to keep them in the Cabinet.

Dawnay, when he was at home, gathered this impression from talking to L. G., B. Law and Carson. He said to the DMO at the time that he thought certain members of the government, without any definite charges to bring forward, felt there ought to be a change of bowling. The DMO asked Dawnay if he thought so too. Dawnay said personally he did.

While Dawnay was in London two things happened:—

A. The Australian Press correspondent Murdoch sent in a letter to (I think) Lloyd George ... giving a very exaggerated account of the bad state of things on the peninsula. This was printed and sent round to all members of CID. Dawnay saw a proof and annotated it pointing out the facts. Kitchener prevented a copy from being sent by Dawnay to I.H. (though the DMO sent one a week later). This in itself was a dirty trick. Further, as Lansdowne told Pollen, no decent people took this letter of Murdoch's for more than it was worth, but certain politicians, i.e. L.G., B. Law, Carson, though knowing its true value, used it to strengthen their brief for the recall of I.H. which it undoubtedly did. When Pollen got home a complete answer was circulated by I.H. to all members of CID.

B. Stopford, on his return, sent in a report to the WO of Suvla landing. Kitchener, without telling I.H. at all, had a kind of private Court of Inquiry on it, which actually produced a finding on this *ex parte* statement without hearing I.H. I.H. only saw this report of Stopford's some time after he got home, when WO sent it for his remarks.

Apropos of Stopford, Pollen produced an instance of K's dirty work. When I.H. returned he went to see various Cabinet ministers, among others L. George: latter said to him at once: "I was one of the strongest in favour of your recall, for this reason—it seemed to me that we could have no further confidence in your judgement when you asked for a man like Stopford to command". Whereupon I.H. was able to show that he repeatedly asked for young and active men, but on K's refusal the choice only lay between Ewart and Stopford, so latter chosen because a few inches less round chest. L. George on hearing this threw down his papers and said: "Well, you say we politicians play dirty tricks. We do! Kitchener was at that meeting all the time and never told us of your telegrams".

They also found when they got home that Hankey, when he was at Imbros, corresponded with Asquith through Admiral behind I.H.'s back.

Finally, when I.H. had got his despatch done K. tried to get him to alter a passage in which he drew attention to the fact that though he got his fresh troops he never got drafts to make up his 45,000 shortness of original units. But on A. Murray's advice I.H. refused, as it was perfectly true and the memo from AG's Dept. on which K's request was based actually said, after giving details of drafts allocated for reinforcements, that though these did not actually sail I.H. had 53rd and 54th Divisions instead of drafts.

Delay about evacuation of Peninsula

[Archibald] Murray decided in favour of it wholesale; while K was away he as CIGS insisted on attending meetings of War Council to give military advice. It was this which began the state of affairs which ended in K's practical fall from power.

Murray convinced the inner Cabinet with aid of Monro's reports etc. Curzon, however, before the meeting of whole Cabinet prepared with Pollen's help a counter paper so good that the reversal of the decision was carried, there was all that bother about getting 5 divisions from Salonica, consulting Byng etc., and 3 weeks delay which might well have ruined all.

As it was the Cabinet predicted their own certain fall if they lost any quantity of men in the withdrawal.

* * *

Annex 1

Staff Duties

By Orlo Williams[1]

The duties of a General Staff
Are probably not more than half
Distinct to any lay mind,
But understanding *quantum stuff*
Is yours if you ascribe enough
Importance to O(a), mind

Chorus

In every martial operation
Devised against a hostile nation
The work of O(a)
Is what carries the day
(Or so I gather from conversation).

Intelligence all comes from 'I'
Who on the enemy do spy
And know whatever *they* do
But anyone can merely *know*
The chief thing is to strike the blow
And that of course O(a) do.

1 This 'ditty' was quoted in Nelson Jonnes' transcription of Orlo's diary.

Chorus repeated

O(b), if they are any use,
    Coordinate what 'a' produce
And simply work like blazes.
    But work like that is simply rot
And most emphatically not
    The noble task O(a)'s is.

Chorus repeat

And if you think that anyone
    Has any finger in the fun
But O(a), then 'I' *may* say
    That C in C and CGS
Do little else but murmur, "Yes",
    And smile at what O(a) say.

Annex 2

The PNTO and the PMLO

By Orlo Williams

Round Tekke Burnu slowly steamed
A British Man-of-War
The guns were slowly booming from
The forts of Sedd-el-Bahr.
With no lights but the fitful gleam
Of searchlights from afar.

The PNTO and the PMLO
Were gazing at the strand,
"Do you suppose," the PNTO said
"That we shall ever land?"
The PMLO said nothing; but
He coughed behind his hand.

"If seven tugs with seven tows
Started at dead of night,"
The PMLO said "I wonder if
They'd land enough to fight."
The PNTO thought abstractedly
And simply said, "They might."

"And will they," said the PMLO,
"Land on the proper beach,
This one on X, that one on Z,
And so on each to each?"
The PNTO held his finger up
Like one about to preach.

"We've thrashed it out with wrinkled brows
And tears," the PNTO said,
"And none will land on W
That ought to land on Z."
The PMLO politely smiled,
The smile of the well-bred.

"At dawn of break," the PNTO said,
"Our ships will open fire,
The gallant troops will then advance
As far as they desire."
The PMLO was indistinct;
I think he muttered "Wire!"

"And what is wire!" the PNTO cried,
"Against a naval shell?
One of us goes there every day
And shoots away like hell."
"And do you," said the PMLO
"Not leave your card as well?"

But when the fateful morning came,
Whose, how, or why, or when,
Are matters little suited for
A merely ribald pen.
The PNTO and PMLO
Both quitted them like men.

In after years, the text book said
To budding G.S.O.'s,
"This is the Golden Rule for both
PNTO's and PMLO's;
'Its no good counting up your hands,
Before you count your tows.'"

Annex 3

"O"

Personalities of the 'O' Section, General Staff

By Orlo Williams [2]

What one notices in 'O'
    Is how people come and go.
Colonel Williams liked the trenches
    Better than the office benches.
Major Grant, too, left O(b)
    For the Royal Artillery.
Baikie, Colonel when he started,
    As a brigadier departed.

Last to leave was Colonel Fuller
    Who would never do his Muller,
Yet one would have praised his figure
    Had his tunic, drill, been bigger.
The most stormy office weathers
    Never ruffled Fuller's feathers.
Even to a bloody fool
    He was affable and cool.

Lion-hearted Aspinall
    Has one grievance, that is all.
He's the only man of note
    K of K will not promote.

2 This 'ditty' was quoted in Nelson Jonnes' transcription of Orlo's diary.

Still, if he's content to wait
        Till his elders meet their fate,
When a *very* ancient stager
        He'll be made a pukka major.

No one could assert of Dawnay
        That his intellect was *borne;*
Poet, critic, strategist,
        Radico-Imperialist,
Pioneer of high finance
        With the Guardsman's brilliance,
He's our perfect specimen
        Of the Soldier-Citizen.

Powell is our Sunny Jim.
        No one could help liking him;
His capacious jovial smile
        Radiates about a mile.
Once to Bolton's Tweedledee
        Tweedledum he played with glee.
Now that Tweedledee is glum
        Thou art lonely, Tweedledum.

Bolton sits about the room
        In an attitude of gloom.
Since he went upon the beach
        He has lost the power of speech;
He was such a cheery lad.
        Why is Bessy now so sad?
Come let's fill the loving cup,
        Bessie, kiss, and make it up.

I should guess that Valentine
        Hasn't mastered Ballantyne;

Possibly when he is twenty
He might just begin on Henty.
Though I shouldn't wonder if
Even that were rather stiff.
Lying very late abed
Is not good for such a head.

(Written some weeks later)

Since this "series at known ranges"
'O' has undergone some changes.
E.g. we have lost our Sailor
And received instead a Taylor.
Taylor is a kindly man
Who does everything he can,
And though that amounts to nil
Taylor does that nil with skill.

Ruthven, since these lines were written
Came and left again for Britain
With one bullet in his thigh
And another in his… Fie!
Then there's Anstey who disdains
Those who hide from aeroplanes.
Bayard, I should really laugh
If you got a thorough straf.

Bessie's gone and Bubblejee
Raucously directs O(b).
Gloating on his precious dak
Like a rather greedy hawk.
How I pity Barttelot,
He must suffer quite a lot.
I could murder Bubblejee
When he croaks for "A… Ahrderly"

Annex 4

MF-999

By Orlo Williams[3]

From: Chief, Medforce.
To: Proemial. October, 1915

Your ninety one sixteen M.O. four five two
Was carefully noted by us.
The following is my deliberate view.
In fact I envisage it thus:—
In case of a very much stronger attack
With German munitions of war,
Having neither munitions nor men to hit back
We'll just carry on as we are.

Each gun will as heretofore proudly let drive
One round — two on Sundays — a day,
And should any ship with munitions arrive,
Why P.N.T.O. will send her away.
The enemy, having 10,000 per gun,
Will counterbat gaily with crumps,
And we shall have drawn all his rounds with our one —
Our singleton drawing the trumps.

The beaches by day will be getting too warm
For landing so much as one tin,
But that after all will not do us much harm,
For the days are now fast drawing in.
By night we can land bully beef tins in tiers,
Men and stores, ammunition and flour,

3 This 'ditty' was quoted in Nelson Jonnes' transcription of Orlo's diary.

And if a bad storm smash the pumps and the piers,
        We'll wire to F.W Four.

The Taubes have hitherto been rather rare,
        And flying too dreadfully high,
But when they are thick we may manage with care
        To hit one in twenty. We'll try.
The bombs they have dropped have been almost too few
        To frighten the General Staff,
But if they successfully straf G.H.Q.
        The troops in the trenches will laugh.

If after sustaining repeated attacks
        Congestion is simply immense
On the hospital ships, we will certainly wax
        Sarcastic at Porter's expense.
And when the survivors can stick it no more,
        And find it unhealthy to stay—
Why Father and Mother who put us ashore
        Will just have to take us away.

Biographies

It has not been possible to find biographical details for all those named in Orlo's diary. Those below are given with the ranks and positions held at the time when first mentioned in the diary.

ADYE, Major-General John. Inspector-General of Communications, British Salonika Army.

AINGER, 2nd Lieutenant Thomas Edward, Berkshire Yeomanry. KIA, 21 August 1915 (Gallipoli).

ALTHAM, Lieutenant-General Sir Edward. Inspector-General of Communications, MEF.

AMERY, Captain the Hon. Leopold Charles Maurice Stennett. Member of Parliament for Birmingham who served as an intelligence officer in the Balkans before returning to the War Cabinet. He had a long and varied political career, including as Secretary of State for India and Burma during the Second World War.

ANGLESEY, Lieutenant Charles Henry Alexander Paget (6th Marquess of Anglesey). Aide-de-Camp to Lieutenant-General Maxwell.

ANSTEY, Captain Edgar Carnegie, Royal Field Artillery, *psc*. GSO2, Operations Section, GHQ MEF.

ARMSTRONG. Either: Colonel John Cecil Armstrong, Paymaster, GHQ MEF; Lieutenant-Colonel St. George Bewes Armstrong, AA&QMG, HQ IGC; or Captain William Maurice (aka Pat) Armstrong, 10th Hussars. Etonian. Initially Aide-de-Camp to Major-General de Lisle, he later served on the staff of 29th Division and was acting staff captain, 88th Brigade, for the evacuation. KIA, Western Front, 1917.

ASHLEY. Orlo's batman. Probably Private James Ashley, 34871, 20th Hussars.

ASHMEAD-BARTLETT, Ellis. War correspondent.

ASPINALL, Captain Cecil Faber, Royal Munster Fusiliers, *psc*. GSO2, Operations Section, GHQ MEF. After adopting his wife's surname to become Aspinall-Oglander, in 1927 he wrote the two Gallipoli volumes of the British official history of the First World War.

ASQUITH, Lieutenant-Commander Arthur Melland, RNVR. Hood Battalion, Royal Naval Division. Son of the Prime Minister.

ASQUITH, Herbert. Prime Minister of the United Kingdom.

BAILLOUD, General Maurice Camille. GOC, French 2nd Division and, from late June, GOC CEO.

BALFOUR, Arthur James. Previously Prime Minister (1902–1905), in May 1915 he replaced Winston Churchill as First Lord of the Admiralty.

BANGOR, Viscount (aka Lieutenant-Colonel Maxwell Richard Crosbie Ward, 6th Viscount Bangor). Deputy Assistant Director Ordnance Services, RND.

BARTTELOT, Captain Sir Walter Balfour, Coldstream Guards. GSO3, Operations Section, GHQ MEF.

BASS, 2nd Lieutenant Walter Alfred Gordon, Royal Garrison Artillery. Cipher officer, Intelligence Section, GHQ MEF. Went to Salonika as cipher officer, October 1917.

BEADON, Lieutenant-Colonel Lancelot Richard, Army Service Corps. Assistant Quartermaster General, GHQ MEF.

BERNARD, Captain Denis John Charles Kirwan, Rifle Brigade. GSO2 Operations Section, GHQ MEF.

BERRY, 2nd Lieutenant Arthur. Cipher Officer, GHQ MEF.

BERTIER DE SAUVIGNY, *Commandant de Cavalerie Breveté* Jean-Marie. French Liaison Officer, GHQ MEF.

BIGHAM, Major the Hon. Charles Clive (2nd Viscount Mersey), Reserve of Officers. Provost Marshal, MEF. In October, after promotion to Lieutenant-Colonel, he was appointed Military Attaché at Cairo.

BIRCH, Captain William. Captain of RMS *Leinster* when she was sunk by a German U-boat on 10 October 1918, killing him.

BIRD. No further details known.

BIRDWOOD, Lieutenant-General Sir William Riddell. GOC ANZAC.

BIRRELL, Augustine. Chief Secretary for Ireland (1907–1916).

BLAKENEY, Lieutenant-Colonel Robert Byron Drury, Royal Engineers. Deputy General Manager, Egyptian State Railways.

BOLTON, Captain Charles A., Manchester Regiment, *psc*. GSO3, Operations Section, GHQ MEF.

BONAR LAW, Andrew. A future Prime Minister, in May 1915 he became Secretary of State for the Colonies.

BONSOR, Major Reginald. Officer Commanding, C Squadron, Surrey Yeomanry.

BOTHA, General the Hon. Louis. Prime Minister of South Africa.

BOWLER, Lieutenant-Colonel Edmund Robert. Assistant Provost Marshal, ANZAC.

BOWMAN-MANIFOLD, Lieutenant-Colonel Michael Graham Egerton. Director of Army Signals, MEF.

BRAITHWAITE, 2nd Lieutenant Valentine Ashworth. Aide-de-Camp to his father, Major-General Braithwaite. Killed on the Somme, 1–2 July 1916.

BRAITHWAITE, Major-General Walter Pipon. Chief of the General Staff, GHQ MEF.

BREEKS, Brigadier-General Richard William. Commander, 29th Divisional Artillery. Breeks was removed from command in late May, on the recommendation of Lieutenant-General Hunter-Weston, for showing signs of a nervous breakdown.

BRIAND, Aristide. Prime Minister of France.

BRIDGES. Possibly Major Roland Harley Bridges, RAMC, who drowned while on service with the Egyptian Expeditionary Force, 22 August 1918.

BRIDGES, Major-General William Throsby. Commander of the Australian Imperial Force and GOC 1st Australian Division. DOW, May 1915.

BRIGGS, Major-General Charles James. GOC, 28th Division.

BRODRICK, Lieutenant the Hon. George St John. Aide-de-Camp to General Hamilton (Brodrick's father, William St John Brodrick, 1st Earl of Midleton, was an MP). Attended Balliol just after Orlo.

BROOKE, Sub-Lieutenant Rupert Chawner, RNVR. Hood Battalion, RND. He died from septicaemia, following an insect bite, on 23 April 1915.

BRUCE, Lieutenant-Colonel Charles Granville. CO, 1st Battalion, 6th Gurkha Rifles. WIA, 30 June 1915.

BRULARD, General Jean-Marie. GOC French 1st Division.

BUCKLEY, Lieutenant-Colonel Basil Thorold, Northumberland Fusiliers, *psc.* GSO1, Head MO2 Section, Directorate of Military Operations, War Office.

BULL. Worked in C2 Section, War Office. No further details known.

BUTLER, Harold Beresford. A friend of Orlo's, they both attended Eton and Balliol. Later in life he was Director-General of the International Labour Office.

BUTLER, Captain Richard Bolger, Indian Army. Aide-de-Camp to General Monro.

BUXTON, 2nd Lieutenant Robert Vere (aka Robin), West Kent Yeomanry. A Special Appointment to GHQ, graded for pay as GSO3, he worked as a liaison officer, Intelligence. Later, CO 2nd Battalion, Imperial Camel Corps.

BYNG, Lieutenant-General Sir Julian. GOC, IX Corps.

CAMERON, Captain John Ewen, RN. Commanding HMS *Phaeton.*

CAMPBELL, Colonel Colin Powys. Orlo's uncle (brother of Helen Cyprian Williams).

CAMPBELL, Major-General Walter. Deputy Quartermaster General, MEF.

CARRUTHERS, Brigadier-General Robert Alexander. Deputy Adjutant & Quartermaster General, ANZAC.

CARSON, Sir Edward Henry. Attorney General for England (May-October 1915), Leader of the Opposition (October 1915-December 1916).

CASS, Lieutenant Hugh. 2nd Battalion, South Wales Borderers. KIA, 19 June 1915.

CHAMBERLAIN, Austen. Secretary of State for India (1915–1917).

CHEATLE, Lieutenant Walter John North. 1st Battalion, King's Own Scottish Borderers, 29th Division. KIA, 26 April 1915, Y Beach, aged 27. Cheatle attended Balliol, 1906–09.

CHERRY, Sub-Lieutenant Lancelot Arthur, RNVR. Drake Battalion, RND. KIA, 11 May 1915. Cherry had attended New College, Oxford.

CHURCHILL, Major John (Jack) Strange Spencer, Queen's Own Oxfordshire Hussars. Camp Commandant, GHQ MEF. Brother of Winston Churchill.

CHURCHILL, Winston Spencer. First Lord of the Admiralty (later Prime Minister).

CLARKE, Brigadier-General Travers Edward. DQMG, British Salonika Army.

CLAYTON, Lieutenant-Colonel Gilbert Falkington. Director of Military Intelligence, British Army Headquarters, Cairo.

COLLET, Flight-Commander Charles Herbert, Royal Naval Air Service. DOW, 19 August 1915.

CORDONA, General Luigi. Chief of Staff of the Italian Army.

COURAGE. No further details known.

COX, Brigadier-General General Herbert Vaughan. Commander 29th Indian Infantry Brigade.

CREEDY, Herbert James. Private Secretary, Secretary of State for War.

CREWE, Robert Offley Ashburton Milnes, 1st Marquess of Crewe. Secretary of State for India (1910–1915).

CUNINGHAME, Lieutenant-Colonel Sir Thomas. Military Attaché at Athens.

CUNLIFFE-OWEN, Lieutenant-Colonel Frederick. GSO2, Intelligence Section, HQ IGC. From November 1915, GSO1, Intelligence Section, HQ, British Army Salonika.

CURLING, Major Bryan James, King's Royal Rifle Corps, *psc*. GSO2, HQ 29th Division (he was DAA&QMG for the division before his promotion).

CURZON, the Hon. George Nathaniel. Lord Privy Seal in Asquith's coalition government.

D'AMADE, General Albert G.L. GOC French *Corps Expéditionaire d'Orient*.

D'ANNUNZIO, Gabriele. Italian poet, politician and soldier.

DARTIGE DU FOURNET, Vice-Admiral Louis. Commander, Allied Dardanelles Squadron.

DAVIES, Lieutenant-General Sir Francis John. GOC VIII Corps, August 1915–January 1916.

DAWNAY, Captain Guy Payan. Reserve of Officers, *psc*. GSO3, Operations Section, GHQ MEF.

DEEDES, Captain Wyndham Henry, King's Royal Rifle Corps. GSO3, Intelligence Section, GHQ MEF.

DE LABORDE, Lieutenant Félix Alexandre Jean Léon. French liaison officer attached to GHQ MEF.

DELACOMBE, Major Addis. Army Pay Corps officer for account of the Intelligence Section, GHQ MEF.

DELCASSÉ, Théophile. French Minister of Foreign Affairs.

DE LISLE, Major-General Henry de Beauvoir, *psc*. GOC 29th Division. Following Stopford's removal, de Lisle was briefly GOC IX Corps.

DELL. No further details known.

DENT, Captain Douglas Lionel, RN. Commander of HMS *Irresistible*, which sunk during the actions of 18 March. Following the loss of his ship, Dent was appointed Principal Naval Transport Officer.

DE PUTRON, Captain Cyril, Lancashire Fusiliers. British liaison officer attached to the French *Corps Expéditionaire d'Orient*).

DORAN, Brigadier-General Walter Robert Butler. Commander, 88th Brigade (29th Division).

DOUGHTY-WYLIE, Lieutenant-Colonel Charles Hotham Montague, Royal Welsh Fusiliers. GSO2, Intelligence Section, GHQ MEF. He was killed while leading an attack through Sedd el Bahr on 26 April 1915. He was awarded a posthumous Victoria Cross for this action.

DOUGLAS, Commander Henry Percy, RN. A surveyor on Admiral de Robeck's staff.

DOUGLAS, Major-General William. GOC, 42nd (East Lancashire) Division.

DRAKE, Major John Hughes, Hertfordshire Yeomanry. Military Landing Officer, Mudros. Attended Eton with Orlo.

DURNFORD, Captain Richard Selby, 9th Battalion, King's Royal Rifle Corps. KIA, 31 July 1915 (Western Front).

EBERHARDT, Admiral Andrei Augustovich, Imperial Russian Navy.

EGERTON, Major-General Granville George Algernon. GOC, 52nd (Lowland) Division until September, when he became Base Commandant, Alexandria.

ELLIOT, Sir Francis Edmund Hugh. His Majesty's Envoy Extraordinary and Minister Plenipotentiary at Athens.

ELLISON, Major-General Sir Gerald Francis, *psc*. Deputy Inspector-General of Communications, MEF, in July; in August he replaced Winter as Deputy Quartermaster General.

EVANS, Major L.I., Royal Engineers. OIC Army Signals, HQ ANZAC.

FAIRHOLME, Colonel William Ernest. British Salonika Army liaison officer with the War Office.

FANSHAWE, Major-General Edward Arthur. Replaced Hammersley as GOC, 11th (Northern) Division.

FARRER, Sub-Lieutenant Harold Marson (aka Bill), Drake Battalion, RND. Had attended Balliol, 1901–05.

FIENNES. *See TWISLETON-WYKENHAM-FIENNES.*

FISHER, Admiral of the Fleet Sir John. Resigned as First Sea Lord in 1915.

FITZGERALD, Lieutenant-Colonel Oswald Arthur Gerald. Personal Military Secretary to Lord Kitchener.

FRANCE, Anatole. French poet, journalist and novelist.

FRENCH, General Sir John. Commander in Chief of the British Expeditionary Force.

FULLER, Brigadier-General Richard Woodfield. Brigadier-General Royal Artillery, MEF

FULLER, Major Cuthbert Graham, Royal Engineers, *psc*. GSO2, Operations Section, GHQ MEF.

GALLIÉNI, Joseph Simon. French Minister for War.

GALLWITZ, General Max von. GOC 12th Army, German Army (Eastern Front).

GAMMELL, Lieutenant James, Royal Artillery. GSO3, Operations Section, GHQ MEF.

GARVIN, James Louis. Editor of *The Observer*.

GASCOIGNE, Major Ernest Frederick Orby, Reserve of Officers. Deputy Assistant Quartermaster General, GHQ MEF.

GASELEE, Sir Stephen. Etonian, British diplomat, writer and librarian.

GASKELL, Fleet Surgeon Arthur. Assistant Director of Medical Services, RND.

GILLMAN, Brigadier-General Webb. Brigadier General, General Staff, GHQ MEF.

GIRODON, Colonel Pierre. Chief of Staff, *Corps Expéditionnaire d'Orient*.

GLYN, Captain Ralph George Campbell, Rifles Brigade. GSO2, Department of the Chief of the Imperial General Staff, War Office.

GODLEY, Major-General Sir Alexander John. Commander, New Zealand Expeditionary Force, and GOC New Zealand and Australian Division.

GORDON, Major-General the Hon. Frederick. GOC 22nd Division (Salonika).

GOUNARIS, Dimitrios. Prime Minister of Greece.

GOURAUD, General Henri. GOC French *Corps Expéditionnaire d'Orient*. WIA, 30 June 1915.

GRANARD, Lieutenant-Colonel Bernard Arthur William Patrick Hastings Forbes (8th Earl of Granard). CO 5th (Pioneer) Battalion, Royal Irish Regiment (10th Division).

GRANT, Major Henry F.L., Royal Artillery, *psc*. GSO3, Operations Section, GHQ MEF.

GRAVES, Sir Robert Wyndham. A career diplomat, he was working in Constantinople when the war began. He was attached to GHQ, though with no formal role, to advise on what to do once Constantinople was captured.

GREGG. Likely in C2 Section, War Office. No further details known.

GREGORY. Probably Brian O'Farrell Gregory, RN. Clerk HMS *Prince of Wales*.

GREY, Sir Edward. Secretary of State for Foreign Affairs.

GROSSMITH, George. English comedian, writer, composer, actor and singer.

GUÉPRATTE, Rear-Admiral Émile Paul Aimable. Commanding French fleet.

HAIG, General Sir Douglas. Commander-in-Chief, British Armies on the Western Front.

HALDANE, Richard Burdon, 1st Viscount Haldane. Previously Secretary of State for War (1905–1912), he was Lord Chancellor until forced to resign in 1915.

HAMILTON, Brigadier-General Alexander Beamish. Supervised the allied landings at Salonika.

HAMILTON, General Sir Ian. Commander-in-Chief, MEF.

HAMMERSLEY, Major-General Frederick. GOC, 11th (Northern) Division.

HANCOCK, Major Mortimer Pawson, Royal Fusiliers. Deputy Assistant Adjutant and Quartermaster General, ANZAC.

HANKEY, Maurice Pascal Alers. Secretary to the Committee of Imperial Defence, and Secretary of the War Council.

HARCOURT, Lewis Vernon, 1st Viscount Harcourt. Secretary of State for the Colonies (1910–1915).

HARDY, Lieutenant Commander Henry Noel Marryat, RN. Commanding Trawler Flotilla.

HARE, Brigadier-General Steuart Welwood. Commander, 86th Infantry Brigade.

HARKE, Lieutenant Sydney Lawrence. Surgeon, Royal Naval Medical Service.

HART DAVIES. No further details known.

HAWKER, Colonel Claude Julian. Camp Commandant, Advanced Base, Imbros Island.

HENDERSON, Arthur. Labour politician and member of Asquith's coalition government.

HENLEY, Sub-Lieutenant the Hon. Francis Robert, RNVR. Drake Battalion, RND.

HERBERT, Brigadier-General Lionel Norton. Commander, 65th Brigade (22nd Division), Salonika.

HIBBEN, Paxton Pattison. Associated Press war correspondent, Athens.

HICKS-BEACH, Lieutenant the Hon. Michael Hugh MP (Viscount Quenington), 1/1st Royal Gloucestershire Hussars. DOW, Egypt, April 1916.

HILL, Brigadier-General Felix Frederick. Commander, 31st Brigade (10th Irish Division).

HODGSON, Captain Charles Basil Mortimer, Royal West Surrey Regiment. Deputy Judge Advocate General, GHQ MEF.

HONY, Lieutenant Henry Charles. Interpreter, Operations Section, GHQ MEF.

HORE-RUTHVEN, Major Alexander, VC, Welsh Guards, *psc*. GSO2, Operations Section, GHQ MEF. Later Governor-General of Australia.

HORNE, Major-General Henry Sinclair. GOC, 2nd Division (Western Front) and later XV Corps.

HOUGH, William. Acting Consul at Jerusalem on war's outbreak, he was imprisoned until November 1914. He then proceeded to Cairo, where he worked in the Registry until appointed as an interpreter in the MEF.

HOWELL, Brigadier-General Philip. Brigadier General, General Staff, British Salonika Army.

HUEFFER, Ford Hermann. English novelist. Known as Ford Maddox Ford after the war.

HUNTER-WESTON, Major-General Aylmer Gould. GOC 29th Division.

HUNTLEY, George Patrick. Irish actor.

INGLEFIELD, Major General Francis Seymour. GOC 54th (East Anglian) Division.

ISTOMIN, Lieutenant-General Nikolai Mikhailovich. Russian corps commander.

JENKS, Captain Maurice Harold. 7th Battalion, Gloucestershire Regiment (39th Brigade, 13th Division).

JOFFRE, General Joseph. Commander-in-Chief of the French Army.

JOLY DE LOTBINIÈRE, Brigadier-General Alain Chartier, RE. Director of Works, MEF.

KAVANAGH, Major-General Charles Toler MacMorrough. GOC 5th Division (Western Front).

KEBLE, Colonel Alfred Ernest Conquer, RAMC. Assistant Director of Medical Services, GHQ MEF.

KEELING, Lieutenant Edward Herbert (aka Eddie), attached to GHQ for cipher work in the Intelligence Section. A graduate of Eton College, which he attended with Orlo, and Oxford University, Keeling was secretary at the Residency in Cairo before the war. Captured and taken prisoner at Kut, he was a POW until escaping. He was later an MP.

KEMP, Lieutenant-Colonel George (Lord Rochdale). CO 1/6th Lancashire Fusiliers (125th Brigade, 42nd Division). In June he was acting Commander, 127th Brigade.

KENNY, Captain William David. Aide-de-Camp to Sultan Hussein Kamel of Egypt, who loaned him to Hamilton.

Kenny then served as another of Hamilton's aides-de-camp.

KERSHAW, Lieutenant Philip Southwell, RNVR, Drake Battalion, RND.

KEYES, Commodore Roger John Brownlow (1st Baron Keyes), RN. Chief of Staff, EMS.

KEYNES, John Maynard (1st Baron Keynes). Economist. Attended Eton with Orlo.

KIGGELL, Lieutenant-General Sir Launcelot Edward. Chief of the General Staff, British Armies in France.

KITCHENER, Field Marshal the Right Hon. Horatio Herbert, 1st Earl. Secretary of State for War.

KNOX, Alfred Dillwyn. British cryptographer and classics scholar. Attended Eton with Orlo.

KÖVESS VON KÖVESSHÁZA, General Hermann. GOC 3rd Army, German Army (Eastern Front).

LAMBERT, Captain St John Murray. Nottinghamshire Battery, Royal Horse Artillery (2nd Mounted Division).

LANSDOWNE, Lord. Minister without portfolio in the Asquith coalition government.

LAWRENCE, Brigadier-General the Hon. Herbert Alexander. Commander, 127th Brigade (42nd Division) until, on promotion to Major-General, he temporarily replaced Lindley as GOC 53rd (Welsh) Division, before in September becoming GOC 52nd (Lowland) Division.

LIMAN VON SANDERS, General Otto, Imperial German Army. GOC, Ottoman 5th Army.

LINDLEY, Major-General the Hon. John Edward. GOC, 53rd (Welsh) Division.

LISTER, Lieutenant the Hon. Charles Alfred, Hood Battalion, RND. Attended Eton and Balliol Colleges. DOW, 28 August 1915.

LLOYD, Captain George Ambrose MP, Warwickshire Yeomanry. Special Service Officer attached to GHQ. Lloyd, who worked in Intelligence at GHQ, later became Lord Lloyd of Dolobran and High Commissioner for Egypt and Sudan.

LLOYD GEORGE, the Right Hon. David, Prime Minister of the United Kingdom, 1916–22.

LOTBINIÈRE. *See JOLY DE LOTBINIÈRE.*

LOWTHER, Captain Lancelot Edward. King's Messenger Service.

LYNDEN-BELL, Major-General Sir Arthur. Chief of General Staff, MEF.

MACKENSEN, Field Marshal August von. Commander-in-Chief, Army Group Mackensen (German 11th Army and Austro-Hungarian 4th Army).

MACKENZIE, Lieutenant Edward Montague Compton, Royal Marines. Author and friend of Orlo's, who joined HQ RND and later worked for the British Secret Service, MI6.

MACKENZIE, Lieutenant-Colonel John, RAMC. OC 25th Casualty Clearing Station, Imbros Island.

MAHON, Lieutenant-General Sir Bryan Thomas. GOC, 10th (Irish) Division and, from October, Salonika Army.

MAITLAND, Captain Frederick Lewis Makgill Crichton, 1st Battalion, Gordon Highlanders. Aide-de-Camp to General Hamilton.

MALCOLM, Lieutenant-Colonel Neill. GSO1, 11th (Northern) Division.

MANIFOLD. *See BOWMAN-MANIFOLD.*

MARQUIS. *See WALLIS.*

MARIX, Flight Commander Reginald Leonard George. Aviator, RNAS.

MARSH, Edward Howard (aka Eddie). Private Secretary to Winston Churchill.

MARSHALL, Major-General William Raine. Commander, 87th Brigade (29th Division). GOC 29th Division when de Lisle shifted to IX Corps.

MASON. No further details known.

MAUDE, Major-General Frederick Stanley. Replaced Shaw as GOC, 13th (Western) Division.

MAXWELL, Lieutenant-General Sir John Grenfell. GOC Force in Egypt.

MAXWELL, Captain William. Censor, GHQ MEF. As a war correspondent he reported from the Sudan, Boer War, Russo-Japanese War, Balkan Wars, and opening stages of the First World War.

McGRIGOR, Brigadier-General Charles Rhoderic. Base Commandant, Alexandria.

McKENNA, the Right Hon. Reginald. Chancellor of the Exchequer.

McLEOD, Captain Donald. Staff Captain, Adjutant General's Branch, GHQ MEF.

McMAHON, Lieutenant-Colonel Sir Athur Henry. British High Commissioner in Egypt, 1915–17.

McMAHON, Lady Mary Evelyn (nee Bland). Married to Lieutenant-Colonel Sir Arthur Henry McMahon.

MERCER, Brigadier-General David, Royal Marines Light Infantry. Commander 1st (Royal Naval) Brigade, RND.

MILLERAND, Alexandre. French Minister for War.

MILWARD, Captain Clement Arthur, *psc*. GSO3, HQ 29th Division and then DAQMG, GHQ MEF.

MITCHELL, Captain Francis Herbert, RN. Attached to GHQ for liaison with EMS.

MOBERLY, Major Bertrand Richard, 56th Punjabi Rifles, *psc*. GSO2, Operations Section, GHQ MEF.

MONRO, General Sir Charles Carmichael. Commander-in-Chief, MEF.

MONTAGU-DOUGLAS-SCOTT, Lieutenant-Colonel Lord Herbert. Military Secretary to General Monro.

MURDOCH, Keith. Australian journalist.

MURRAY, Lieutenant-General Sir Archibald James. Chief of the Imperial General Staff. Later, Commander-in-Chief, Egyptian Expeditionary Force.

NAPIER, Lieutenant-Colonel the Hon. Henry Dundas. Military Attaché at Sofia, Bulgaria.

NEAVE, Captain Richard. 1st Battalion, Essex Regiment.

NEWCOMBE, Major Stewart Francis, Royal Engineers. An associate of T.E. Lawrence, Newcombe worked in Egypt until joining the 2nd Australian Division at Gallipoli in September 1915.

NORTHCLIFFE, Lord Alfred (aka Alfred Charles William Harmsworth). British newspaper and publishing magnate.

O'BEIRNE, Hugh James. Acting Chargé d'Affaires, Sofia, July–October 1915.

ONSLOW, Lieutenant Brian Walton, 11th King Edward's Own Lancers. Aide-de-Camp to Lieutenant-General Birdwood. Aged 22, he was KIA by an artillery shell while sleeping outside his dugout above Anzac Cove, 28 July 1915. He is buried at Beach Cemetery.

ORR. No further details known.

PALLIS, Alexander Anastasius. Attended Eton and Balliol with Orlo. Civil servant, Greek politician, author.

PALLIS, Lieutenant-Colonel Konstantinos. Staff Officer, Greek Army.

PARIS, Major-General Archibald. GOC Royal Naval Division.

PEASE, the Right Hon Joseph Albert (aka Jack). Liberal politician and member of Asquith's Cabinet.

PEEL, Lieutenant-Colonel E.J.R., Royal Artillery. Commanding 147th Brigade, RFA.

PEEL, Major the Hon. Arthur George Villiers, Royal Marines. Assistant Provost Marshal, RND.

PELISSIER, Harry Gabriel. Theatrical producer and Compton Mackenzie's brother-in-law.

PELLIOT, Lieutenant Paul. French Liaison Officer, GHQ MEF.

PEYTON, Captain Henry Sydney Charles, Rifle Brigade. GSO3, Intelligence Section, GHQ MEF.

PEYTON, Major-General William Eliot. GOC, 2nd Mounted Division.

PIRIE-GORDON, Lieutenant Charles Harry Clinton, RNVR. Naval Intelligence officer on HMS *Doris*, including during its raid on Alexandretta.

PITCAIRN, Captain George Simpson, 8th Battalion, Royal Sussex Regiment. A mining engineer before the war, he was attached to GHQ on Special Appointment, graded for pay as GSO3.

POLLEN, Captain Stephen Hungerford, Reserve of Officers. Aide-de-Camp and military secretary to General Hamilton.

PORSON, Richard. Classical scholar.

POTTS, Lieutenant-Commander Thomas Moffett, RNR. HMS *Imogene.*

POWELL, Captain Eden Bernard, Rifle Brigade, *psc.* GSO3, Intelligence Section, GHQ MEF.

PRIOR, Captain Edward Foss, 8th Battalion, Rifle Brigade. An Etonian, he was WIA, July 1915, and KIA on the Western Front, 15 September 1916.

RADCLIFFE, Captain John Douglas Henderson, 7th Battalion, King's Royal Rifle Corps. DOW, 30 July 1915 (Western Front).

RENDEL, George William. 3rd Secretary, British Embassy, Athens.

REYNOLDS, Louis George Stanley. Private Secretary to Quartermaster-General of the Forces, War Office. Attended Balliol with Orlo.

ROBERTSON, Lieutenant-General Sir William. Chief of Staff, British Expeditionary Force, until late December 1915, when appointed Chief of the Imperial General Staff.

ROBERTSON, Major A.B., Cameron Highlanders. GSO2, Operations Section, GHQ MEF.

ROPER, Brigadier-General Alexander William. Brigadier-General Royal Engineers, MEF.

RUSSELL, Brigadier-General Andrew Hamilton. Commander, New Zealand Mounted Rifles Brigade.

SALMON, Major William Henry, Reserve of Officers. Interpreter, GHQ MEF.

SAMAIN, Albert Victor. French poet.

SAMSON, Wing Commander Charles Rumney. Commanding No. 3 Wing, RNAS.

SARRAIL, General Maurice Paul Emmanuel. He was meant to be GOC of a reinforced *Corps Expéditionnaire d'Orient*, but was instead sent to Salonika as GOC French Army of the Orient.

SCHOOLING. Worked in C2 Section, War Office. No further details known.

SHAW, Major-General Frederick Charles. GOC, 13th (Western) Division.

SHEEPSHANKS, Captain Arthur Charles, 8th Battalion, Rifle Brigade. He was WIA, July 1915 (Western Front).

SIMPSON-BAIKIE, Brigadier-General Hugh Archie Dundas, Royal Artillery. GSO1, Operations Section, GHQ MEF. He is better known for commanding the artillery of 29th Division and later VIII Corps.

SITWELL, Brigadier-General William Henry. Commander, 34th Brigade (11th Northern Division).

SKEEN, Colonel Andrew, *psc.* GSO1 and Chief of Staff, HQ ANZAC.

SMITH, Sir Frederick Edwin. Solicitor General.

SMITH, Captain Ian Mackintosh (aka Jan), Somerset Light Infantry. Special Service Officer GHQ, attached to HQ ANZAC for intelligence work during the landings. A linguist, he was Military Consul at Van when the war began.

SMITH, Brigadier-General Sydenham Campbell Urquhart. Brigadier General Royal Artillery, IX Corps until October, when appointed BGRA MEF.

STOPFORD, Lieutenant-General Sir Frederick William. GOC IX Corps.

STORR, Major Charles Lancelot. Private Secretary to Lord Kitchener.

STRANGE. Probably Lieutenant Jack Ronald Stewart Strange, RNR.

STREET, Brigadier-General Harold Edward, *psc*. Chief of Staff, VIII Corps.

STRIEDINGER, Major Oscar, Army Service Corps. Assistant Director of Transport, MEF.

SUTTON, Lieutenant Francis Arthur, Royal Engineers. He was WIA and awarded a Military Cross for his service at Gallipoli. On account of losing his hand during battle, he was known as 'One-Arm Sutton' (it was the title of his 1933 autobiography). He attended Eton with Orlo.

SYKES, Colonel Frederick Hugh. As Chief of Staff, Royal Flying Corps, he visited Gallipoli in June 1915 to investigate and report on the Royal Naval Air Service. He returned to Gallipoli in August and commanded the RNAS.

TAYLOR, Major Oswald James, Royal Marines. OC RND Ordnance Depot.

TAYLOR, Lieutenant-Colonel Reginald O'Bryan, *psc*. Was a Special Service Officer attached to GHQ in August. On promotion, appointed inaugural Brigadier-General General Staff, GHQ MEF, which sat atop the Operations and Intelligence sections. Appointed Commander, 159th Brigade (53rd Division) in November, and acting GOC 53rd Division in December 1915.

TENNANT, Lieutenant William George, RN. HMS *Chatham*.

THROCKMORTON, Lieutenant Geoffrey William Berkeley, Berkshire Yeomanry.

THURSBY, Rear-Admiral Cecil Fiennes, RN. Commanding the 2nd Squadron during the landings at Z Beach (Anzac).

TWISLETON-WYKENHAM-FIENNES, Lieutenant-Colonel Eustace Edward, Oxfordshire Hussars. GSO3, RND. Previously Parliamentary Private Secretary to Winston Churchill.

TYRRELL, Lieutenant-Colonel Gerald Ernest, Royal Artillery. GSO1, Intelligence Section, GHQ MEF (Head of the Intelligence Section at GHQ).

UNWIN, Captain Edward, RN. Commanded SS *River Clyde* during the landing at V Beach on 25 April. He was awarded a Victoria Cross for his actions on that day.

VENIZELOS, Eleftherios. Prime Minister of Greece.

VITALE DE PONTAGIO, Captain Umberto. Italian liaison officer, GHQ.

WAGSTAFF, Major Cyril Mosley, Royal Engineers, *psc*. GSO2 (Operations), HQ ANZAC.

WALFORD, Lieutenant William. Aide-de-Camp to Lieutenant-General Maxwell.

WALLACE, Major-General Alexander. Inspector General of Communications, MEF, until replaced in July.

WALLIS, Lieutenant Harry Bernard, Royal Marines. RND Ordnance Depot. Orlo, who attended Balliol with Wallis, refers to him throughout the diary as both 'Marquis' and 'Wallis'.

WARD, Captain John Hubert. King's Messenger Service.

WARD, Lieutenant-Colonel Montagu Charles Pearson, Royal Artillery, *psc*. GSO1, Intelligence Section, GHQ MEF (Head of the Intelligence Section at GHQ).

WATSON, Major Hugh Wharton Myddleton, King's Royal Rifle Corps. GSO3, Operations Section, GHQ MEF.

WEBER, Major General Erich. GOC XV Corps, Ottoman 5th Army.

WEDGWOOD, Lieutenant-Commander Josiah Clement, MP, RNVR. OC No. 3 Armoured Car Squadron, RNAS.

WEMYSS, Vice-Admiral Rosslyn Erskine. Senior Naval Officer, Mudros (later Governor of Mudros Harbour). Wemyss was the second most senior British naval officer at the Dardanelles. In 1917 he replaced Admiral Jellicoe as First Sea Lord at the Admiralty.

WILLIAMS (new cipher officer mentioned on 24 October). No further details known.

WILLIAMS, Alice Isabella (née Pollock). Orlo's wife.

WILLIAMS, Lieutenant-Colonel Weir de Lancey. Hampshire Regiment, *psc*. GSO1, Operations Section, GHQ MEF (Head of Operations Section at GHQ).

WILSON, Captain the Hon. Arthur Stanley. King's Messenger Service.

WILSON, Lieutenant-General Sir Henry Fuller Maitland. GOC XII Corps (Salonika).

WINTER, Brigadier-General Samuel Henry. Deputy Quartermaster General, GHQ MEF.

WOLLEY-DOD, Colonel Owen Cadogan, *psc*. GSO1, 29th Division. Later commanded the 86th Brigade (29th Division) at Gallipoli.

WOODWARD, Brigadier-General Edward Mabbott, *psc*. Deputy Adjutant General, GHQ MEF.

YOUNGHUSBAND, Major-General Sir George. Commander, 28th Indian Brigade (10th Indian Division).

ZAIMIS, Alexandros. Greek Prime Minister after Venizelos.

* * *

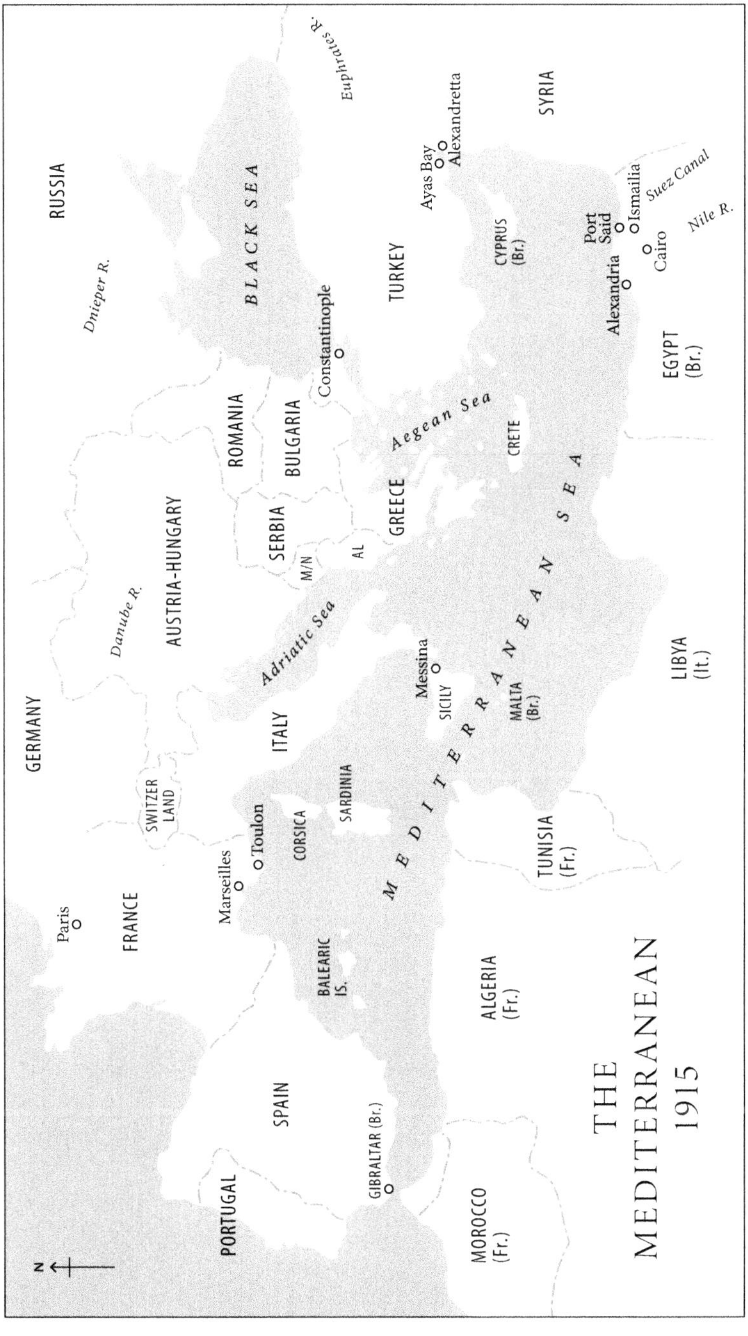
THE MEDITERRANEAN 1915
N
RUSSIA
Dnieper R.
BLACK SEA
Euphrates R.
Constantinople
TURKEY
Ayas Bay
Alexandretta
SYRIA
CYPRUS (Br.)
Port Said
Ismailia
Suez Canal
Nile R.
Cairo
Alexandria
EGYPT (Br.)
ROMANIA
BULGARIA
Aegean Sea
CRETE
GREECE
SERBIA
M/N
AL
AUSTRIA-HUNGARY
Danube R.
Adriatic Sea
GERMANY
ITALY
Messina
SICILY
MALTA (Br.)
MEDITERRANEAN SEA
LIBYA (It.)
SWITZER LAND
Toulon
CORSICA
SARDINIA
Marseilles
TUNISIA (Fr.)
Paris
FRANCE
BALEARIC IS.
ALGERIA (Fr.)
SPAIN
GIBRALTAR (Br.)
PORTUGAL
MOROCCO (Fr.)

N
AUSTRIA-HUNGARY
BALKANS & AEGEAN SEA
Belgrade
ROMANIA
Bucharest
SERBIA
Danube R.
Nish
Varna
MONTE-NEGRO
Sofia
BULGARIA
BLACK SEA
Burgas
Strumnitza
Maritza R.
ALBANIA
Uskub
Adrianople
Constantinople
Monastir
MACEDONIA
Dedeagatch
Salonica
Stavros
Panderma
Mt Olympus
Chanak
AEGEAN SEA
GREECE
TURKEY
Smyrna
Athens
Key
1 GALLIPOLI PENINSULA
2 TENEDOS
3 LEMNOS (Mudros)
4 IMBROS
5 MITYLENE
DODECANESE (It.)
CRETE
MEDITERRANEAN SEA
LIBYA (It.)
Alexandria
EGYPT (Br.)

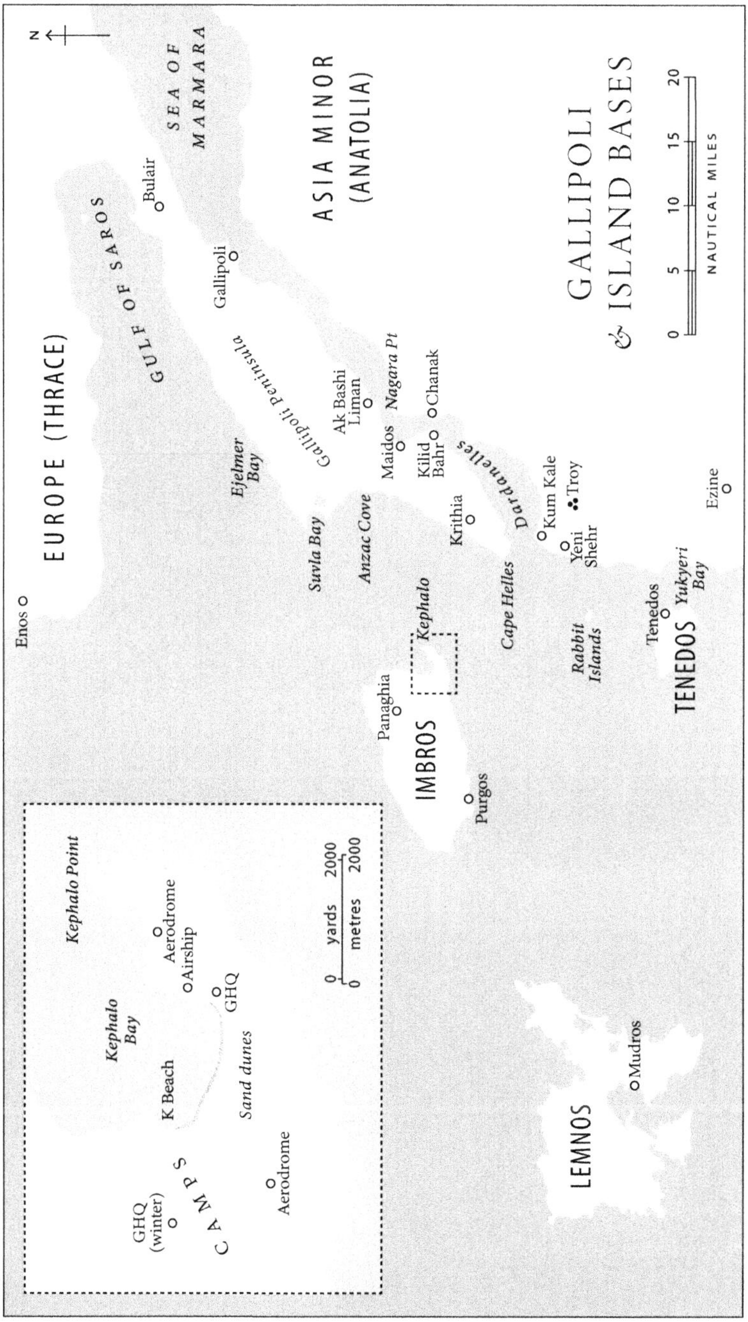
GALLIPOLI
& ISLAND BASES
EUROPE (THRACE)
ASIA MINOR
(ANATOLIA)
GULF OF SAROS
SEA OF
MARMARA
N
Enos
Bulair
Gallipoli
Gallipoli Peninsula
Ejelmer
Bay
Suvla Bay
Anzac Cove
Ak Bashi
Liman
Maidos
Nagara Pt
Chanak
Kilid
Bahr
Dardanelles
Krithia
Kum Kale
Troy
Yeni
Shehr
Ezine
Cape Helles
Kephalo
Panaghia
IMBROS
Purgos
Rabbit
Islands
Tenedos
TENEDOS
Yukyeri
Bay
LEMNOS
Mudros
0
5
10
15
20
NAUTICAL MILES
Kephalo Point
Kephalo
Bay
Aerodrome
Airship
GHQ
K Beach
Sand dunes
CAMPS
GHQ
(winter)
Aerodrome
0
yards
2000
0
metres
2000

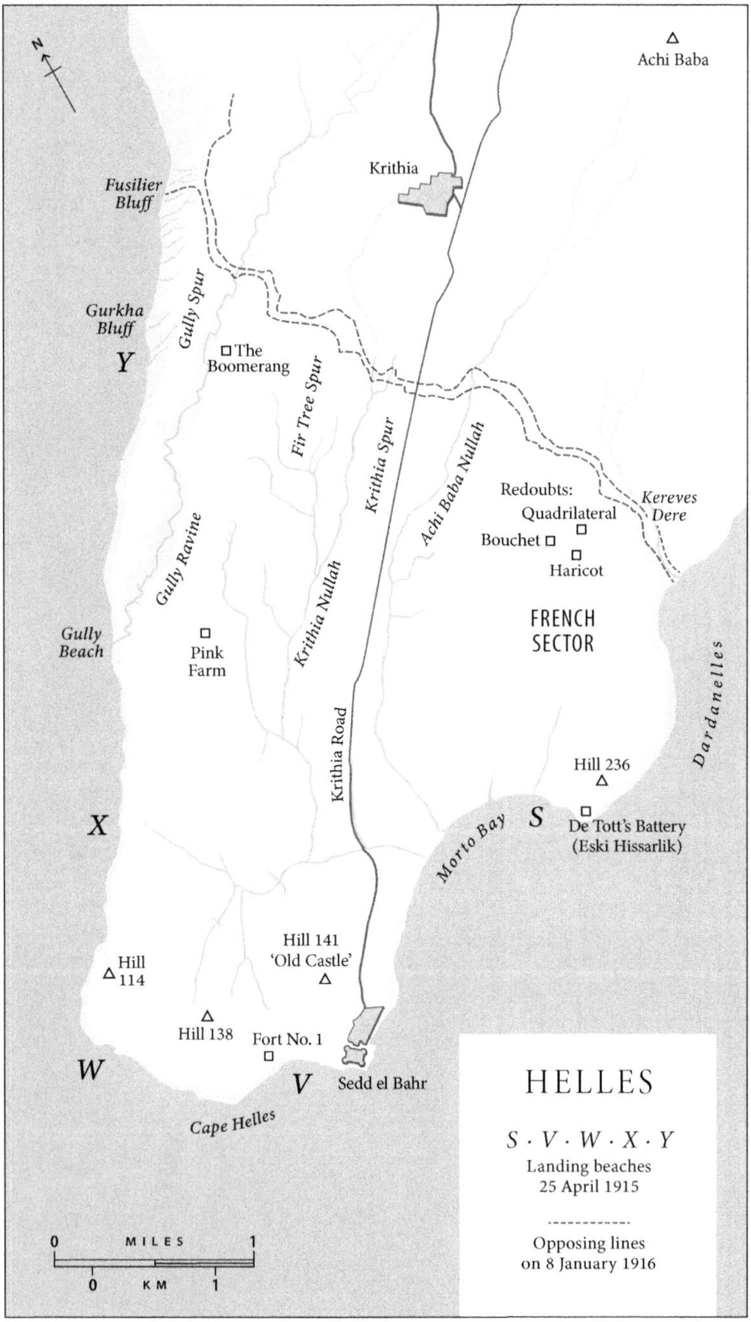
N
Achi Baba
Krithia
Fusilier Bluff
Gurkha Bluff
Gully Spur
The Boomerang
Y
Fir Tree Spur
Krithia Spur
Achi Baba Nullah
Redoubts:
Quadrilateral
Bouchet
Haricot
Kereves Dere
Gully Ravine
Krithia Nullah
Gully Beach
Pink Farm
FRENCH SECTOR
Dardanelles
Krithia Road
Hill 236
X
S
Morto Bay
De Tott's Battery (Eski Hissarlik)
Hill 141 'Old Castle'
Hill 114
Hill 138
Fort No. 1
W
V
Sedd el Bahr
Cape Helles
HELLES
S · V · W · X · Y
Landing beaches
25 April 1915
Opposing lines
on 8 January 1916
0 MILES 1
0 KM 1

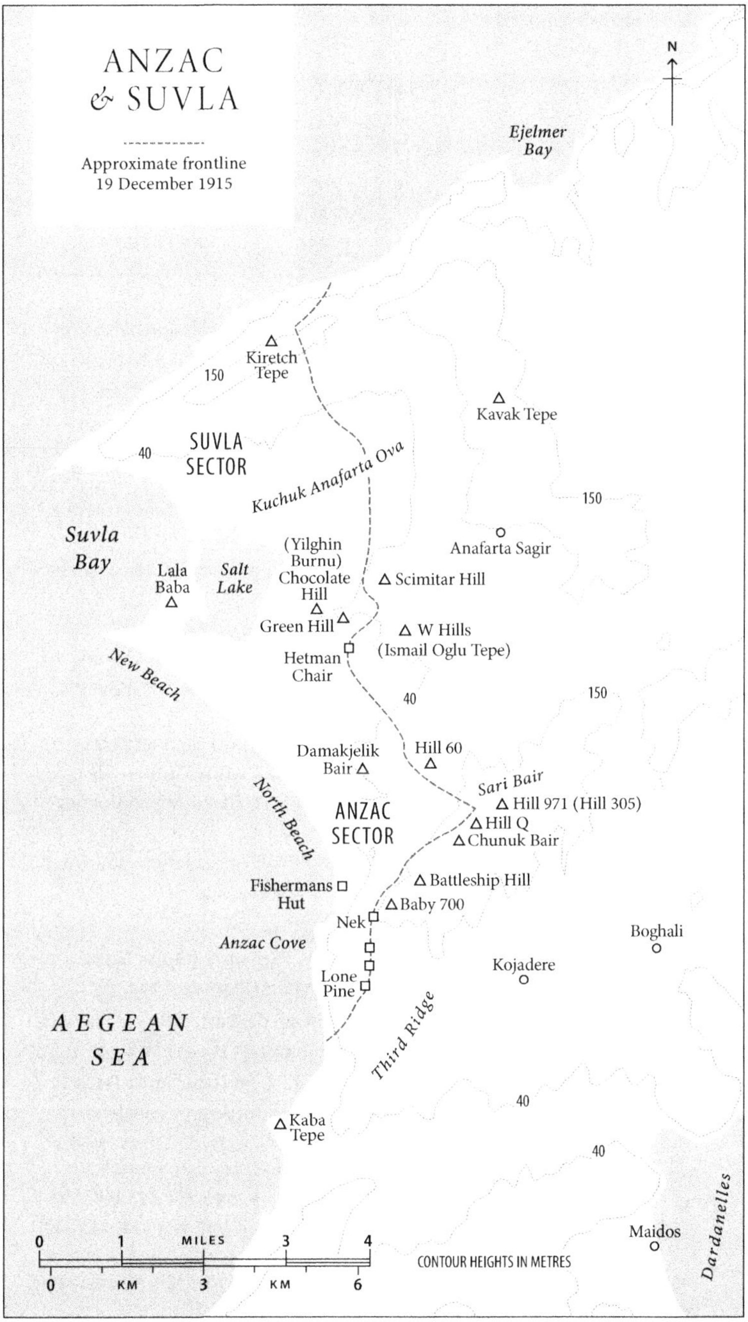
ANZAC
& SUVLA
Approximate frontline
19 December 1915
N
Ejelmer
Bay
Kiretch
Tepe
150
Kavak Tepe
40
SUVLA
SECTOR
Kuchuk Anafarta Ova
150
Suvla
Bay
Anafarta Sagir
Lala
Baba
Salt
Lake
(Yilghin
Burnu)
Chocolate
Hill
Scimitar Hill
Green Hill
W Hills
(Ismail Oglu Tepe)
New Beach
Hetman
Chair
40
150
Damakjelik
Bair
Hill 60
Sari Bair
Hill 971 (Hill 305)
North Beach
ANZAC
SECTOR
Hill Q
Chunuk Bair
Fishermans
Hut
Battleship Hill
Baby 700
Nek
Anzac Cove
Boghali
Kojadere
Lone
Pine
Third Ridge
AEGEAN
SEA
40
Kaba
Tepe
40
Dardanelles
Maidos
0
1
MILES
3
4
0
KM
3
KM
6
CONTOUR HEIGHTS IN METRES

Index

INDEX

Printed in Dunstable, United Kingdom

64294788R10245